LEARNING AID

for use with

BASIC MARKETING

Seventh Canadian Edition

E. Jerome McCarthy
Michigan State University

Stanley J. Shapiro
Simon Fraser University

William D. Perreault, Jr.
The University of North Carolina

IRWIN

©Richard D. Irwin, Inc., 1975, 1979, 1983, 1986, 1989, 1992, and 1994

Printed in the United States of America.

ISBN 0-256-12814-6

1 2 3 4 5 6 7 8 9 0 ML 0 9 8 7 6 5 4 3

Contents

Introduction

This *Learning Aid* is designed to help you organize and learn all of the material that is presented in *Basic Marketing*, Seventh Canadian Edition. Feedback from marketing instructors—and students—indicates that students who use the *Learning Aid* regularly do tend to learn the material better—and also tend to do better on examinations.

Please note, however, that the *Learning Aid* is intended to be used along with *Basic Marketing*. *It is not a substitute for reading and carefully studying the text!*

How the Learning Aid Is Organized

The *Learning Aid* is divided into 22 chapters—one chapter for each corresponding chapter in *Basic Marketing*. There are also separate chapters for Appendix A: Economics Fundamentals and Appendix C: Marketing Arithmetic.

Each chapter in the *Learning Aid* contains the following five sections:

     A. What this chapter is about
     B. Important terms
     C. True-false questions
     D. Multiple-choice questions
     E. Application exercises

The purpose of each of these sections is explained below. Please note that some sections are designed to be used *before* you read each chapter in *Basic Marketing*.

What This Chapter Is About

This section provides a brief introduction to each chapter in *Basic Marketing*. It should be read *before* you read the text—to help you focus on the important points in each chapter.

Important Terms

This section lists the important new terms introduced in each chapter of *Basic Marketing*—and the page on which each term first appears. (These terms are shown in blue in the text to help you find them.)

You should look over the list of important terms *before* reading each chapter—to help you focus on the key points in the chapter. *After* reading each chapter, you should review the list of important terms to make sure you understand each term. If you have any doubts about what a particular term means, use the indicated page number to find and restudy its definition in the text—or look up the term's definition in the Glossary at the end of the text. Some students even write out the definitions of each important term on 3 x 5 cards—to help them study for exams.

True-False Questions

This section provides a series of *self-testing* true-false questions—to test your understanding of the material presented in *Basic Marketing*. The correct answer for each question is given at the end of the test—along with a page number showing where the correct answer can be found in the text.

After reading each chapter in the text and reviewing the important terms, try to answer all of the true-false questions *before* looking at the correct answers. Then check your answers—and for each question that you answered wrong, review the related text material to find out *why* your answer is wrong. This is an important step! Simply memorizing the correct answers is *not* likely to improve your exam performance!

Multiple-Choice Questions

This section contains a series of *self-testing* multiple-choice questions—to further test your understanding and comprehension of the material presented in *Basic Marketing*. Again, the correct answer for each question is given at the end of the questions—along with a page number showing where the correct answer can be found in the text.

Ideally, you should take the multiple-choice tests only *after* you have read the text, reviewed the important terms, and tried the true-false questions. Again, you should try to answer all of the questions *before* looking at the correct answers—and make sure you review the text material to learn *why* your wrong answers were wrong!

Finally, keep in mind that the self-testing true-false and multiple-choice questions are just a *sample* of what you might expect on an exam. They do not cover every single concept discussed in the text—nor do they cover every possible type of question that might be asked. In other words, *simply answering these self-testing questions is not adequate preparation for exams*. You must also read and study the text!

Application Exercises

This section includes two or more exercises for each of the chapters in *Basic Marketing* (not including the appendices). Each exercise is designed to illustrate and apply some of the more important concepts and analytical approaches introduced in the text.

Although these exercises are designed mainly to be discussed in class and/or assigned as homework—*you can still benefit from doing them even if your instructor does not assign them*. Many students find the "Introductions" to each exercise quite helpful in understanding the related text material. And many of the exercises contain short "caselets" which show how concepts discussed in the text can be applied in the "real world." Doing these exercises will not only improve your understanding of the text material—but will also better prepare you for more advanced marketing and business case courses.

How to Study for Examinations

While no study routine works best for everyone, the following suggestions are based on proven learning principles and should be of benefit to most students. *For every chapter your instructor assigns in Basic Marketing:*

1. **Read the** *what this chapter is about* **section in the** *Learning Aid*.

2. **Look over the** *important terms* **section in the** *Learning Aid*.

3. **Read the learning objectives listed at the beginning of the chapter.**

4. **Read the chapter from beginning to end without any interruptions—and** *without doing any underlining or note-taking*. **(Underlining key points while you read interrupts your flow of thought and tends to reduce reading comprehension.)**

5. **Read the chapter again—this time underlining key points and/or writing notes in the page margins. Look at the exhibits and illustrations, and think about how they relate to the text material.**

6. **Review the** *important terms* **section in the** *Learning Aid* **to make sure you can define each term.**

7. **Take the self-testing true-false test in the** *Learning Aid*—**and go back to the text to study any questions you answered incorrectly.**

8. **Take the self-testing multiple-choice test in the** *Learning Aid*—**and go back to the text to study any questions you answered incorrectly.**

9. **Take detailed classroom lecture notes**—**and review them** *immediately after class* **to make sure that they are complete and that you understand everything your instructor said.**

10. **Do any** *application exercises* **that your instructor assigns.**

11. *Optional:* **Do the** *application exercises* **that were not assigned.**

12. **Just before the examination—review:**
    a. the points you underlined in the text and/or your notes in the page margins.
    b. the *important terms* in the *Learning Aid*.
    c. the self-testing true-false and multiple-choice questions in the *Learning Aid*—especially the questions you answered wrong the first time.
    d. any *application exercises* that were assigned.
    e. your lecture notes. Good luck!

Acknowledgements

All the exercises in this edition of the *Learning Aid* were updated and/or revised, but the continuing influence of the creative abilities of Professor Andrew Brogowicz (of Western Michigan University) will be obvious to previous users. Really good ideas endure!
The *Learning Aid* exercises were revised for the Seventh Canadian Edition by Ann Porter.

E. Jerome McCarthy
Stanley J. Shapiro
William D. Perreault, Jr.

Chapter 1

Marketing's role in the global economy

What This Chapter Is About

Chapter 1 introduces the concept of marketing. First, we show how marketing relates to production--and why it is important to you and to the global economy. Then the text shows that there are two kinds of marketing--micro-marketing and macro-marketing. The importance of a macro-marketing system in any kind of economic system is emphasized. Six stages of economic development are discussed--to suggest the varying marketing opportunities in different economies.

The vital role of marketing functions is discussed. It is emphasized that producers, consumers, *and* marketing specialists perform marketing functions. You will learn that responsibility for performing the marketing functions can be shifted and shared in a variety of ways, but that from a macro viewpoint all of the functions must be performed by someone. No function can be completely eliminated.

The main focus of *this chapter* is on macro-marketing--to give you a broad introduction. But the focus of *this text* is on management-oriented micro-marketing--beginning in Chapter 2.

Important Terms

marketing, p. 4
production, p. 4
utility, p. 6
form utility, p. 6
task utility, p. 6
possession utility, p. 6
time utility, p. 7
place utility, p. 7
micro-marketing, p. 9
macro-marketing, p. 11
economic system, p. 13
planned economic system, p. 13
market-directed economic system, p. 14
micro-macro dilemma, p. 15
pure subsistence economy, p. 13
market, p. 17
central markets, p. 17

middleman, p. 18
tariffs, p. 23
quotas, p. 23
countertrade, p. 23
economies of scale, p. 24
universal functions of marketing, p. 25
buying function, p. 26
selling function, p. 26
transporting function, p. 26
storing function, p. 26
standardization and grading, p. 26
financing, p. 26
risk taking, p. 26
market information function, p. 26
facilitators, p. 27
innovation, p. 29
marketing ethics, p. 29

True-False Questions

___ 1. According to the text, marketing means "selling" or "advertising."

___ 2. Production is a more important economic activity than marketing.

___ 3. Actually making goods or performing services is called marketing.

___ 4. Form and task utility are provided by production with the guidance of marketing.

___ 5. Marketing provides time, place, and possession utility.

___ 6. It is estimated that marketing costs about 50 percent of each consumer's dollar.

___ 7. Marketing is both a set of activities performed by organizations and a social process.

___ 8. Micro-marketing is the performance of activities that seek to accomplish an organization's objectives by anticipating customer or client needs and directing a flow of need-satisfying goods and services from producer to customer or client.

___ 9. Micro-marketing activities should be of no interest to a nonprofit organization.

___ 10. Macro-marketing is a set of activities that direct an economy's flow of goods and services from producers to consumers in a way which effectively matches supply and demand and accomplishes the objectives of society.

___ 11. Macro-marketing emphasizes how the whole system works, rather than the activities of individual organizations.

___ 12. Only market-directed societies need an economic system.

___ 13. In a market-directed economy, government planners decide what and how much is to be produced and distributed by whom, when, to whom, and why.

___ 14. In a market-directed economy, the prices of consumer goods and services serve roughly as a measure of their social importance.

___ 15. Sometimes micro-macro dilemmas arise because what is "good" for some producers and consumers may not be "good" for society as a whole.

___ 16. The Canadian economy is entirely market-directed.

___ 17. A pure subsistence economy is an economy in which each family unit produces everything it consumes.

___ 18. Marketing takes place whenever a person needs something of value.

___ 19. The term marketing comes from the word market--which is a group of potential customers with similar needs who are willing to exchange something of value with sellers offering various ways of satisfying those needs.

Learning aid for use with

___ 20. While central markets facilitate exchange, middlemen usually complicate exchange by increasing the total number of transactions required.

___ 21. More effective macro-marketing systems are the result of greater economic development.

___ 22. Without an effective macro-marketing system, the less-developed nations may be doomed to a "vicious circle of poverty."

___ 23. A nation in the first stage of economic development offers little or no market potential.

___ 24. An excellent market for imported consumer products exists among countries or regions which are experiencing the second (preindustrial or commercial) stage of economic development.

___ 25. When a nation reaches the primary manufacturing stage of economic development, it will begin to export a large portion of its domestic production of consumer products.

___ 26. Once a nation reaches the fourth stage of economic development, it will usually manufacture most of its consumer durables--such as autos and televisions.

___ 27. When a nation reaches the stage of capital equipment and consumer durable products manufacturing, industrialization has begun--but the economy still depends on exports of raw materials.

___ 28. A nation which reaches the sixth stage of economic development normally exports manufactured products which it specializes in producing.

___ 29. Tariffs are simply quotas on imported products.

___ 30. Quotas set the specific quantities of products that can move into or out of a country.

___ 31. When PepsiCo trades its Canadian made soft-drink concentrate for Russian vodka, it is using countertrade.

___ 32. "Economies of scale" means that as a company produces larger numbers of a particular product, the cost for each of these products goes down.

___ 33. Achieving effective marketing in an advanced economy is simplified by the fact that producers are separated from consumers in only two ways: time and space.

___ 34. The "universal functions of marketing" consist only of buying, selling, transporting, and storing.

___ 35. In a market-directed economy, marketing functions are performed by producers, consumers, and a variety of marketing specialists.

___ 36. Marketing facilitators are any firms which provide the marketing functions of buying and selling.

___ 37. Responsibility for performing the marketing functions can be shifted and shared in a variety of ways, but no function can be completely eliminated.

_ 38. Our market-directed macro-marketing system discourages the development and spread of new ideas and products.

_ 39. The moral standards that guide marketing decisions and actions are called marketing ethics.

Answers to True-False Questions

1. F, p. 5	14. T, p. 15	27. T, p. 21
2. F, p. 5	15. T, p. 15	28. T, p. 21
3. F, p. 4	16. F, p. 16	29. F, p. 23
4. T, p. 6	17. T, p. 17	30. T, p. 23
5. T, p. 6	18. F, p. 17	31. T, p. 23
6. T, p. 7	19. T, p. 17	32. T, p. 24
7. T, p. 8	20. F, p. 17	33. F, p. 25
8. T, p. 9	21. F, p. 19	34. F, p. 25
9. F, p. 9	22. T, p. 19	35. T, p. 27
10. F, p. 11	23. T, p. 20	36. F, pp. 27-28
11. T, p. 11	24. F, p. 20	37. T, p. 28
12. F, p. 13	25. F, p. 20	38. F, p. 29
13. F, pp. 14-15	26. F, p. 21	39. T, p. 29

Multiple-Choice Questions (Circle the correct response)

1. According to the text:
   a. marketing is much more than selling or advertising.
   b. the cost of marketing is about 25 percent of the consumer's dollar.
   c. production is a more essential economic activity than marketing.
   d. only marketing creates economic utility.
   e. all of the above are true statements.

2. When a "fruit peddler" drives his truck through residential neighborhoods and sells fruits and vegetables grown by farmers, he is creating:
   a. form utility.
   b. time and place utility.
   c. possession utility.
   d. all of the above.
   e. all of the above, *except* a.

3. Tam Furniture Stores recently purchased several rail carloads of dining room tables. The tables were distributed to their retail outlets in the Northeast, where they sold rapidly to customers. In this situation, Tam Furniture Stores created:
   a. both task and possession utility.
   b. both place and time utility.
   c. place, time, and possession utility.
   d. only place utility.
   e. both form and place utility.

Learning aid for use with

4. The text stresses that:
   a. advertising and selling are not really part of marketing.
   b. marketing is nothing more than a set of business activities performed by individual firms.
   c. marketing techniques have no application for nonprofit organizations.
   d. marketing is a social process and a set of activities performed by organizations.
   e. a good product usually sells itself.

5. *Micro*-marketing:
   a. is concerned with need-satisfying goods, but not with services.
   b. involves an attempt to anticipate customer or client needs.
   c. is primarily concerned with efficient use of resources and fair allocation of output.
   d. includes activities such as accounting, production, and financial management.
   e. is the process of selling and distributing manufactured goods.

6. *Macro*-marketing:
   a. is not concerned with the flow of goods and services from producers to consumers.
   b. seeks to match homogeneous supply capabilities with homogeneous demands for goods and services.
   c. refers to a set of activities performed by both profit and nonprofit organizations.
   d. focuses on the objectives of society.
   e. All of the above are true statements.

7. Which of the following statements about economic decision making is *true*?
   a. In a market-directed system, the micro-level decisions of individual producers and consumers determine the macro-level decisions.
   b. Government planning usually works best when economies become more complex and the variety of goods and services produced is fairly large.
   c. Canada may be considered a pure market-directed economy.
   d. Planned economic systems usually rely on market forces to determine prices.
   e. All of the above are true statements.

8. Which of the following is an example of the micro-macro dilemma?
   a. Sulfites help to keep restaurant salads looking fresh, but some people have a dangerous allergic reaction to sulfites.
   b. Your hair spray may hold your hair in place, but cause air pollution in the apartment you share with a roommate.
   c. Children like to ride bicycles, but accidents are common.
   d. All of the above.
   e. A and B, but not C.

9. Marketing cannot occur unless:
   a. an economy is market-directed rather than planned.
   b. producers and consumers can enter into face-to-face negotiations at some physical location.
   c. an economy has a money system.
   d. there are two or more parties who each have something of value they want to exchange for something else.
   e. middlemen are present to facilitate exchange.

10. The development of marketing middlemen:
    a. tends to make the exchange process more complicated, more costly, and harder to carry out.
    b. usually reduces the total number of transactions necessary to carry out exchange.
    c. tends to increase place utility but decrease time utility.
    d. becomes less advantageous as the number of producers and consumers, their distance apart, and the number and variety of products increase.
    e. All of the above are true statements.

11. In the "primary manufacturing" stage of economic development,
    a. almost all the people are above the "subsistence" level.
    b. there is strong demand to keep local manufacturers in business.
    c. the country no longer imports capital products and consumer durable products.
    d. the country begins to export manufactured products.
    e. there is some processing of raw materials that once were shipped out of the country in raw form.

12. What stage of economic development is a country in when small local manufacturing of products such as textiles has begun and the dependence on imports for nondurable products is declining?
    a. Capital equipment and consumer durable products manufacturing stage
    b. Exporting manufactured products stage
    c. Nondurable and semidurable consumer products manufacturing stage
    d. Commercial stage
    e. Primary manufacturing stage

13. A multinational manufacturer will usually find the biggest and most profitable foreign markets for its products in countries that are in which stage of economic development?
    a. Primary manufacturing
    b. Capital equipment and consumer durable products manufacturing
    c. Preindustrial or commercial
    d. Nondurable and semidurable consumer products manufacturing
    e. Exporting manufactured products

14. In advanced economies:
    a. mass production capability is a necessary and sufficient condition for satisfying consumer needs.
    b. exchange is simplified by discrepancies of quantity and assortment.
    c. the creation of time, place, and possession utilities tends to be easy.
    d. both supply and demand tend to be homogeneous in nature.
    e. exchange between producers and consumers is hampered by a separation of values and information.

15. Which of the following is *not* one of the "universal functions of marketing"?
    a. Production
    b. Standardization
    c. Financing
    d. Buying
    e. Transporting

16. Which of the following is a *true* statement?
    a. Since marketing is concerned with many thousands of different products, there is no one set of marketing functions that applies to all products.
    b. Responsibility for performing marketing functions can be shifted and shared, but no function can be completely eliminated.
    c. From a micro viewpoint, every firm must perform all of the marketing functions.
    d. Marketing functions should be performed only by marketing middlemen or facilitators.
    e. Many marketing functions are not necessary in planned economies.

Answers to Multiple-Choice Questions

1. a, p. 4
2. e, pp. 6-7
3. c, pp. 6-7
4. d, p. 8
5. b, p. 9
6. d, p. 11

7. a, pp. 14-15
8. d, p. 15
9. d, p. 17
10. b, p. 18
11. e, p. 20
12. c, p. 21

13. e, p. 21
14. e, p. 25
15. a, pp. 25-26
16. b, p. 28

Exercise 1-1

What is marketing?

Introduction

Society ignored or even criticized the contributions of marketing until the beginning of the 20th century. At that time, economies once marked by a scarcity of goods began to enjoy an abundance of goods. Marketing skills were needed to solve the distribution problems that resulted. Thus, it was not until the early 1900s that the importance of marketing was realized--and that marketing was accepted as a separate academic subject in schools and colleges.

Today, countries that operate with market-directed economies have achieved genuine improvements in standards of living--while many planned economies have collapsed or are "on the ropes." Even today, however, many people do not have a very clear understanding of marketing. No one single definition of marketing will satisfy everyone. Many people--including some students and business managers--tend to think of marketing as just "selling" or "advertising." Others see marketing as an all-inclusive social process that can solve all the world's problems. Some critics, meanwhile, seem to blame marketing for most of society's ills!

This exercise is intended to help you see more clearly what marketing is all about. One way to learn about marketing is to study the definitions in the text. Another way is to use these definitions. This is the approach you will follow in this exercise.

Assignment

Listed below are some commonly asked questions about marketing. Answer each of these questions in a way which shows your understanding of marketing.

1.   What activities does marketing involve besides selling?

Learning aid for use with

2.   How would you respond to the criticism "Marketing just adds unnecessary costs to the price of everything we buy"?

3.   Is marketing useful for nonprofit organizations? Explain.

4.   Why do we need middlemen? Don't they just add to the cost of distributing products to consumers?

5.   How do consumers in a market-directed economy influence what products will be produced and by whom?

6.   Why is effective marketing needed in an advanced economy? Isn't mass production--with its economies of scale--the real key to meeting consumer needs at the lowest cost?

Question for Discussion

Should marketing be viewed as a set of activities performed by business and nonprofit organizations, or alternately as a social process? Why is it important to make this distinction?

Exercise 1-2

How marketing functions create economic utility

Introduction

Marketing has been defined as the "creation and delivery of a standard of living." In economic terms, marketing contributes to the consumer welfare through the creation of three of the five basic kinds of economic utility--*time*, *place*, and *possession* utility. Further, marketing may also guide development of *form* and *task* utility.

The marketing process does not take place automatically. It requires that certain marketing functions or activities be performed by various marketing institutions--and by *consumers* themselves. The following eight functions are essential to the marketing of all goods: buying, selling, transporting, storing, standardization and grading, financing, risk-taking, and market information. No matter how simple or complex the marketing process is these functions must be performed. Some functions may be performed several times to facilitate the marketing of a given product, while others may be performed only once. At times, the performance of a function may be shifted from one member of a marketing system to another. For example, some modern wholesalers and retailers shift the burden of storing goods back to manufacturers. But, the fact remains that each of the eight functions must be performed by someone at least once before any good can be marketed—none can be eliminated.

Assignment

This assignment illustrates how the performance of marketing functions creates economic utility. Read the following case carefully and then answer the questions that follow in the space provided.

RICARDO'S RIVERSIDE DELI

Tom and Anne Malthus are a young couple who work in Montreal and live in a small apartment downtown. They shop for most of their food—including meat—at Ricardo's Riverside Deli, a small grocery store located near their apartment. The Malthuses inspect the packages of meat and select the amount and type of meat they want for their meals that week. They have always been happy with the quality and selection of meat at Ricardo's—and they like the store's "satisfaction or your money back" guarantee.

The Riverside Deli is too small to have a full butcher department and meat freezer. Instead, the owner, Dave Ricardo, buys fresh meat from Meat Distribution Co., a wholesale butcher. The wholesaler keeps a large quantity of bulk meat in cold storage--and then cuts grade-A stew beef, steaks, roasts, hamburger, and other selections to fill orders from the Riverside Deli and its other grocery store customers. The wholesaler delivers the meat to Ricardo each morning before the store opens. At the end of the month the wholesaler bills Riverside Deli for its purchases.

This arrangement seems to work well. Although Ricardo doesn't keep computerized records, he knows his customers' preferences and he orders carefully. He knows that steaks sell well when the weather allows even apartment dwellers to barbecue on their balconies, but he cuts back on big steaks as soon as cold weather hits. He packages the meat in convenient serving sizes and makes up more small packages than most grocery stores because many apartment dwellers live alone. With a day or two's notice, he can also handle special requests. As a result, Ricardo's Riverside Deli can offer a selection that meets most customers' needs. If Ricardo orders too much of a certain type of meat and it has not sold within a few days, he marks down the price--to prompt a quicker sale.

Based on your analysis of this description, answer the following questions.

1. Does the Riverside Deli help to resolve discrepancies of quantity between food producers and consumers? Briefly explain your answer.

    _____

    _____

    _____

2. What kind(s) of economic utility is created by Ricardo's Riverside Deli for its customers?

    _____

    _____

    _____

3. The eight basic marketing functions are listed below. Check Yes or No whether each function is performed by someone in this description. If "Yes," explain *when* and *by whom* each function was performed. If "No," explain why not.

    a) Buying: Yes _____ No _____ Explain.

    _____

    _____

    _____

    b) Selling: Yes _____ No _____ Explain.

    _____

    _____

    _____

c)   Transporting: Yes _____ No _____ Explain.

_____

_____

_____

d)   Storing: Yes _____ No _____ Explain.

_____

_____

_____

e)   Grading: Yes _____ No _____ Explain.

_____

_____

_____

f)   Financing: Yes _____ No _____ Explain.

_____

_____

_____

g)   Risk-taking: Yes _____ No _____ Explain.

_____

_____

_____

h)   Market information: Yes _____ No _____ Explain.

_____

_____

_____

Like most young couples, Tom and Anne Malthus are always interested in ways to make their budget stretch further. An article in the Sunday newspaper on cutting grocery costs suggests buying meat directly from downtown wholesalers. According to the article, some meat wholesalers will sell direct to consumers—if the consumer buys a whole side of beef. The article described it this way: The customer calls the meat company and agrees on a price and time to pick up the purchase. The meat packing plant then cuts the side of beef into large pieces and wraps them in freezer paper. The wholesaler requires customers to pay with cash when they pick up the meat. The newspaper article says that on a per pound basis the price is about 25 percent cheaper that the same selection of meat would be at a grocery store.

4.   If the Malthuses were to buy meat directly from the wholesaler, they would probably need to perform some of the basic marketing functions themselves. Each of the basic marketing functions is listed below. For each function, check Yes or No to indicate if the Malthuses would need to perform this function. In addition, briefly explain any difficulties you think they might face in trying to perform the function.

a)   Buying: Yes _____ No _____ Explain:

_____

_____

_____

b)   Selling: Yes _____ No _____ Explain:

_____

_____

_____

c)   Transporting: Yes _____ No _____ Explain:

_____

_____

_____

d)   Storing: Yes _____ No _____ Explain:

_____

_____

_____

e)   Standardization and Grading: Yes ___ No ___ Explain:

_____

_____

_____

f) Financing: Yes _____ No _____ Explain:

_____

_____

_____

g) Risk-taking: Yes _____ No _____ Explain:

_____

_____

_____

h) Market information: Yes _____ No _____ Explain:

_____

_____

_____

Question for Discussion

Name a product for which all eight marketing functions do *not* need to be performed by someone somewhere in the marketing system.

Exercise 1-3

Ethical challenges in marketing

Introduction

Marketing managers face many challenges--including difficult decisions in areas of social responsibility and ethics. Some guidelines in these areas are provided by the laws of our society. Clearly, a marketing manager must know and obey laws that govern marketing actions. But, there are many decision areas in marketing where laws do not exist, and where the question of what is "right" or "wrong" is not so clear-cut. Usually, these are decision areas where the marketing manager must deal with trade-offs or conflicts--situations where what is good for some customers, stockholders, employees, other channel members, or society in general is not good for someone else. These are situations where the marketing manager must weigh all of the facts--and make a personal judgment about what to do.

Throughout the text, you will be alerted to many of the decision areas where a marketing manager must be sensitive to ethical decisions. This exercise provides an opportunity for you to start thinking about some of these issues. Later in the course you may want to look at your answers again--to see if you've changed your mind about any of them.

Assignment

Listed below are short descriptions of situations which *might* be classified as "ethical" dilemmas. For each situation, identify which person or group has the ethical dilemma and state what action you would recommend in their position--and why. Be sure to write down any assumptions you are making. Keep in mind that different people might have a very different reaction to what is a "correct" or "incorrect" answer for most of the situations in this exercise. So, the objective is for you to analyze the situation-- and think about what *you* would do.

1.   Connor Peale has been shopping for a new sofa for his living room and is very impressed with the price quoted by Good Furniture Co. for a brand-name sofa he has seen advertised in a decorating magazine. Good Furniture Co. is able to offer customers deeply discounted prices on brand-name furniture because it sells by phone. It has no warehouse or showroom and has eliminated those costs. Instead, telephone orders are passed along to manufacturers who ship furniture directly to consumers by contract truck carriers. Although the price is good, Mr. Peale is reluctant to order the sofa because it might not be as comfortable as it looks. To help close the sale, the Good Furniture telephone salesman tells Mr. Peale the name of a retailer in Peale's area that carries the same sofa--and suggests "Why don't you go over there and try the sofa and then call me back to order it if it's what you want."

Recommendation (and reason):

2. A large retail chain is considering opening a store in a small city. The chain's low prices will almost certainly drive many of the existing local retailers out of business. They simply can't buy in large enough quantities to be cost competitive. There are equally profitable opportunities for new stores in other, more competitive markets. On the other hand, if the chain does not move into the small city it is likely that sooner or later some other competitor will--and the market is not large enough for two chains.

    Recommendation (and reason):

3. Jim Shue is very flattered to be invited for a second round of interviews for a job as assistant marketing manager with Capital Construction Company. As a new graduate, he's eager to get a position with Capital, which has done well developing new designs for houses aimed at the "executive" market. Shue has some background in the business because he has worked each summer as a junior salesman for similar housing developments run by his uncle's company. In fact, on several occasions he has been in direct competition with Capital to sell customers a home. The managers at Capital Construction know about his family connection and Shue has told them that he wants to be hired on his own merits. In the last interview of the day, the president of Capital asks Shue: "So what do you think are going to be the "hot" trends in high-end homes this coming year?" Shue thinks that this is a great opportunity to demonstrate his knowledge, but also worries that the whole interview process may be part of an effort to get inside information about his uncle's marketing plans.

    Recommendation (and reason):

4. A company that sells airplanes to foreign governments is working on an important sale in a developing nation. The company's local agent middleman in the country has explained that competitor firms from other countries are paying influential local citizens to serve as "consultants." The agent has pointed out that "this is how business is done here--it's who you know that counts. Without consultants, someone else will definitely get the business." The agent has asked for $50,000 to hire consultants. As director of international sales, Bill Smith worries that some of the money paid to consultants might be used to bribe the foreign government officials involved in the purchase. On the other hand, he believes that the company will lose out on the sale if it does not have the help of the local consultants who know how decisions will be made--and by whom.

Recommendation (and reason):

5.	A company that sells bottled "pure mineral water" has just found that a problem in its filtering process has resulted in trace amounts of chemicals in some of the bottles it has already shipped. The small levels of chemicals involved are not a health hazard, and no law has been violated. Further, it is very unlikely that anyone else would detect the problem. On the other hand, the company has always promoted its product as "pure and of the highest quality." The only way to correct the problem is to recall all of the bottles that are already in retailer and wholesaler inventories--which would be very costly and also generate bad publicity in a very competitive market. What should the company do?

Recommendation (and reason):

6.	Two different advertising agencies were doing the advertising planning work for two competing computer manufacturers—Euro Computers and Maple-Leaf Computing. However, the larger of the two advertising agencies, Worldwide Advertising recently bought out the other agency. The acquired agency had been doing the work for Maple-Leaf Computing. The president of the newly merged agency wrote a letter to the marketing manager at Maple-Leaf and said "Because there may be the appearance of a conflict of interest in our handling both your account and Euro Computers the most ethical thing for us to do is resign from your account." The marketing manager at Maple-Leaf immediately telephoned to say: "Ethical? You're going to leave me high and dry looking for a new agency and in the meantime all the people who used to work on my account will be telling Euro Computers the details about my marketing plans."

Recommendation (and reason):

7.	Physicians at University Hospital were awarded a very large contract to conduct research on the weight-loss effects of a diet supplement. Because the doctors are on the staff of the medical school, all the money from the study goes to a special fund to provide scholarships for needy medical students. When the physicians agreed to the contract, they were pretty sure that sooner or later they'd see their results in an advertisement which would begin: "Doctors at a major research hospital proved that significant weight-loss . . ." So, they were especially careful in their research and set up a controlled study in which the researchers did not know which patients were taking the supplement and which weren't. The results were clear-cut and showed that most patients taking the supplement lost more than 10 pounds during the study. In the final report, the researchers noted that almost all of the patients regained their excess weight when they stopped using the supplement. However, advertisements for the supplement do not mention the weight regain.

Recommendation (and reason):

8.   Industrial Products Company has for many years made strong rubber tie-down straps. The straps are very useful for securing loads on large commercial trucks and they are sold directly to large trucking companies and through cash-and-carry wholesalers to smaller firms. Last summer, sales of the straps picked up suddenly and Industrial Products found from newspaper articles that they were being used by inner-city youths for a game of "bungee jumping" from overpasses and railroad bridges. Concerned about the possibility of being held liable if any accidents occurred, Industrial Products sent a memo to all its customers asking them not to sell the straps to youngsters and the president of the company appeared on TV interview shows expressing his disapproval of using the tie-down straps for anything other than securing loads on trucks. The media attention has only heightened the craze and an influential consumer rights group has written to Industrial Products to ask them to withdraw the tie-down straps from the market.

Recommendation (and reason):

Question for Discussion

Are the ethical challenges faced by a marketing manager any different--in a basic way--than the challenges faced by businesspeople in other types of jobs? Why or why not?

Chapter 2

Marketing's role within the firm or nonprofit organization

What This Chapter Is About

Chapter 2 shows how important micro-marketing can be within a business firm or a nonprofit organization. In particular, the "marketing concept" and the evolution of firms from a production to a marketing orientation is explained. Then, the importance of understanding the difference between a production orientation and a marketing orientation is discussed. The differences between for-profit and nonprofit organizations are also included.

The nature of the marketing management process is introduced--and the importance of marketing strategy planning is explained. The four Ps--Product, Price, Place, and Promotion--are introduced as the controllable elements which the marketing manager blends into a marketing mix to satisfy a particular target market. It is very important for you to understand the four Ps--because planning the four Ps is the major concern of the rest of the text.

This chapter gives a very necessary overview to what is coming. Study it carefully so you can understand how the material in the following chapters will fit together.

Important Terms

simple trade era, p. 35
production era, p. 36
sales era, p. 36
marketing department era, p. 36
marketing company era, p. 36
marketing concept, p. 37
production orientation, p. 37
marketing orientation, p. 37
social responsibility, p. 44
marketing management process, p. 47
strategic (management) planning, p. 48
marketing strategy, p. 48
target market, p. 48

marketing mix, p. 48
target marketing, p. 48
mass marketing, p. 49
channel of distribution, p. 57
personal selling, p. 51
mass selling, p. 51
advertising, p. 51
publicity, p. 51
sales promotion, p. 52
marketing plan, p. 54
implementation, p. 54
operational decisions, p. 54
marketing program, p. 55

True-False Questions

___ 1. The simple trade era was a time when families traded or sold their "surplus" output to local middlemen who resold these goods to other consumers or distant middlemen.

___ 2. Marketing departments are usually formed when firms go from the "production era" to the "sales era."

3. A company has moved into the "marketing company era" when, in addition to short-run marketing planning, the total company effort is guided by the marketing concept.

4. The marketing concept says that a firm should aim all its efforts at satisfying customers, even if this proves to be unprofitable.

5. The term "marketing orientation" means making products which are easy to produce and then trying to sell them.

6. The three basic ideas included in the definition of the marketing concept are: a customer orientation, a total company effort, and sales as an objective.

7. There are no functional departments in a firm that has adopted the marketing concept.

8. The marketing concept was very quickly accepted, especially among producers of industrial commodities like steel and pipe.

9. In the 1980s, service industries adopted the marketing concept more and more.

10. Because they don't try to earn a profit, the marketing concept is not very useful for nonprofit organizations.

11. A nonprofit organization does not measure profit in the same way as a firm.

12. A firm's obligation to improve its positive effects on society and reduce its negative effects is called fiscal responsibility.

13. The marketing management process consists of (1) planning marketing activities, (2) directing the implementation of the plans, and (3) controlling these plans.

14. Strategic (management) planning is a managerial process of developing and maintaining a match between the resources of the production department and its product opportunities.

15. Marketing strategy planning is the process of deciding how best to sell the products the firm produces.

16. A marketing strategy specifies a target market and a related marketing mix.

17. A target market consists of a group of consumers who are usually quite different.

18. A marketing mix consists of the uncontrollable variables which a company puts together to satisfy a target market.

19. Target marketing aims a marketing mix at some specific target customers.

20. The mass marketing approach is more production-oriented than marketing-oriented.

21. The terms "mass marketing" and "mass marketer" mean the same thing.

22. The problem with target marketing is that it limits the firm to small market segments.

23. The four "Ps" are: Product, Promotion, Price, and Personnel.

_ 24. The customer should not be considered part of a "marketing mix."

_ 25. The Product area is concerned with developing the right physical good, service, or blend of both for the target market.

_ 26. A channel of distribution must include several kinds of middlemen and specialists.

_ 27. Personal selling and advertising are both forms of sales promotion.

_ 28. Price is the most important of the four Ps.

_ 29. The marketing mix should be set before the best target market is selected.

_ 30. A marketing plan and a marketing strategy mean the same thing.

_ 31. Implementation means putting the marketing plan into operation.

_ 32. Short-run decisions that stay within the overall guidelines set during strategy planning are called implementation decisions.

_ 33. A marketing program may consist of several marketing plans.

_ 34. An extremely good marketing plan may be carried out badly and still be profitable, while a poor but well-implemented plan can lose money.

_ 35. The watch industry has become much more marketing-oriented.

_ 36. Well-planned marketing strategies usually can ignore the marketing environment variables.

Answers to True-False Questions

1. T, p. 35	13. T, p. 47	25. T, p. 50
2. F, p. 36	14. F, p. 48	26. F, p. 51
3. T, p. 36	15. F, p. 48	27. F, p. 51
4. F, p. 37	16. T, p. 48	28. F, p. 52
5. F, p. 37	17. F, p. 48	29. F, p. 53
6. F, p. 37	18. F, p. 48	30. F, p. 54
7. F, p. 37	19. T, p. 48	31. T, p. 54
8. F, p. 40	20. T, p. 49	32. F, p. 54
9. T, p. 40	21. F, p. 49	33. T, p. 55
10. F, p. 42	22. F, p. 49	34. T, p. 56
11. T, p. 42	23. F, p. 49	35. T, p. 58
12. F, p. 44	24. T, p. 50	36. F, p. 60

Multiple-Choice Questions (Circle the correct response)

1. A firm that focuses its attention primarily on "selling" its present products in order to meet or beat competition is operating in which of the following "management eras"?
   a. Production era
   b. Sales era
   c. Marketing department era
   d. Marketing company era
   e. Advertising era

2. Based on the following company statements, which company is most likely to be in the marketing company era?
   a. "Our sales force was able to sell middlemen more of our new product than they can resell in all of this year."
   b. "Our marketing manager is coordinating pricing, product decisions, promotion and distribution to help us show a profit at the end of this year."
   c. "The whole company is in good shape--demand exceeds what we can produce."
   d. "Our long range plan--developed by our marketing manager--is to expand so that we can profitably meet the long-term needs of our customers."
   e. "Our new President previously led our marketing effort as Vice President of Sales."

3. Which of the following best explains what the "marketing concept" means:
   a. Firms should spend more money on marketing than they have in the past.
   b. A firm's main emphasis should be on the efficient utilization of its resources.
   c. All of a firm's activities and resources should be organized to satisfy the needs of its customers--at a profit.
   d. A company's chief executive should previously have been a marketing manager.
   e. A firm should always attempt to give customers what they need regardless of the cost involved.

4. The difference between "production orientation" and "marketing orientation" is best explained as follows:
   a. there are no separate functional departments in a marketing-oriented firm.
   b. in a marketing-oriented firm, the total system's effort is guided by what individual departments would like to do.
   c. production-oriented firms usually do not have a marketing manager.
   d. in a marketing-oriented firm, every department's activities are guided by what customers need and what the firm can deliver at a profit.
   e. all major decisions are based on extensive marketing research studies in marketing-oriented firms.

5. Which of the following statements about nonprofits is *false*?
   a. Marketing is being more widely accepted by nonprofit organizations.
   b. The marketing concept is as important for nonprofit organizations as it is for business firms.
   c. In business firms and in nonprofit organizations, support comes from satisfied customers.
   d. A nonprofit organization does not measure profit in the same way as a firm.
   e. The marketing concept provides focus in both business firms and nonprofit organizations.

6. Which of the following is one of three basic marketing management jobs?
    a. To direct the implementation of plans
    b. To control the plans in actual operation
    c. To plan marketing activities
    d. All of the above

7. The marketing management process:
    a. includes the on-going job of planning marketing activities.
    b. is mainly concerned with obtaining continuous customer feedback.
    c. involves finding opportunities and planning marketing strategies, but does not include the management tasks of implementing and control.
    d. is called "strategic planning."
    e. Both a and d are true statements.

8. A marketing strategy consists of two interrelated parts. These are:
    a. selection of a target market and implementing the plan.
    b. selection of a target market and development of a marketing mix.
    c. selection and development of a marketing mix.
    d. finding attractive opportunities and developing a marketing mix.
    e. finding attractive opportunities and selecting a target market.

9. Marketing strategy planners should recognize that:
    a. target markets should not be large and spread out.
    b. mass marketing is often very effective and desirable.
    c. firms like General Electric, Eaton's and Procter & Gamble are too large to aim at clearly defined markets.
    d. target marketing is not limited to small market segments.
    e. the terms "mass marketing" and "mass marketers" mean essentially the same thing.

10. A marketing mix consists of:
    a. policies, procedures, plans, and personnel.
    b. the customer and the "four Ps."
    c. all variables, controllable and uncontrollable.
    d. product, price, promotion, and place.
    e. none of the above.

11. Which of the following statements about marketing mix variables is *false*?
    a. "Promotion" includes personal selling, mass selling, and sales promotion.
    b. The term "Product" refers to services as well as physical goods.
    c. A channel of distribution does not have to include any middlemen.
    d. Generally speaking, "Price" is more important than "Place."
    e. The needs of a target market virtually determine the nature of an appropriate marketing mix.

12. A "marketing plan":
    a. is just another term for "marketing strategy."
    b. consists of several "marketing programs."
    c. includes the time-related details for carrying out a marketing strategy.
    d. is a strategy without all the operational decisions.
    e. ignores implementation and control details.

13. Which of the following statements about operational decisions is FALSE?
    a. They sometimes take up a good part of an advertising manager's time.
    b. They are made regularly, sometimes on a daily basis.
    c. They usually require ongoing changes in the basic strategy to be effective.
    d. They sometimes take up a good part of a sales manager's time.
    e. They help to carry out a marketing strategy.

14. A "marketing program":
    a. is another name for a particular marketing mix.
    b. blends several different marketing plans.
    c. consists of a target market and the marketing mix.
    d. is primarily concerned with all of the details of implementing a marketing plan.
    e. must be set before a target market can be selected.

15. The watch industry example in the text serves to illustrate that:
    a. good implementation and control is usually more important than good planning.
    b. there are a limited number of potential target markets.
    c. an effective marketing strategy guarantees future success.
    d. consumers want only high-quality products.
    e. creative strategy planning is needed for survival.

Answers to Multiple-Choice Questions

1. b, p. 36	6. d, p. 47	11. d, p. 52
2. d, p. 36	7. a, p. 47	12. c, p. 54
3. c, p. 37	8. b, p. 48	13. c, p. 54
4. d, p. 37	9. d, p. 49	14. b, p. 55
5. c, p. 42	10. d, p. 49	15. e, p. 58

Exercise 2-1

Marketing-oriented vs. production-oriented firms

Introduction

Business firms can be classified as either "production-oriented" or "marketing-oriented," depending on whether they have adopted the "marketing concept." The marketing concept is a modern philosophy which simply states that a firm should aim all its efforts at satisfying its customers--at a profit. This philosophy implies a total management commitment to (1) a customer orientation, (2) a total company effort, and (3) profit, not just sales, as an objective of the firm. The same idea applies to nonprofits, but some measure of long-term success other than profit may serve as an objective.

In general, a production-oriented organization tries to get customers to buy what the firm has produced, while a marketing-oriented firm tries to produce and sell what customers need. Actually, the terms "production-oriented" and "marketing-oriented" should be viewed as opposite ends of a continuum along which different firms could be placed. But it is often useful to classify a firm as being *mainly* production- or marketing-oriented.

In practice, however, there is no simple way of identifying the two types of firms. Instead, one must look for subtle "clues" to help decide whether a firm is production-oriented or marketing-oriented. These clues can take many forms, such as the attitudes of management toward customers, the firm's organization structure, and its methods and procedures.

Assignment

This exercise gives you some practice in identifying production-oriented and marketing-oriented firms. You will be given pairs of firms--and a "clue" about each firm. On the basis of these clues, you must decide which one of the two firms is more marketing-oriented and which is more production-oriented.

For each pair of firms, print an *M* before the firm that you think is marketing-oriented and a *P* before the firm that is production-oriented--and then briefly explain your answers. (Note: each set should have an *M* and a *P*--you *must* make a choice.) The first pair is answered for you as an example.

Orientation		Clues

1. _P_   Firm A: "Our goal is to run at full capacity and sell everything that we make."

    _M_   Firm B: "Our goal is to build customer loyalty by designing products that they want to buy."

Firm A is interested in "doing its own thing," while Firm B has focused its efforts on producing what customers want and need.

2. ___   **Firm A:**   "How much money will we save if we wait a year before buying an additional delivery truck?"

   ___   **Firm B:**   "How much will it improve our customer service if we buy an additional delivery truck?"

3. ___   **Firm A:**   "As sales manager, my job is to hire salespeople who can "move" as many units as we can produce. After all, the higher the sales, the higher the profits."

   ___   **Firm B:**   "As finance manager, my job is to determine how many units it will be profitable for us to sell at the price customers are willing to pay."

4. ___   **Firm A:**   "What competitive advantage would the proposed new product have in satisfying consumer needs?"

   ___   **Firm B:**   "Our competitor's new product is a great idea. Let's see if we can produce and sell it at a lower price."

5. ___   **Firm A:**   "Our sales are too low. Perhaps we could use our most persuasive salespeople to recruit some new middlemen."

   ___   **Firm B:**   "Our sales have dropped. Let's ask our middlemen why customers have stopped buying our product."

6. ___   **Firm A:**   "Sure our inventory costs are high. But how many customers would we lose if we were frequently unable to fill orders immediately?"

   ___   **Firm B:**   "Our inventory costs are too high. We'll have to reduce our inventory, even if it means that it will take customers longer to get their orders."

7. ___   **Firm A:**   "People today want the convenience of one-stop shopping and we've got to go where the customers are. It will cost us more to construct a building in the shopping center, but we'll attract more regular customers and that's the key to profit for a bank."

     ___   **Firm B:**   "It would cost us too much to build a bank in the shopping center. We'll locate our bank a few blocks away where the land is cheaper. We can depend on our low prices and good selection to bring the customers to us."

8. ___   **Firm A:**   "Our sales have nearly doubled since the advertising manager was promoted to president. He's tripled the amount we spend on advertising and personal selling, and he's told the accountants to stick to their balancing the books and leave the marketing budget to him."

     ___   **Firm B:**   "It helps to have an accountant as president. When he took over the company, he found that it was too expensive for a salesperson to visit many of our smaller customers, and now our sales force concentrates its efforts on satisfying those larger accounts that contribute the most to our profits."

9. ___   **Firm A:**   "Our profits have been declining. Perhaps we should search for ways to cut costs and make more efficient use of our resources."

     ___   **Firm B:**   "Our profits have been declining. Perhaps we should search for new opportunities to satisfy unfulfilled needs."

10. ___   **Firm A:**   "We're getting killed by overseas competitors. We need to improve our quality control and do a better job of meeting customers' expectations."

     ___   **Firm B:**   "Overseas producers compete unfairly with cheap labor. We need to have our public relations department lobby for tighter import quotas so that we can make a profit."

11. ___   Firm A: "We've given the people in this city one of the finest symphony orchestras in the world, but hardly anyone attends the concerts. It's a case of misplaced social values--and something must be done about it."

___   Firm B: "We've got to find out what it is about our concert series that turns people away. It's a case of needing to do a better job of meeting people's needs-- rather than sitting back and waiting for people to see the light."

Question for Discussion

If, as the text emphasizes, it is so important that firms be marketing-oriented, how is it that many production-oriented firms are not only surviving but apparently operating profitably?

Exercise 2-2

Mass marketing vs. target marketing

Introduction

A marketing manager's planning job is to find attractive market opportunities and develop effective marketing strategies. A "marketing strategy" consists of two interrelated parts: (1) a *target market*--a fairly homogeneous group of customers to whom a company wishes to appeal, and (2) a *marketing mix*--the controllable variables which the company puts together to satisfy this target group.

Here, it is important to see the difference between *mass marketing* and *target marketing* in planning marketing strategies.

Production-oriented firms typically assume that everyone's needs are the same. They try to build universal appeals into a marketing mix which--it is hoped--will attract "everyone." This approach we will call "mass marketing." Marketing-oriented firms, on the other hand, recognize that different customers usually have different needs--so they try to satisfy the needs of some particular group of customers--whose needs are fairly similar--rather than trying to appeal to everyone. This "target marketing" approach--a logical application of the marketing concept--simply means that a marketing strategy should aim at *some* target market.

Assignment

This exercise is designed to illustrate the difference between mass marketing and target marketing. Read each of the following cases carefully, and then (1) indicate in the space provided whether each firm is following a mass-marketing or a target-marketing approach and (2) briefly explain your answers.

1. Consumers may eventually enjoy "personalized" cable TV channels—with shows that are tailored to each individual viewer's interests in both entertainment and advertising content. By combining detailed survey information about respondents with Can/Stat Inc.'s computerized cable switching system, producers of news, comedy, and other types of shows may be able to combine them into personalized broadcasts. Every show and ad in these personalized broadcasts will appeal to each reader's self-identified interests. Thus, people who drink beer will see shows with beer ads, but non-beer drinkers never will. And antique collectors can look forward to special shows on antiques, while bicycle racers can look forward to documentaries about the sport. But because of equipment limitations, for the next four or five years the "personalized" broadcasts will be limited to markets with no more than 300,000-500,000 potential viewers.

   a) Mass marketing _____ Target marketing _____

   b) Comments: _____

   _____

   _____

   _____

   _____

   _____

   _____

2. Technology Design Corporation has just introduced a new product called the "Ultra Chaise Lounge," which is being promoted as the "ultimate in lawn and patio furniture." According to David Robinson, the company president, the Ultra Chaise Lounge is "absolutely guaranteed to be rust-proof, mildew-proof, and weatherproof." Moreover, "it features revolutionary new materials and a design that makes it the most comfortable folding chaise lounge on the market." Available in several models ranging in price from $30 to $55, the "Ultra Chaise Lounge" is expected to sell "in the millions." "This product is so superior," says Mac Williams, "that no household in North America will want to be without one."

   a) Mass marketing _____ Target marketing _____

   b) Comments: _____

   _____

   _____

   _____

   _____

   _____

3. Maria Costana recently retired after 20 years of service as a chef for a luxury cruise line. During her career, she worked on ships that took her to almost every part of the world. In the process, she learned to prepare the favorite dishes of many different countries. Maria and her husband-- also an outstanding cook--have decided to use their savings to open an "ethnic" restaurant, but with a difference. Each week they will feature the cuisine of a different region. Maria is sure that their restaurant will be an outstanding success. "We want to be a destination restaurant," she says, "a place where adventurous folks want to come for special meals and service to celebration special occasions. Our prices won't be cheap, but that will help us afford special promotional mailings to the upscale professionals who live within driving distance of the restaurant."

a) Mass marketing _____ Target marketing _____

b) Comments: _____

   _____

   _____

   _____

   _____

   _____

   _____

4. Precision Product Corporation, one of the world's largest producers of keyboards for personal computers, recently introduced a new keyboard design under its "Excel" label. The premium-priced keyboard includes all of the keys found on a typical keyboard, but there is an extra set of special function keys. These keys can be programmed to "remember" a series of key strokes—so that pressing one key executes a complicated series of key strokes. The special function keys will be especially attractive to business analysts, engineers, and others who regularly use the very popular LOTUS 1-2-3 spreadsheet software—since it will make it easier and faster to set up and run analyses. Tests also show that it takes a new computer-user less time to learn to use LOTUS with the new keyboard. The company estimates that within two years 10 percent of current business users of LOTUS will buy the product—because of the productivity savings. The company is working on a new model that offers similar advantages to users of desktop publishing software—one of the fastest growing applications of personal computers.

a) Mass marketing _____ Target marketing _____

b) Comments: _____

   _____

   _____

   _____

Question for Discussion

A marketing strategy should aim at some target market. But does "target marketing" guarantee that a firm's marketing strategy will be successful?

Exercise 2-3

Developing a unique marketing mix
for each target market

Introduction

Developing a marketing strategy consists of two *interrelated* tasks: (1) selecting a target market and (2) developing the best marketing mix for that target market.

Marketing-oriented firms recognize that not all potential customers have the same needs. Thus, rather than first developing a marketing mix and *then* looking for a market to sell that mix to, marketing-oriented firms first try to determine what kind of mix each possible target market may require. Then they select a target market based on their ability to offer a good marketing mix at a profit.

Assignment

This exercise assumes that different groups of customers in a general market area may have different needs--and therefore may require different marketing mixes. Three possible target markets and alternative marketing mixes are described below for each of four different product types. For each product type, select the marketing mix which would be best for each target market. (*All alternatives must be used, i.e., you cannot use one alternative for two target markets.*) Indicate your selection by writing the letter of the marketing mix in front of the target market you select.

Note: To make it easier for you, each target market consists of only one individual or family, but it should be clear that each individual or family really represents a larger group of potential customers who have similar needs.

1. Product type: Automobile

Possible Target Markets

___ (1) Middle-aged couple with two children who have just purchased a mountain cabin for use as a family "retreat."

___ (2) A manager of a real estate firm who uses his company car to show clients the community--and convey a successful business image.

___ (3) A student who needs a car to commute to the college campus--and to work a paper route.

Alternative Marketing Mixes

(a) A five-year-old, "for sale by owner" Honda Civic listed in the classified ads of a local newspaper.

(b) A Buick Park Avenue with luxury features--on a one-year lease from the Buick dealer in a nearby city.

(c) A Ford Explorer purchased with financing arranged by the salesman at a local car dealer--and backed with an extended service warranty.

2. Product type: Food

Possible Target Markets

___ (1) Airline pilot who has just arrived from an out-of-town flight at 8:30 p.m.

___ (2) Middle-aged low-income housewife concerned with feeding her large family a well-balanced meal, while operating on a tight budget.

___ (3) Young mother who has spent the day at the office and has to rush to get her children dinner before going to a business dinner.

Alternative Marketing Mixes

(a) A large, hamburger pizza and some soft drinks delivered to the house--purchased at "2.00 off the regular price" with a coupon from an insert in the newspaper.

(b) Nationally advertised brand of frozen "gourmet" dinner on display in the frozen-food case of a "7-Eleven" convenience food store.

(c) "Market basket" of perishables and canned goods purchased at a large supermarket that advertises "low everyday prices."

3.   Product type: Computer

Possible Target Markets

___ (1)   Young working couple who want their child to learn about computers by using educational game programs.

___ (2)   Sales rep who wants to keep records of his sales calls and prepare short reports for the home office while he travels.

___ (3)   A local Savings and Loan that has to constantly update deposit and withdrawal information--and prepare a variety of company records and reports.

Alternative Marketing Mixes

(a)   A portable laptop computer from Dell with pre-loaded software--sold with an "on-site or on-the-road" service agreement.

(b)   Powerful mini-computer leased from a manufacturer--such as Digital Equipment--that uses knowledgeable salespeople to help the customer decide on the right equipment.

(c)   Inexpensive Packard Bell computer sold by a mass-merchandiser that advertises its discount prices.

4.   Product type: Clothing for Vacations

Possible Target Markets

___ (1)   Wealthy couple planning to go on a winter cruise in the Mediterranean.

___ (2)   Young college student planning to go to Florida for Spring Break.

___ (3)   Middle-income, family planning to go to Disney World for a week with their two young children.

Alternative Marketing Mixes

(a)   Discount clothier that spends most of its advertising budget on radio spots and features "final markdowns" on last season's fashions.

(b)   Mail order catalog sent to subscribers of "Architectural Digest" which features high-priced "resort wear" in exotic prints.

(c)   Department store with women's, men's and children's clothing departments with moderate prices that advertises through inserts in the local paper.

5. Product type: Stereo Equipment

Possible Target Markets	*Alternative Marketing Mixes*
___ (1) Middle-class married couple who are looking for a stereo that will blend in with their living room furniture.	(a) Popular brand of an AM/FM console stereo with an attractive wood cabinet purchased on credit at a large department store.
___ (2) Affluent young executive who wants to install a stereo in her penthouse, but doesn't know much about stereo equipment.	(b) Expensive component stereo system, manufactured by a firm with a reputation for high quality and sold by a dealer who specializes in stereo equipment.
___ (3) Do-it-yourself enthusiast who wants to add a stereo to the basement recreation room he has just built.	(c) Build-it-yourself component stereo kit featured in a catalog published by a large mail-order distributor of electronic equipment.

Question for Discussion

Assuming that a firm cannot satisfy all the needs of all potential customers, what factors should a marketing manager consider before selecting a target market?

Learning aid for use with

Appendix A

Economics fundamentals

What This Chapter Is About

Appendix A is important to understanding how buyers and sellers look at products and markets. Some of the economist's tools are shown to be useful. In particular, demand and supply curves, and their interaction are discussed. Also, elasticity of demand and supply are explained. They help us understand the nature of competition. Three kinds of market situations are discussed: pure competition, oligopoly, and monopolistic competition.

The material in this Appendix is not easy--but it is very important. A good marketing manager does not always "win" in every market because consumers' attitudes are continually changing. But an understanding of the nature of demand and competition in different markets will greatly increase your chances for success. Careful study of this appendix will build a good economics base for this text (especially Chapters 3, 4, 18, and 19).

Important Terms

law of diminishing demand, p. 63
demand curve, p. 64
inelastic demand, p. 66
elastic demand, p. 66
substitutes, p. 68
supply curve, p. 69
inelastic supply, p. 70

elastic supply, p. 70
equilibrium point, p. 71
consumer surplus, p. 72
pure competition, p. 73
oligopoly, p. 74
monopolistic competition, p. 75

True-False Questions

___ 1. Economists usually assume that customers evaluate a given set of alternatives in terms of whether they will make them feel better (or worse) or in some way improve (or change) their situation.

___ 2. "The law of diminishing demand" says that if the price of a product is raised, a greater quantity will be demanded--and if the price of a product is lowered, a smaller quantity will be demanded.

___ 3. A demand schedule may indicate that as prices go lower, the total unit sales increase, but the total revenue decreases.

___ 4. A demand curve is a graph of the relationship between price and quantity in a market.

___ 5. Most demand curves slope upward.

___ 6. If total revenue would decrease if price were raised, then demand is said to be elastic.

___ 7. If total revenue would increase if price were lowered, then demand is said to be inelastic.

___ 8. Unitary elasticity of demand means that total revenue remains the same when prices change, regardless of whether price is increased or decreased.

___ 9. A demand curve must be entirely elastic or inelastic; it cannot be both.

___ 10. Whether a product has an elastic or inelastic demand depends on many factors including the availability of substitutes, the importance of the item in the customer's budget, and the urgency of the customer's need in relation to other needs.

___ 11. When only a small number of good "substitutes" are available, demand tends to be quite inelastic.

___ 12. A supply curve shows the quantity of products that will be offered at various possible prices by all suppliers together.

___ 13. An extremely steep or almost vertical supply curve is called elastic because the quantity supplied would not change much if the price were raised.

___ 14. The intersection of demand and supply determines the size of a market and the market price.

___ 15. A market is at the equilibrium point if the quantity and the price that sellers are willing to offer are equal to the quantity and the price that buyers are willing to accept.

___ 16. "Consumer surplus" is the difference between the value of a purchase and the price the consumer has to pay.

___ 17. In pure competition, both the industry demand curve and the individual firm's demand curve are horizontal.

___ 18. Except for oligopolies, most markets tend to become more competitive--that is, move toward pure competition.

___ 19. Oligopoly situations develop when a market has a few sellers of essentially homogeneous products and a fairly elastic industry demand curve.

___ 20. In oligopoly situations, individual firms are faced with a "kinked" demand curve.

___ 21. In monopolistic competition, there is only one seller and that seller has complete control over the price of its unique product.

1. T, p. 63	8. T, p. 66	15. T, p. 71
2. F, p. 63	9. F, p. 67	16. T, p. 71-72
3. T, p. 64	10. T, p. 68	17. F, p. 73
4. T, p. 64	11. T, p. 68	18. T, p. 73-74
5. F, p. 64	12. T, p. 69	19. F, p. 74
6. T, p. 66	13. F, p. 70	20. T, p. 74
7. F, p. 66	14. T, p. 71	21. F, p. 75

Multiple-Choice Questions (Circle the correct response)

1. The "law of diminishing demand" says that:
   a. if the price of a product were lowered, a greater quantity would be demanded.
   b. if the price of a product were raised, a greater quantity would be demanded.
   c. the demand for any product will tend to decline over time.
   d. if the price of a product were lowered, a smaller quantity would be demanded.
   e. the more of a product a person buys, the less utility that particular product offers him.

2. A demand curve:
   a. is generally up-sloping from left to right.
   b. is formed by plotting the points from a supply schedule.
   c. shows what quantities would be demanded by potential customers at various possible prices.
   d. shows how total revenue increases as prices decrease.
   e. All of the above are true statements.

3. If a firm's total revenue increases when the price of its product is reduced from $15 to $10, the demand for this product is:
   a. elastic.
   b. inelastic.
   c. unitary elastic.
   d. cannot be determined without looking at the demand curve.

4. Study the following demand schedule:

PRICE	QUANTITY DEMANDED	TOTAL REVENUE
$500	1,000	$500,000
400	2,000	800,000
300	3,000	900,000
200	4,000	800,000
100	5,000	500,000

This demand schedule shows that the demand for this product is:
   a. elastic.
   b. inelastic.
   c. unitary elastic.
   d. both elastic and inelastic.
   e. This demand schedule cannot be correct because it violates the "law of diminishing demand."

5. The elasticity of demand for a particular product does *not* depend upon:
   a. the availability of substitutes.
   b. the importance of the item in the customer's budget.
   c. the urgency of the customer's need.
   d. how much it costs to produce the product.
   e. All of the above affect the elasticity of demand.

6. Which of the following products would have the most *inelastic* demand for most potential customers?
   a. A home computer
   b. A vacation trip to France
   c. A one-pound package of salt
   d. A pair of designer jeans
   e. A "Big Mac" hamburger

7. A supply curve:
   a. is generally flatter than its supply schedule.
   b. is not affected by production costs.
   c. is generally up-sloping from left to right.
   d. is a picture of the quantities of goods that would be demanded at various possible prices.
   e. All of the above are true statements.

8. Which of the following statements about elasticity of supply is *true*?
   a. If a product's demand curve is elastic, then its supply curve also must be elastic.
   b. A product's elasticity of supply determines its elasticity of demand.
   c. In the short run, the supply curve for most agricultural products is highly elastic.
   d. In the long run, the supply curve for most products is highly inelastic.
   e. None of the above statements are true.

9. Which of the following statements about demand and supply interaction is *true*?
   a. Demand is the sole determiner of price.
   b. A market is said to be in equilibrium when the elasticity of demand equals the elasticity of supply.
   c. The interaction of supply and demand determines the size of the market and the market price.
   d. For a market to be in equilibrium, the price and quantity that buyers are willing to accept must be greater than the price and quantity that suppliers are willing to offer.
   e. All of the above statements are true.

10. Given a situation where there is elastic demand and elastic supply, an *increase* in the quantity suppliers are willing to supply at all possible prices will:
   a. decrease price, but not change quantity demanded.
   b. increase price and decrease quantity demanded.
   c. lower price and increase quantity demanded.
   d. increase price and increase quantity demanded.

11. The term "consumer surplus" means that:
    a. consumers never get their money's worth in any transaction.
    b. there are more needs than there are products to satisfy them.
    c. consumers don't consume all the products they buy.
    d. some consumers would be willing to pay more than the market equilibrium price if they had to.
    e. there are more consumers than there are producers.

12. Which of the following is *not* a factor affecting competition?
    a. the number of the firm's competitors.
    b. the uniqueness of the firm's marketing mix.
    c. the size of the firm's competitors.
    d. the elasticity of the firm's demand curve.
    e. All of the above are factors that do affect competition.

13. In which of the following situations would an individual firm be most likely to face a flat demand curve?
    a. Oligopoly
    b. Pure competition
    c. Monopoly
    d. Monopolistic competition
    e. None of the above--demand is always downward sloping.

14. Oligopoly situations are generally characterized by:
    a. essentially heterogeneous products.
    b. relatively few sellers, or a few large firms and perhaps many smaller firms.
    c. fairly elastic industry demand.
    d. a and b above--but not c.
    e. All of the above.

15. In an oligopoly situation:
    a. an individual firm's demand is inelastic above the "kink" and elastic below the kink.
    b. the market price is usually somewhere above the "kink."
    c. price wars usually increase profits for all competitors.
    d. price fluctuations may occur despite the kinked demand curve faced by each firm.
    e. All of the above are true statements.

16. A particular market is characterized by different (heterogeneous) products in the eyes of some customers and sellers who feel they do face some competition. This product-market is an example of:
    a. oligopoly.
    b. monopoly.
    c. monopolistic competition.
    d. pure competition.
    e. It could be any of the above.

17. Which of the following statements about the competitive environment is *true*?
    a. The industry demand curve in a pure competition situation is horizontal.
    b. Monopolistic competition is characterized by downsloping demand curves due to the lack of any substitute products.
    c. In a pure competition situation, an individual firm is faced with a very inelastic demand curve.
    d. Since a monopolistic competitor has a downsloping demand curve just like a pure monopolist, it has some control over its price.
    e. All of the above are true statements.

Answers to Multiple-Choice Questions

1. a, p. 63
2. c, p. 64
3. a, p. 66
4. d, p. 67
5. d, p. 67-68
6. c, p. 68

7. c, p. 69
8. e, p. 70
9. c, p. 71
10. c, p. 71-72
11. d, p. 71-72
12. e, p. 72-75

13. b, p. 73
14. b, p. 74
15. d, p. 74
16. c, p. 75
17. d, p. 75

Exercise A-1

Estimating and using demand elasticity

Introduction

"Demand elasticity" is a very useful concept for analyzing the nature of demand and competition in markets. As explained in Appendix A in the text, demand elasticity can be defined in terms of what happens to total revenue when the price of a product is lowered.

a.   If total revenue would increase if the price were lowered, then demand is said to be *elastic*.
b.   If total revenue would decrease if the price were lowered, then demand is said to be *inelastic*.
c.   If total revenue would stay the same if the price were lowered, or raised then we have a special case called *unitary elasticity of demand.*

Different products have different demand elasticities because of factors such as the availability of substitutes, the importance of the item in the customer's budget, and the urgency of the customer's need in relation to other needs.

The elasticity of a firm's demand curve is extremely important to a marketing strategy planner. It provides a shorthand description of the nature of competition and demand facing a firm--often suggesting necessary changes in strategies. For example, a firm with a highly elastic demand curve might have many competitors and would have very little control over the price it could charge for its product. In this case, perhaps the firm should plan a new strategy--one aimed at a different target market with fewer competitors and less elastic demand.

Assignment

This exercise has three parts and is designed to increase your understanding of demand elasticity. The first part focuses on the relationship of demand elasticity to changes in total revenue. The second part shows how demand elasticity can vary in different market situations. The third part shows how product and price are related through demand elasticity.

1.   Demand elasticity was defined above in terms of what happens to total revenue when price is lowered. Now complete the following table--showing what happens to total revenue *(TR)* when price is *raised* instead of lowered.

	Elastic _demand_	Inelastic _demand_	Unitary elasticity _of demand_
Price lowered	TR increases	TR decreases	TR remains the same
Price raised	_____	_____	_____

2.   Figure A-1 shows three demand curves--each with a different degree of elasticity. Each of the demand curves represents *one* of the following situations:

   a)   The demand for an individual farmer's lettuce crop.
   b)   The demand for fuel oil during a harsh winter.
   c)   The demand for one firm's "quality" stereo CD changer.

In the space provided, state which of the three situations each demand curve most likely represents. Then briefly explain each answer in terms of the factors which can cause demand elasticity to vary in different market situations.

FIGURE A-1

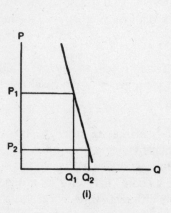 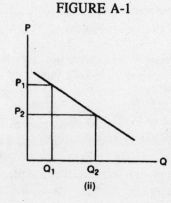 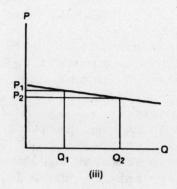

Graph (i) Situation: _____

   Explanation: _____

   _____

   _____

   _____

Graph (ii) Situation: _____

   Explanation: _____

   _____

   _____

   _____

Graph (iii) Situation: _____

        Explanation: _____

_____

_____

3.   Read the following paragraph and then answer questions (a) through (c).

IntelliCorp produces and sells computer-controlled instruments that are used by industrial firms to control manufacturing equipment. The firm's management is seeking a larger share of the market. Thus, its objective for the coming year is to increase both its dollar sales volume and its market share for the instruments--which are currently priced at $1,600. IntelliCorp's estimated demand curve for the next year is shown in Figure A-2.

FIGURE A-2

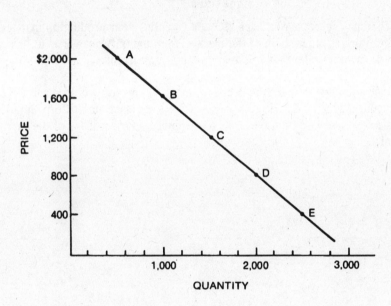

a)   Use Figure A-2 to complete the following table:

Demand Schedule of IntelliCorp's Computer-Controlled Instruments

Points on Graph	Price per unit	Quantity Demanded per unit	Total Revenue per year
A	$2,000	500	$1,000,000
B	1,600	_____	_____
C	1,200	_____	_____
D	800	_____	_____
E	400	_____	_____

b) Looking at IntelliCorp's demand curve and demand schedule, would you describe the demand for the firm's instruments as (a) elastic, (b) inelastic, (c) unitary elastic, or (d) both elastic and inelastic? Explain your answer.

_____

_____

c) As marketing manager for IntelliCorp, you have called a meeting of top management to discuss the firm's pricing for the coming year. After explaining the purpose of the meeting, you have asked for comments and suggestions.

"The obvious thing to do is cut our price as low as possible," says the sales manager, "so we can increase market share."

"That's nonsense," says the chief accountant. "If we want to increase our dollar sales revenue, then we must raise our selling price."

"That may increase our sales revenue," replies your production manager, "but if we want to capture a larger share of the market, then the only answer is to increase our production to its maximum level--while maintaining our current price."

Since you have to make the decision, explain how you would resolve the conflicting advice of your department managers. Then state what price IntelliCorp should charge to increase sales revenue on the instruments *and* capture a larger share of the market by selling more units.

Question for Discussion

Consider the three market situations in Question 2. If a firm's demand curve is elastic, does the demand curve for the industry also have to be elastic? What if the firm's demand curve is inelastic?

Learning aid for use with

Exercise A-2

Analyzing the competitive environment

Introduction

Marketing managers do not always enjoy a full range of alternatives when planning a marketing mix. Their choices may be limited--or largely determined--by the nature of the competitive environment.

For example, a firm might be able to use almost any marketing mix in a *pure monopoly* situation, while a firm's mix might be entirely determined by market forces in a *pure competition* situation. In an *oligopoly* situation, a firm would have some control over its marketing mix, but it might find it difficult to differentiate its product and any price-cutting could lead to a "price-war." Of course, most firms find themselves in a *monopolistic competition* situation where their control over their marketing mix can range from a lot to a little--depending on how competitive the monopolistic competition is.

It is not always easy to identify the nature of a firm's competitive environment. In general, one must consider many factors—besides the elasticity of a firms demand curves—. Other factors that should be considered include: (a) the number and size of competitors, (b) the similarity of competing products and marketing mixes—as seen be target customers, and (c) ease of entry for new firms.

Assignment

This exercise will give you some practice in analyzing the competitive environment. Read the following cases carefully and for each of them:

a)   Indicate the nature of the competitive environment, taking into consideration the probable target market.

Use the following terms to identify the nature of competition: pure competition, monopolistic competition, monopoly, and oligopoly.

b)   Briefly explain your answer, taking into account the various factors which were discussed above.

The first case has been answered for you as an example.

1.   Don's Truck Stop is a combination gasoline station-restaurant-motel which caters to long-distance truck drivers. It is located at the intersection of two major highways near a city of about 150,000 people. There are no other truck stops in the immediate area.

   a)   Nature of competition: *Monopolistic competition*.

   b)   Explanation: *Although Don's Truck Stop probably gets a large share of the long-distance truckers' business, it does not have a pure monopoly because truckers can go into the city or on to the next truck stop. Further, there is nothing to prevent a potential competitor from locating nearby--which may very well happen if Don's is enjoying unusually high profits.*

2.   Tom Knappe is one of the thousands of farmers who grow large crops of sunflower seeds to use in making cooking oil, baked goods, and snack foods—as well as for birdfeeding. Tom's crop is just a very small fraction of the nation's total crop of sunflower seeds. But like other farmers, he has increased the size of his crop in recent years as increasing demand has raised market prices. Now he plans to increase his crop even more, given the strong likelihood of rising international demand for sunflower seeds.

   a)   Nature of competition: _____

   b)   Explanation: _____

   _____

   _____

   _____

   _____

   _____

3.   Acura Dry Cleaning specializes in dry cleaning of clothing and other household items--as well as operating a shirt laundry. It operates a central processing plant and 10 conveniently located branches where dry cleaning can be dropped off and picked up a day or two later. This company is located in a city of 1,000,000 where there are about 100 other dry cleaners (some of whom also have multiple-outlet operations). All these cleaners charge approximately the same "low" prices for basically the same services--because a steady influx of new dry cleaners has tended to keep prices at a fairly low level. Further, some firms have not been able to attract enough business to cover their rising labor costs and have been forced out of business.

   a)   Nature of competition: _____

   b)   Explanation: _____

   _____

_____

_____

_____

_____

4. The trend toward cholesterol-free diets has been a problem for Maxine Claude, who owns a cattle ranch in Alberta. Like thousands of other ranchers in Canada, she raises the beef that is used to produce the steaks and hamburgers that end up on the dinner tables of Canada, that are used by restaurants in preparing meals, and that are used in producing a variety of packaged foods. Maxine Claude's herd flock has always been a very small portion of the millions of beef cattle raised in Canada. But like most other ranchers, she has had to decrease the size of her herd in recent years as consumer demand for red meat has declined.

a) Nature of competition: _____

b) Explanation: _____

_____

_____

_____

_____

_____

5. The Toronto metropolitan area is supplied by five regional manufacturers of bricks. The bricks are used in constructing homes and office buildings as well as for other purposes (decorative walls, patios). Three of these firms account for more than 80 percent of all the bricks sold in the area. The bricks are purchased either in standardized sizes or according to buyer specifications, and all five firms charge almost identical prices. When bricks are in short supply, a few buyers have purchased some bricks from other firms located outside the region, but high transportation cost make this an extremely expensive alternative. Two manufacturers have announced plans to boost their production capacity, and all five manufacturers have announced price increases of at least 6 percent for the coming year.

a) Nature of competition: _____

b) Explanation: _____

_____

_____

_____

_____

6.   Indoor Sports, Inc. operates the only privately-owned indoor racket ball court facility in Monument City--a northern city with a population of 340,000. It runs a full program of racket ball lessons, tournaments, and public play. It is also the "sponsor" of local "high school racket ball"--trading practice time for a share of the gate. Its only "indoor" competition is from the state university courts--which are only three miles away. The university athletic department does not run competing programs--because its primary role is to serve the students and intramural teams. However, it does have a large amount of "extra time" and regularly sells blocks of time to groups (for example, businessmen who come to town for conferences at local hotels). The athletic department usually charges such groups prices that are below Indoor Sports's prices (by 10-40 percent) and probably way below its variable costs of operating the facility.

a)   Nature of competition: _____

b)   Explanation: _____

_____

_____

_____

_____

_____

Question for Discussion

For each of the five cases described above, discuss (a) whether the firm(s) in the case achieved and any "competitive advantage" over their competitors, and (b) if not, what steps might be taken to achieve some competitive advantage.

Chapter 3

Finding target market opportunities with market segmentation

What This Chapter Is About

In this chapter you will learn how alert marketers find attractive market opportunities—ones that enable them to get a competitive advantage. Creatively defining a firm's markets (product-markets) can suggest many possibilities—and how to do this should be studied carefully. The focus is on how you can use market segmentation to identify possible target markets. Segmenting markets is vital to marketing strategy planning. You will also see how sophisticated segmentation approaches—like clustering and perceptual mapping—are used to make better market segmentation decisions.

To improve your understanding, try to apply the segmentation approach to a market in which you actually buy something. Then see how the dimensions in your own market segment affect the marketing mix which is offered to you. There is a logic to marketing strategy planning—marketing mixes flow directly from the characteristics of target markets. Try to get a feel for this interaction as you learn how to segment markets.

This chapter makes it clear why it is important to understand markets—and customers. In later chapters, you will build on this base—as you learn more about the demographic and behavioral dimensions of the consumer market and the buying behavior of intermediate customers.

This is a very important—if difficult—chapter, and deserves careful study. It is difficult because it requires *creative* thinking about markets—but this can also be a challenge, and help you learn how to find your own "breakthrough opportunity."

Important Terms

breakthrough opportunities, p. 81
competitive advantage, p. 81
market penetration, p. 82
market development, p. 82
product development, p. 83
diversification, p. 83
market, p. 86
generic market, p. 86
product-market, p. 86
market segmentation, p. 90
market segment, p. 91

single target market approach, p. 93
multiple target market approach, p. 93
combined target market approach, p. 93
combiners, p. 93
segmenters, p. 94
qualifying dimensions, p. 97
determining dimensions, p. 97
clustering techniques, p. 104
trade-off analysis, p. 105
conjoint analysis, p. 105
perceptual maps, p. 105

True-False Questions

____ 1. Often, attractive opportunities are fairly close to markets the firm already knows and has some chance of doing something about—given its resources and objectives.

____ 2. "Breakthrough opportunities" are ones which help innovators develop hard-to-copy marketing strategies that will be very profitable for a long time.

____ 3. A firm with a "competitive advantage" has a marketing mix that the target market sees as better than a competitor's mix.

____ 4. Marketing opportunities involving present markets and present products are called "market penetration" opportunities.

____ 5. A "market development" opportunity would involve a firm offering new or improved products to its present markets.

____ 6. When it comes to choosing among different types of opportunities, most firms tend to be production-oriented and usually think first of diversification.

____ 7. A market consists of a group of potential customers with similar needs.

____ 8. A generic market is a market with broadly similar needs and sellers offering various and often diverse ways of satisfying those needs.

____ 9. A product-market is a market with very similar needs and sellers offering various close substitute ways of satisfying those needs.

____ 10. A generic market description looks at markets narrowly—and from a producer's viewpoint.

____ 11. A firm's "relevant market for finding opportunities" should be bigger than its present product-market—but not so big that the firm couldn't expand and be an important competitor in this market.

____ 12. Just identifying the geographic boundaries of a firm's present market can suggest new marketing opportunities.

____ 13. A generic market description should include both customer-related and product-related terms.

____ 14. A segmenter is usually attempting to satisfying a sub-market with its own unique demand curve—and therefore must settle for a smaller sales potential than a combiner.

____ 15. Customer-related segmenting dimensions are always more effective than situation-related dimensions.

____ 16. When segmenting markets, "good" market segments are ones which are heterogeneous within, homogeneous between, substantial, and operational.

____ 17. The multiple target market approach combines two or more homogeneous sub-markets into one larger target market as a basis for one strategy.

_____ 18. The determining dimensions may help identify the "core features" which will have to be offered to everyone in the broad product-market.

_____ 19. Clustering techniques try to find similar patterns within sets of customer-related data.

Answers to True-False Questions.

1. T, p. 80	8. T, p. 86	15. F, pp. 91-92
2. T, p. 81	9. T, p. 86	16. F, pp. 92-93
3. T, p. 81	10. F, p. 86	17. F, p. 93
4. T, p. 82	11. T, p. 87	18. F, p. 97
5. F, p. 82	12. T, p. 89	19. T, p. 104
6. F, p. 84	13. F, p. 89	
7. T, p. 86	14. F, p. 91	

Multiple-Choice Questions (Circle the correct response)

1. Breakthrough opportunities:
   a. are so rare that they should be pursued even when they do not match the firm's resources and objectives.
   b. seldom occur within or close to a firm's present markets.
   c. are especially important in our increasingly competitive markets.
   d. are those which a firm's competitors can copy quickly.
   e. are best achieved by trying to hold onto a firm's current market share.

2. When a firm tries to increase sales by selling its present products in new markets, this is called:
   a. market penetration.
   b. market development.
   c. product development.
   d. diversification.
   e. market integration.

3. A market consists of:
   a. a group of potential customers with similar needs.
   b. various kinds of products with similar characteristics.
   c. sellers offering substitute ways of satisfying needs.
   d. all the firms within a particular industry.
   e. both a and c.

4. A market in which sellers offer various close substitute ways of satisfying the market's needs is called a:
   a. generic.
   b. relevant market.
   c. product-market.
   d. central market.
   e. homogeneous market.

5. Which of the following is the best example of a "generic market"?
   a. The expensive ten-speed bicycle market.
   b. The Canadian college student creative expression market.
   c. The photographic market.
   d. The pet food market.
   e. The teen-age market.

6. A firm's "relevant market for finding opportunities":
   a. should be as large as possible.
   b. should have no geographic limits.
   c. should be no larger than its present product-market.
   d. should always be named in product-related terms.
   e. None of the above is a true statement.

7. Market segmentation:
   a. tries to find heterogeneous sub-markets within a market.
   b. means the same thing as marketing strategy planning.
   c. assumes that most sub-markets can be satisfied by the same marketing mix.
   d. assumes that any market is likely to consist of sub-markets.
   e. All of the above are true statements.

8. Naming broad product-markets is:
   a. an assorting process
   b. a disaggregating process
   c. a segmenting process
   d. an accumulating process
   e. an aggregating process

9. Segmenting:
   a. is essentially a disaggregating or "break it down" process.
   b. assumes that all customers can be grouped into homogeneous and profitable market segments.
   c. tries to aggregate together individuals who have similar needs and characteristics.
   d. usually results in firms aiming at smaller and less profitable markets.
   e. assumes that each individual should be treated as a separate target market.

10. "Good" market segments are those which are:
    a. heterogeneous within.
    b. operational.
    c. homogeneous between.
    d. substantial—meaning large enough to minimize operating costs.
    e. all of the above.

11. Having segmented its market, the Stuart Corp. has decided to treat each of two sub-markets as a separate target market requiring a different marketing mix. Apparently, Stuart is following the _____ target market approach.
    a. single
    b. combined
    c. multiple

12. Segmenting and combining are two alternate approaches to developing market-oriented strategies. Which of the following statements concerning these approaches is *true*?
    a. Combiners treat each sub-market as a separate target market.
    b. Segmenters try to develop a marketing mix that will have general appeal to several market segments.
    c. A combiner combines the demand curve in several markets into one demand curve.
    d. A segmenter assumes that the whole market consists of a fairly homogeneous group of customers.
    e. Both segmenters and combiners try to satisfy some people very well rather than a lot of people fairly well.

13. Customer-related (rather than situation-related) segmenting dimensions include:
    a. benefits offered.
    b. buying situation.
    c. brand familiarity.
    d. family life cycle.
    e. consumption or use patterns.

14. Which of the following types of dimensions would be the most important if one were particularly interested in why some target market was likely to buy a particular brand within a product-market?
    a. Primary dimensions
    b. Secondary dimensions
    c. Qualifying dimensions
    d. Determining dimensions
    e. Both a and c above.

15. Which of the following statements about clustering techniques is *true*?
    a. Clustering techniques try to find dissimilar patterns within sets of customer-related data.
    b. Computers are usually needed to search among all of the data for homogeneous groups of people.
    c. Computers identify the relevant dimensions and do the analysis.
    d. A cluster analysis of the toothpaste market indicated that most consumers seek the same benefits.
    e. All of the above are true.

16. "Perceptual Mapping":
    a. involves a packaged-goods manufacturer's attempt to obtain the best possible shelf space for its product in retail outlets.
    b. in useful for segmenting but not combining.
    c. helps strategy planners see how customers view various brands or products in relation to each other.
    d. applies only to existing products, not new products.
    e. eliminates the need for subjective decision making in product planning.

17. "Perceptual Mapping" is concerned with
    a. how current target customers view the products available from one company.
    b. how customers view the competing brands in a market.
    c. an analysis of the design strengths and weaknesses of products in a market.
    d. the economic factors that affect consumer choices among alternative brands.
    e. None of the above is true.

Answers to Multiple-Choice Questions

1. c, p. 81
2. b, p. 82
3. e, p. 86
4. c, p. 86
5. b, p. 86
6. e, p. 87

7. d, p. 90
8. b, p. 90
9. c, p. 91
10. b, pp. 92-93
11. c, p. 93
12. c, p. 93

13. d, pp. 96-97
14. d, p. 97
15. b, p. 104
16. c, p. 105
17. b, p. 105

Exercise 3-1

Product-markets vs. generic markets

Introduction

A practical first step in searching for breakthrough opportunities is to define the firm's present (or potential) markets. Markets consist of potential customers with similar needs and sellers offering various ways of satisfying those needs.

Markets can be defined very broadly or very narrowly—with either extreme being a potential threat to effective strategy planning. For example, defining its market too broadly as "transportation" could result in General Motors seeing itself in direct competition with manufacturers of airplanes, ships, elevators, bicycles, little red wagons, and perhaps even spaceships! On the other hand, a definition such as "the market for six-passenger motor vehicles with gasoline-powered internal-combustion engines" would be too narrow—and doesn't even identify "potential customers."

While there is no simple and automatic way to define a firm's *relevant* market, marketers should start by defining the relevant generic market and product-market using the 3 and 4 part definitions discussed on pages 88-90 of the text and shown below:

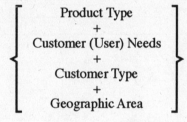

Generic Market Definition
$$\left\{ \begin{array}{c} \text{Product Type} \\ + \\ \text{Customer (User) Needs} \\ + \\ \text{Customer Type} \\ + \\ \text{Geographic Area} \end{array} \right\}$$
Product Market Definition

It often requires a lot of creativity to think in terms of generic markets and product-markets—but failure to do so can cause strategy planners to overlook breakthrough opportunities—and leave themselves exposed to new forms of competition. Just ask the manufacturers of kerosene lamps, buggy whips, and mathematical slide rules!

Assignment

This exercise will give you some practice in naming product-markets and generic markets. It will also require you to be creative and apply your marketing intuition.

Listed below are several generic markets and brand-name products. Using the 3 and 4 part definitions of generic markets and product-markets, suggest possible market names in the blanks. Note: There are no "right answers," but they should be logical and consistent. Generic markets should *not* include any product-related terms. A generic market can have several related product-markets.

And a product is offered to a product-market which is a part of a larger generic market. Question 1 is answered to help you get started.

1. Generic market: Security for families in the world
   a. Product-market: <u>Homeowner's insurance for financial security for home-owning families in Canada.</u>
   b. Product-market: <u>Guards for physical security for wealthy families in the world.</u>
   c. Product-market: <u>Smoke alarms for mental security for families in the developed countries.</u>

2. Generic market: Communications systems.
   a. Product-market: _____
   b. Product-market: _____
   c. Product-market: _____

3. Product: Duncan Hines chewy chocolate-chip cookies.
   a. Product-market: _____
   b. Product-market: _____
   c. Product-market: _____

4. Generic market: Entertainment for lower income individuals in Canada.
   a. Product-market: _____
   b. Product-market: _____
   c. Product-market: _____

5. Product: Calvin Klein (label on back pocket) jeans.
   a. Product-market: _____
   b. Product-market: _____

6. Product: Pioneer hi-fi stereo components (medium to high quality and price).
   a. Product-market: _____
   b. Product-market: _____
   c. Product-market: _____

Questions for Discussion

1. How can a firm decide which and how many markets to enter?

2. With the use of the product-market grid illustrated below, explain what strategies gourmet cookie companies in major cities might undertake due to problems of increased competition and decreased sales.

	Present Products	New Products
Present Markets	Market Penetration	Product Development
New Markets	Market Development	Diversification

Exercise 3-2

Using perceptual mapping to evaluate marketing opportunities

Introduction

Finding target market opportunities is a continuing challenge for all marketers. Understanding how customers view current or proposed market offerings is often a crucial part of this challenge. And understanding customer perceptions is more difficult when different segments of the market have different needs and different views of how well current or proposed products meet those needs. Developing insights requires that you try to answer questions such as: Are there customer segments with needs which no existing products are satisfying very well? Could our existing product be modified to do a better job of satisfying the needs of some segment? Could promotion be used to communicate to consumers about aspects of the product—so that target customers would "see" it in a different way?

There are no easy answers to such questions, but Perceptual Mapping approaches can help. As explained in the text (pages 105-107) Perceptual Mapping uses marketing research techniques which measure customer views of products or brands according to several product features (e.g., do consumers think of a brand of detergent as "gentle" or "strong" relative to other brands?). Usually, customers are also asked to decide the amount of each feature than would be "ideal" (e.g., how strong a detergent do you want?)

The results are plotted on a two- or three-dimensional diagram—called a "product space." Each dimension represents a product feature which the customers feel is important. The diagram shows how each product or brand was rated on each of the dimensions. In other words, it shows how the various products or brands are "positioned" relative to each other—and relative to the "ideal" products or brands of different segments of customers. Usually, circles are used to show segments of customers with similar "ideal points" along the dimensions.

The mechanics of how all this is done are beyond the scope of this course. But you should know that perceptual mapping research techniques produce a very useful graphic aid to help marketing managers do their job better. Looking at a product space for a market, a marketing planner may see opportunities to "reposition" existing products or brands through product and/or promotion changes. Or he may spot an empty space which calls for the introduction of a new product. Often, he may be quite surprised to see that customer views of market offerings differ a great deal from his own ideas.

Assignment

Figure 3-2 is a fictional "perceptual map" for ready-to-eat breakfast cereal. The diagram shows how target customers rated several brands of cereal along two product dimensions which have been identified only as Dimension A and Dimension B, respectively. The diagram also shows 8 segments of customers grouped together on the basis of similar "ideal points." For example, customers in segment #8 desire a lot of both attribute A and B).

Study Figure 3-2 carefully and then answer the following questions.

FIGURE 3-2
Perceptual Map of Ready-to-Eat Breakfast Cereal

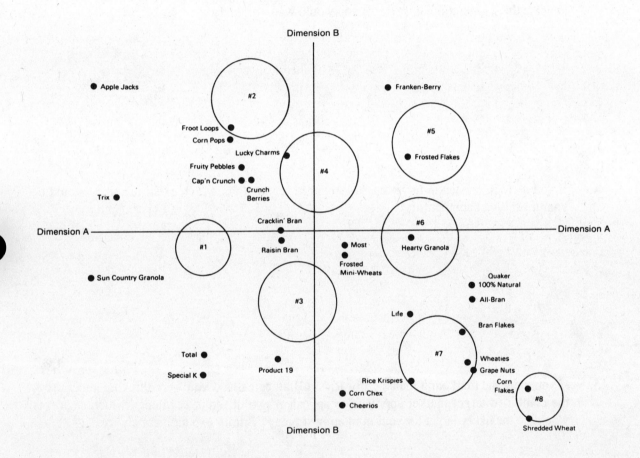

1. a) Based on your interpretation of Figure 3-2, what product feature does Dimension A appear to represent?

    b) Based on your interpretation of Figure 3-2, what product feature does Dimension B appear to represent?

2.   What opportunities for "repositioning" *existing* products do you see in Figure 3-2? Be specific, and indicate the segment(s) to which you want to target your appeal(s).

3.   What opportunities for introducing *new* products do you see in Figure 3-2? Be specific, and indicate the segment(s) whose needs you would want to satisfy.

4.   If you were interested in targeting customers in segment #6, which existing brands would be your most direct competitors?

5.   If you were the marketing manager for Raisin Bran cereal and you were thinking about using the combined target market approach to appeal to two different segments, which segments would be the likely target for your marketing strategy? Briefly explain your choice.

Learning aid for use with

6. In Figure 3-2 there are already many competing product offerings in the upper left and lower right quadrants. Why doesn't an innovative producer offer a new product to the far left and bottom of the space—where there is currently no product?

7. Are the two product dimensions shown in Figure 3-2 the two most important dimensions in choosing a brand of breakfast cereal? If not, what dimensions are most important?

8. Do all potential customers agree as to which two dimensions are the most important dimensions in choosing a brand of breakfast cereal? If not, what are the implications for using "perceptual mapping" as an aid in evaluating market opportunities?

Questions for Discussion

Is perceptual mapping an art or a science? Why?

Exercise 3-3

Segmenting multidimensional markets

Introduction

Marketing-oriented business managers realize that what is often considered as the mass market may actually consist of many smaller more homogeneous market segments. Thus, market segmentation becomes a crucial step in the development of a successful marketing strategy.

Market segmentation can be illustrated graphically through the use of "market grids." The grid approach pictures a market as a large box that is divided up into smaller boxes on the basis of the relevant needs and characteristics of potential customers. Each smaller box within the larger box represents a smaller, more homogeneous market segment—and a potential target market.

For example, a watch manufacturer who believed that sex and social class were the most relevant customer dimensions for his product-market might construct the following market grid.

FIGURE 3-3
Market Grid for the Watch Market

Male			
Female			
	Upper-Class	Middle-Class	Lower Class

In looking at Figure 3-3 however, you should keep in mind that sex and social class are only two of many possible dimensions that might be used to segment the watch market. As discussed in the text, possible segmenting dimensions include geographic dimensions, demographic dimensions, need or attitude dimensions, life-style dimensions, benefit dimensions, usage patterns, brand familiarity, and buying situations.

In other words, market segmentation is complicated by the fact that markets can be defined in many different ways. In keeping with the marketing concept, markets should be defined in terms of the needs and characteristics of potential customers. But this still remains a difficult task because customers are *multi-dimensional* and typically display many similarities and differences—only some of which may be relevant for a particular market situation.

The task of deciding which dimensions are relevant for segmenting a particular market is further complicated by the need to distinguish between qualifying and determining dimensions. *Qualifying dimensions* include *any factors which qualify one as a potential customer*, while *determining dimensions* include only those factors which *determine which type of product or even which brand may be purchased*. For example, any person who needs to know the correct time and can afford the price of a watch presumably would quality as a potential customer. But these dimensions would not be sufficient to determine which type of watch (e.g., calendar watch, digital watch, pocket watch, etc.) or which brand a person might purchase.

This exercise is designed to familiarize you with some of the different types of dimensions that are often used to segment markets—and to emphasize the need for considerable management judgment in deciding which dimensions are most relevant for a particular market.

FIGURE 3-4
Alternative Dimensions for the Canadian Instant Breakfast Food Market

Under $10,000
$10,000 - $19,999
$20,000 - $29,999
$30,000 - $39,999
$40,000 - $49,999
$50,000 or over

a. Based on family income levels of potential customers.

Atlantic Provinces – Urban	Rural
Ontario – Urban	Rural
Quebec – Urban	Rural
West – Urban	Rural

b. Based on geographic location of potential customers.

Strong brand loyalty
Weak brand loyalty
No brand loyalty

c. Based on "brand loyalty" of potential customers.

Extroverted conformists	Extroverted nonconformists
Introverted conformists	Introverted nonconformists

d. Based on personality traits of potential customers.

Harried Commuters	Working Mothers
Snack Servers	Calorie Counters

e. Based on potential customers' needs and benefits sought*

Harried commuters—Busy career people who need a source of energy and nutrition—but who don't have time to prepare and eat a complete breakfast.

Working mothers—The women whose work schedules prevent them from making sure their children eat a full and nutritious breakfast.

Snack servers—Homemakers who see to it that their children eat a full and balanced breakfast—but who also want to provide them with nutritious and good-tasting snacks.

Calorie counters—Dieters looking for tasty, filling, and nutritious meal substitutes.

Assignment

Assume you are the marketing manager for a firm that has decided to enter the Instant Breakfast Food Market. The firm feels that an opportunity exists to introduce a new product which is superior to anything already on the market in terms of taste and convenience.

As marketing manager, it is your job to develop a successful marketing strategy for the new product—starting with the selection of a target market. Therefore, you have asked your marketing research staff to analyze the breakfast food market and describe the various market segments that make up the overall market. However, as it turned out, there was considerable disagreement among the researchers as to which dimensions should be used to segment the market. Unable to reach any consensus among themselves, they therefore submitted five different dimensions for the instant breakfast food market—as shown in Figure 3-4.

1. Of the five dimensions shown in Figure 3-4, which two do you think would be most relevant and effective for segmenting the instant breakfast food market? Why?

2. Draw a grid based on the two dimensions you selected in Question 1. Based on your grid, which of the following approaches would you recommend in selecting a target market for the instant breakfast food market: (a) the single target market approach, (b) the multiple target market approach, or (c) the combined target market approach. In answering this question, specify your recommended target market and explain why you selected it.

3.   Assume your firm was able to acquire the rights for an instant breakfast food product from another country. This product comes in a relatively expensive multiple-unit package, looks and tastes like a chocolate brownie, requires no preparation, and can be used either as a nutritious meal substitute, a snack or a diet food. Would this product meet the needs of your recommended target market? If not, how would it have to be changed?

Question for Discussion

What criteria should marketing managers use to judge whether or not the segmenting dimensions they are using are relevant and effective for marketing strategy planning?

Chapter 4

Evaluating opportunities in the changing marketing environment

What This Chapter Is About

In the last chapter, you learned that finding opportunities takes a real understanding of customers. But marketing managers can not select target markets or plan strategies in a vacuum. Uncontrollable environments affect the attractiveness of possible opportunities. And opportunities need to be carefully evaluated and screened—to identify the really attractive ones.

A company's objectives can guide this process—and its resources may limit the search for opportunities, or alternatively give the firm a competitive advantage.

This chapter treats the competitive environment in some depth (building on the economic concepts reviewed in Appendix A, which follows Chapter 2). The marketing manager can't control competitors—but he can try to avoid head-on competition—or plan for it when it is inevitable. The economic and technological environment can change rapidly. These shifts may require changes in marketing strategies.

The political and legal environment is given special attention because of its possible impact on the marketing manager. Further, the evolution of legislative thinking is outlined as a foundation for discussion in later chapters.

The cultural and social environment concerns the number of people and how they live and behave. A marketing manager must understand his markets—and cultural and social environments affect the way people buy.

Finding *attractive* opportunities requires screening and evaluation—and various approaches are presented towards the end of the chapter.

Important Terms

company objectives, p. 113
company resources, p. 116
competitive environment, p. 118
competitor analysis, p. 119
competitive barriers, p. 120
economic and technological environment p. 123
technological base, p. 126
gross domestic product (GDP) p. 127

political environment, p. 128
nationalism p. 128
consumerism, p. 130
legal environment, p. 132
cultural and social environment, p. 137
strategic business unit (SBU), p. 145
portfolio management, p. 146

True-False Questions

___ 1. Consumerism is a social movement seeking to give sellers as much power and legal rights as buyers and consumers.

___ 2. Ownership of patients, loyalty of customers and financial strength are some of the many resources of a firm which should be evaluated when searching for new opportunities.

___ 3. A business firm's only objective should be to earn enough profit to survive.

___ 4. Trying to maximize short-run return on investment may not be good in the long run.

___ 5. Winning a larger market share necessarily leads to greater profitability.

___ 6. Company objectives should lead to a hierarchy of marketing objectives.

___ 7. Attractive opportunities should make use of a firm's resources and its unique strengths.

___ 8. A large producer with economies of scale always has a competitive advantage over smaller firms.

___ 9. A patent owner has a 20-year monopoly to develop and use its new product, process, or material as it sees fit.

___ 10. Although the marketing manager cannot control the competitive environment, he can choose strategies that will avoid head-on situations.

___ 11. The technological base includes the technical skills and equipment which affect the way the resources of an economy are converted to output.

___ 12. Changes in the technological environment could be rejected by the cultural and social environment—through the political and legal environment—even though such changes might help the economic environment.

___ 13. Nationalism may affect marketing strategy planning by determining to whom and how much a firm may sell.

___ 14. The political environment may either block or promote new marketing opportunities.

___ 15. Recent trends indicate a major shift in traditional thinking about buyer-seller relations from "let the seller beware" to "let the buyer beware."

___ 16. Because the cultural and social environment tends to change slowly, firms should try to identify and work with cultural attitudes rather than trying to encourage big changes in the short run.

___ 17. Product-market screening criteria should be mainly quantitative in nature, because qualitative criteria are too subjective.

___ 18. Forecasts of the probable results of implementing whole strategic plans are needed to apply quantitative screening criteria.

— 19. The profit potentials of alternative strategic plans can be evaluated at the same time only if the plans are very similar.

— 20. The General Electric "strategic planning grid" forces company managers to make three-part judgments (high, medium, and low) about the business strengths and industry attractiveness of all proposed or existing products of businesses.

— 21. The G.E. "stop-light" evaluation method is a very objective approach because G.E. feels there are too many possible errors if it tries to use subjective criteria for judging "attractiveness" or "strength."

— 22. The G.E. approach favors opportunities which are high in industry attractiveness and low in business strengths over opportunities which are high in business strengths and low in industry attractiveness.

— 23. SBU's are small businesses which try to compete with major divisions of larger multiproduct companies.

— 24. Portfolio management tends to emphasize current profitability and return on investment, often neglecting the long run.

Answers to True-False Questions

1. F, p. 130	9. F, p. 117	17. F, p. 141
2. T, p. 116	10. T, p. 118	18. T, p. 142
3. F, p. 113	11. T, p. 126	19. F, p. 143
4. T, p. 114	12. T, p. 126	20. T, p. 144
5. F, p. 114	13. T, p. 128	21. F, p. 145
6. T, pp. 115-116	14. T, p. 131	22. F, p. 145
7. T, p. 116	15. F, p. 136	23. F, p. 145
8. F, p. 116	16. T, pp. 137-138	24. T, p. 146

Multiple-Choice Questions (Circle the correct response)

1. In the short run at least, which of the following is usually *beyond* the control of the marketing manager?
   a. Political and legal environment
   b. Economic and technological environment
   c. Cultural and social environment
   d. Competitive environment
   e. All of the above.

2. The recent decline in the Canadian birth rate has forced manufacturers of baby food, clothing, and toys to reconsider their marketing strategies. Which of the following uncontrollable variables does this trend illustrate?
   a. Economic and technological environment
   b. Cultural and social environment
   c. Existing business situation
   d. Political and legal environment
   e. Resources and objectives of the firm

3. Which of the following was *not* included in Bill C2?
   a. Existing federally-incorporated cooperatives were provided with a legal framework.
   b. Matters pertaining to competition policy were brought under civil jurisdiction.
   c. Protection for the consumer in the area of warranties was increased.
   d. Services were brought under the Combines Investigation Act.
   e. Bid-rigging was made an indictable offense.

4. In Canada, provincial and city laws are in existence to regulate:
   a. minimum prices and the setting of prices.
   b. the conditions necessary for setting up a business.
   c. the granting of credit.
   d. the rights of the consumer against deceptive trade practices.
   e. all of the above.

5. The purpose of provincial "trade practices" legislation is to:
   a. reduce price-cutting practices at the retail level.
   b. protect consumers from price-discrimination practices.
   c. create inter-provincial standards for trade practices.
   d. protect the consumer from unconscionable and deceptive practices.
   e. allow price-fixing arrangements between manufacturers and small retailers.

6. Which of the following objectives of a business is the *most* important?
   a. To engage in some specific business activity which will perform a socially and economically useful function.
   b. To develop an organization to carry on the business and implement its strategies.
   c. To earn enough profit to survive.
   d. All three of the above are equally important, because a failure in any one could lead to a total failure of the business.

7. Of the following, the *last* objectives that a firm should specify are its:
   a. company objectives.
   b. marketing objectives.
   c. promotion objectives.
   d. advertising objectives.
   e. price objectives.

8. A first step in evaluating marketing opportunities is to:
   a. decide which markets the firm wishes to enter.
   b. consider the objectives and resources of the firm.
   c. hire a "futurist" as a marketing consultant.
   d. estimate market and sales potentials.
   e. find out if potential competitors are larger.

9. Which of the following is *not* an example of how the economic and technological environment may affect marketing strategy planning?
   a. The price of bicycles is rising because of inflation.
   b. Bicycle manufacturers are finding it difficult to keep up with the growing demand for bicycles because of raw material shortages.
   c. Because of exchange rates, imported bikes are cheaper than those made in Canada.
   d. Computer-controlled assembly lines can turn out a new bike every three and one-half seconds.
   e. The demand for bikes is increasing because consumers are becoming more health conscious.

10. Product-market screening criteria should be:
    a. quantitative.
    b. qualitative.
    c. realistic and achievable.
    d. all of the above.
    e. all of the above *except* b.

11. Which of the following is a quantitative screening criteria?
    a. increase sales by $100,000.
    b. earn 25 percent return on investment.
    c. break even within one year.
    d. all of the above are quantitative criteria.

12. General Electric's "strategic planning grid":
    a. substitutes precise quantitative estimates for management judgment and intuition.
    b. places too much emphasis on industry attractiveness, almost ignoring the firm's own business strengths.
    c. emphasizes market share and market growth rate.
    d. is oversimplified in that it assumes all opportunities must be either "good" or "bad."
    e. None of the above is a true statement.

13. GE's Planning Grid approach to evaluating proposed and existing plans and businesses
    a. considers how profitable opportunities are likely to be.
    b. reflects the corporation's objectives.
    c. helps managers see why some ideas are supported and others are not.
    d. can use quantitative data but it is basically a qualitative approach.
    e. All of the above are true.

14. Organizational units within a larger company which focus their efforts on selected product-markets and are treated as separate profit centers are called:
    a. portfolios.
    b. strategic business units.
    c. BTUs.
    d. functional departments.
    e. basing points.

Answers to Multiple-Choice Questions

1. e, pp. 118-123
2. b, pp. 137-141
3. a, pp. 133-134
4. e, p. 134
5. d, pp. 134-135
6. d, p. 113
7. d, p. 113

8. b, pp. 116-118
9. e, p. 123-125
10. d, p. 142
11. d, p. 142
12. e, pp. 144-145
13. e, e, pp. 144-145
14. b, T, pp. 145-146

Name: _____   Course & Section: _____

Exercise 4-1

How marketing environment variables affect strategy planning

Introduction

Marketing managers are not free to choose *any* marketing strategy they please. On the contrary, their choice of strategies is usually affected by variables related to the:

1.   Objectives and resources of the firm

2.   Competitive environment

3.   Economic and technological environment

4.   Political and legal environment

5.   Cultural and social environment

These variables are sometimes called "uncontrollable" because, in the short run, they are beyond the control of marketing managers—although in the long run, marketing managers may be able to influence some or all of these variables.

In the short run, at least, these marketing environment variables may force marketing managers to change their present strategies—or even to choose less-than-ideal strategies. On the other hand, trends in the marketing environments often create new opportunities for alert marketing strategy planners.

Assignment

This exercise is intended to stimulate your thinking about how the marketing environment variables *might* affect marketing strategy planning. Read each of the following situations carefully and answer the questions that follow each situation.

1.   The number of single-adult households in Canada continues to increase. This has had a big impact on some industries. How do you think a food manufacturer's marketing strategy might be influenced by this trend?

   _____

   _____

   _____

2. The economic environment also affects the choices made in marketing strategy planning. A marketing manager must attempt to anticipate, understand and deal with such changes, as well as changes in the technological base underlying this economic environment. Compare and contrast the marketing strategies of firms facing the following situations:

   a. The manufacturer of Mercedes Benz cars during a recession versus a period of economic growth.

   b. A chain grocery store during a recession versus a period of economic growth.

   c. A fashion designer in a recession versus a period of economic growth.

3. In recent years, various federal and local agencies, environmental groups, and consumer advocates have been promising greater concern for the environmental impact of solid waste, especially disposable products and packaging. Consequently, many communities now have active "recycling" programs, and some consumers have begun to switch away from products or packages that are not biodegradable. What effect do you think these trends might have on the marketing efforts of a fast-food restaurant? On a consumer package goods company like Procter and Gamble?

4. Choices made in marketing strategy planning are also affected by aspects of the political and legal environments.

   a. In the past decade, the government of Quebec issued a law prohibiting advertisements directed at children. Describe how this change would affect the marketing strategy planning of a firm such as Fisher-Price in Quebec.

   b. How would it affect the marketing strategy of a cereal manufacturer in the same province?

5. Comment on the purpose of the Consumer Packaging and Labeling Act. Do you agree with the viewpoint that Canadian consumers are rational and capable of deciding what are deceptive marketing activities without government interference? Justify your position.

6. In 1991, the former East Germany and West Germany were reunited—and trade barriers with many formerly communist countries of eastern Europe fell. How do these changes affect marketing opportunities for Volkswagen? For Ford?

    _____

    _____

    _____

Question for Discussion

How can marketers deal effectively with changing trends and developments in their marketing environments?

Learning aid for use with

Exercise 4-2

Analyzing competitors' strategies

Introduction

The competitive environment affects the number and types of competitors a marketing manager must face—and how the competitors may behave. Although a marketing manager usually can't control what a competitor does, it is possible to plan for competition—and where possible to avoid head-on competition by finding new or better ways to satisfy customers' needs. Thus, the search for a breakthrough opportunity—and some sustainable competitive advantage—requires an understanding not only of customers but also of competitors. That's why marketing managers often turn to competitor analysis to evaluate the strengths or weaknesses of competitors' marketing strategies.

As discussed on pages 119-121 of the text, competitor analysis is simply a logical extension of the marketing strategy planning framework that focuses on identifying a target market and the marketing mix to meet that market's needs. It also considers competitive barriers—conditions that may make it difficult or impossible for a firm to compete in a market. A careful competitor analysis may help a marketing manager see opportunities to serve new markets—ones which play to a firm's strengths while avoiding its weaknesses, including competitive weaknesses.

Doing a complete competitor analysis is a real challenge. You will be better equipped to take on that challenge at the end of the course when you know more of the details of marketing strategy planning. But, this exercise gets you started with this type of thinking.

Assignment

The following case describes a retail hardware store and its competitive environment. Read and analyze the case carefully—to better understand the company's marketing strategy strengths and weaknesses. Then, complete the competitor analysis table and answer the questions—being sure to support your ideas with facts from the case.

Miller's Home Hardware

Miller's Home Hardware is located in an affluent suburb of a medium sized city. The store is in a neighborhood shopping center that also includes a grocery store, drugstore, dry cleaners and a pet store. It is between two of the city's largest private schools—and the area is favored as a place to live by doctors, lawyers, and other high-income families.

Mary Miller bought the store five years ago in partnership with her brother, Bob Miller. Mary quit her job as rate analyst with the Provincial Public Utilities commission to try her hand at retailing, and Bob had retired after 20 years in the military. When the Millers took it over, the store had been in business for ten years. At first they made few changes except that Mary used skills developed at her previous job to computerize inventory and ordering.

Miller's is a typical Home Hardware with more than 15,000 items kept regularly in stock. Almost all the stock is ordered through the regional Home Hardware warehouse, which is about three hours away. With computer links and UPS delivery, most items can be restocked within two days to a week. Because the store is small, Miller's often orders in small quantities.

To meet customers' needs, Miller's has added more decorating items than many similar stores. One employee is regularly assigned to a van which will go to customers' houses to measure and install blinds and match existing paint colors. Over the years, the Millers have also added locksmithing, glass cutting, and lawnmower engine repair to the services they offer.

The Millers found that most customers tend to come to the store at the beginning or end of the day and that mid-day business is very slow. Two full-time employees operate cash registers at the front of the store but most of the sales staff are part-timers. The Millers hired several retired tradesmen to work a three-hour shift in the morning. In the afternoon and on week-ends, high-school students assist customers. The Millers try to have enough salespeople "on the floor" to greet almost all customers as soon as they enter the store and help them find and select what they need.

Until recently, Miller's competition came from Hites, a builders' supply house and lumber yard, and from another neighborhood hardware store, Northside Sentry Hardware, which is on a country road about three miles away. Last year, however, Builders Square—a subsidiary of a national retailer—opened a large warehouse store. It is located on an abandoned railroad switching yard two miles towards the center of town. The Builders Square store is huge—more than 5 times the size of the local builder's supply and more than 20 times the size of Miller's.

When Builders Square opened, Bob Miller said: "This'll probably be the end of us. There's hardly an item that we sell that the warehouse store doesn't sell—and at a deep discount too. There's no way we can match their prices! When they sell lawn mowers, they bring in a truck load." But after a year, Mary was not so pessimistic. As she said to Bob, "We've had our best year ever. I wish I understood it. I hear that the Sentry Hardware is about to close its doors—and one of our part-timers says that Hites Builders Supply is like a ghost town."

Complete the table on the following page—with specific emphasis on aspects of strategy that are different from its competitors. Some of the blanks have been partially filled in for you. However, more information may have to be added to some parts of the table.

Learning aid for use with

	Miller's Home Hardware	Hites Builders' Supply	Builders Square
Target Market (Who are the customers; how do they shop)		Builders and contractors; some walk-in homeowner business; most customers are probably knowledgeable and know specifically what they want	
Product (focus of product line, including service; branding; guarantees			very broad product line of hardware and lumber; some well-known brands; mainly self-service with some help available at front-desk
Place (channel relationships with suppliers; transportation and storing considerations	Tied to Regional Home Hardware Wholesaler		National purchasing; truck-load direct deliveries from manufacturers
Price (price level; credit terms; special sales; etc.)	High compared to competition	Discounts to big customers or on large orders, and free delivery for large items	Very low everyday prices; delivery available at extra cost; modest discounts and credit to contractors who are regular customers
Promotion		Ads in newspaper & in local real estate mag.; Yellow pages; some telemarketing and personal selling (out of store) to big developers and contractors	National TV ads and local newspaper inserts; special sales desk for contractors to place special orders
Competitive Barriers			Chain's large volume purchases give it a cost advantage; large facility supports product availability

1. What are some of the key ways that the Home Hardware wholesaler might help Miller's to compete with the other competitors?

2. Do you think that Miller's competes most directly with Hites or with Builders Square? Explain your reasons.

3. Why do you think that Miller's could have a profitable year even when Sentry Hardware and Hites are having real problems?

4. Is there anything that Miller's could do if another local hardware store were to open nearby (or if Sentry Hardware were to make changes) and offer a similar marketing mix designed to serve the same target customers?

Question for Discussion

If head-on competition makes it more difficult to develop a successful marketing strategy, why do so many firms continue to compete in markets that are characterized by pure (or nearly pure) competition?

Learning aid for use with

Chapter 5

Getting information for marketing decisions

What This Chapter Is About

Marketing managers need information to plan effective marketing strategies. Chapter 5 stresses that getting good information for marketing decisions involves much more than just surveys.

Many managers now rely on marketing information systems to help meet their recurring information needs. But marketing managers must also deal with ever-changing needs in dynamic markets. So you should understand how marketing research can help marketing managers solve problems--and make better decisions.

A scientific approach to marketing research is explained and illustrated. This approach can help marketing managers solve problems--not just collect data.

This chapter also shows that the text's strategy planning framework is especially helpful in identifying marketing problems. This framework, along with a "scientific approach," can be very helpful in solving real problems. Often, small bits of information available *now* are far more valuable than an extensive research report which cannot be available for several months.

Try to understand how to go about a scientific approach to problem solving--just finding the right problem is sometimes half the job. This is something you should be able to do by the end of the text-- even though you do not have all the tools and skills needed to do a formal research project. Specialists can be hired to do that part of the job if you--as the marketing manager--have correctly identified what information is needed to make the marketing strategy decisions.

Important Terms

marketing information system (MIS), p. 154
decision support system (DSS), p. 155
marketing model, p. 155
marketing research, p. 157
scientific method, p. 160
hypotheses, p. 160
marketing research process, p. 161
situation analysis, p. 163
secondary data, p. 164
primary data, p. 164
syndicated data, p. 164
research proposal, p. 166

qualitative research, p. 166
focus group interview, p. 166
quantitative research, p. 168
response rate, p. 168
consumer panel, p. 171
experimental method, p. 172
statistical packages, p. 173
population, p. 174
sample, p. 174
random sampling, p. 174
confidence intervals, p. 175
validity, p. 176

True-False Questions

__ 1. A marketing information system is an organized way of using "one-shot" research projects to gather and analyze information that will help marketing managers make better decisions.

__ 2. The key advantage in using an MIS is that it makes available information accessible.

__ 3. A decision support system (DSS) is a computer program that makes it easy for a marketing manager to get and use information as he or she is making decisions.

__ 4. Decision support systems that include marketing models allow the manager to see how answers to questions might change in various situations.

__ 5. Marketing research is best defined as a set of techniques applied by specialists in survey design or statistical methods.

__ 6. Marketing research details may be handled by staff or outside specialists, but the marketing manager must know how to plan and evaluate research projects.

__ 7. Unethical practices among researcher make consumers unwilling to participate in any research.

__ 8. The scientific method is a decision-making approach that focuses on being objective and orderly in testing ideas before accepting them.

__ 9. Hypotheses are statements of fact about relationships between things or what will happen in the future.

__ 10. The marketing research process is a five-step application of the scientific method that includes: defining the problem, analyzing the situation, getting problem-specific data, interpreting the data, and solving the problem.

__ 11. Defining the problem--although usually the easiest job of the marketing researcher--is also the most important job.

__ 12. Developing a list that includes all possible problem areas is a sensible start to the situation analysis step.

__ 13. Gathering primary data about the problem area is part of analyzing the situation.

__ 14. Secondary data is information which is already collected or published.

__ 15. The Canada Year Book is a good source of primary data.

__ 16. A written research proposal is a plan that specifies what marketing research information will be obtained and how.

__ 17. The two basic methods for obtaining information about customers are questioning and observing.

__ 18. Qualitative research seeks in-depth, open-ended responses.

___ 19. A focus group interview involves interviewing 6 to 10 people in an informal group setting.

___ 20. It is typical to use quantitative research in preparation for doing qualitative research.

___ 21. Quantitative research seeks structured responses that can be summarized in numbers--like percentages, averages, or other statistics.

___ 22. A common quantitative research approach to summarize consumers' opinions and preferences is to have respondents indicate how much they agree or disagree with a questionnaire statement.

___ 23. The response rate is the percent of people contacted who complete a questionnaire.

___ 24. Mail surveys are economical per questionnaire--if a large number of people respond.

___ 25. A mail survey is the best research approach if you want respondents to expand on particular points and give in-depth information.

___ 26. With the observation method, the researcher avoids talking to the subject.

___ 27. The use of computer scanners to observe what customers actually do is changing research methods for many firms.

___ 28. A consumer panel is a group of consumers who provide information occasionally--whenever a meeting of the group is called.

___ 29. With the experimental method, the responses of groups which are similar, except on the characteristic being tested, are compared.

___ 30. The experimental method is the most widely used marketing research method because managers want and need quantitative information to make better decisions.

___ 31. Syndicated data is a blend of primary and secondary data available from private research firms.

___ 32. Statistical packages are easy-to-use computer programs that help analyze data.

___ 33. In regard to marketing research, *population* means the total group that responds to a survey.

___ 34. In most marketing research studies, only a sample--a part of the relevant population--is surveyed.

___ 35. Random sampling is sampling in which each member of the population does not have the same chance of being included in the sample.

___ 36. With random samples, researchers can narrow confidence intervals by increasing sample sizes.

___ 37. Validity concerns the extent to which data measures what it is intended to measure.

___ 38. Conducting and interpreting a marketing research project should be left entirely to the researcher because most marketing managers have no training in this area.

___ 39. One should always seek to obtain as much marketing information as possible before making a decision.

Answers to True-False Questions

1. F, p. 154	14. T, p. 164	27. T, p. 171
2. T, p. 154	15. T, p. 165	28. F, p. 171
3. T, p. 155	16. T, p. 166	29. T, pp. 172-173
4. T, p. 155	17. T, p. 166	30. F, p. 173
5. F, p. 157	18. T, p. 166	31. T, p. 164
6. T, p. 157	19. T, p. 166	32. T, p. 173
7. T, p. 159	20. F, p. 168	33. F, p. 174
8. T, p. 160	21. T, p. 168	34. T, p. 174
9. F, p. 160	22. T, p. 168	35. F, p.174
10. T, p. 161	23. T, p. 168	36. T, p. 174
11. F, p. 162	24. T, p. 168	37. T, p. 176
12. T, p. 163	25. F, p. 168	38. F, p. 176
13. F, p. 164	26. T, p. 170	39. F, p. 177

Multiple-Choice Questions (Circle the correct response)

1. Which of the following statements about marketing information systems is *true*?
   a. Marketing information systems are used to gather and analyze data from intracompany sources, while marketing research deals with external sources.
   b. Decision support systems allow managers to see how answers to questions might change in different situations.
   c. Computerized marketing information systems tend to increase the quantity of information available for decision making but not without some corresponding decrease in quality.
   d. The value of decision support systems is limited because the manager can't use them while he is actually making his decisions.
   e. All of the above are true statements.

2. Marketing research:
   a. requires a market research department in the company.
   b. consists mainly of survey design and statistical techniques.
   c. should be planned by research specialists.
   d. is needed to keep isolated marketing planners in touch with their markets.
   e. All of the above are true.

3. In small companies,
   a. there is no need for marketing research.
   b. there should be a marketing research department--or there will be no one to do marketing research.
   c. the emphasis of marketing research should be on customer surveys.
   d. salespeople often do what marketing research gets done.

4. The scientific method is important in marketing research because it:
   a. forces the researcher to follow certain procedures, thereby reducing the need to rely on intuition. 盲肓)
   b. develops hypotheses and then tests them.
   c. specifies a marketing strategy which is almost bound to succeed.
   d. Both a and b are correct.
   e. All of the above are correct.

5. The most important--and often the most difficult step--of the marketing research process is:
   a. analyzing the situation.
   b. collecting data.
   c. observation.
   d. defining the problem.
   e. interpreting the data.

6. When analyzing the situation, the marketing analyst:
   a. sizes up the situation by talking with executives in competitive companies.
   b. seeks information that is already available in the problem area.
   c. begins to talk informally to a random sample of customers.
   d. talks to experts in data analysis at trade association meetings.
   e. All of the above.

7. A small manufacturing firm has just experienced a rapid drop in sales. The marketing manager thinks that he knows what the problem is and has been carefully analyzing secondary data to check his thinking. His next step should be to:
   a. conduct an experiment.
   b. develop a formal research project to gather primary data.
   c. conduct informal discussion with outsiders, including middlemen, to see if he has correctly defined the problem.
   d. develop a hypothesis and predict the future behavior of sales.
   e. initiate corrective action before sales drop any further.

8. Which of the following is a good source for locating secondary data:
   a. a focus group interview.
   b. personal interviews with customers.
   c. the Canada Year Book
   d. a marketing research survey.
   e. none of the above.

9. A research proposal
   a. should be written by the marketing manager--not the researcher--since the manager knows what needs to be done.
   b. usually can't provide much information about how data will be collected, since it is hard to tell until the research is started.
   c. might lead a marketing manager to decide that the proposed research will cost more than it is worth.
   d. is a plan developed during the problem definition stage of research.
   e. All of the above are true.

10. A marketing analyst would *not* use which of the following research methods when gathering primary data?
a. Observation
b. Experiment
c. Mail survey
d. Library search
e. Personal interviews

11. With regard to getting problem-specific data:
a. the observation method involves asking consumers direct questions about their observations.
b. telephone surveys are declining in popularity.
c. focus group interviews are usually more representative than a set of personal interviews.
d. mail surveys are limited to short, simple questions--extensive questioning cannot be done.
e. None of the above is a true statement.

12. To be effective, marketing research should be:
a. quantitative.
b. qualitative.
c. either or both--depending on the situation.

13. A marketing researcher wants to do a survey to probe in-depth consumer attitudes about their experiences with the company's products. He is LEAST likely to get what he wants if he uses
a. personal interviews.
b. the focus group approach.
c. a telephone interview approach.
d. a mail survey.
e. None of the above is very useful for getting in-depth information about consumer attitudes.

14. Experimental method research:
a. is often hard to use in "real world" markets.
b. can use either questioning or observing.
c. is less popular than focus group interviews.
d. is used to compare groups for differences.
e. all of the above.

15. A statistical package is most likely to be used for a marketing research project that:
a. used focus group interviews.
b. relied on secondary data.
c. included a mail survey.
d. consisted of open-ended questions in a personal interview.
e. was based on qualitative research.

16. Using random samples:
a. guarantees that the findings will be valid.
b. is stressed by theoretical statisticians--but usually is unnecessary in marketing research.
c. guarantees that the sample will have the same characteristics as the population.
d. allows the researcher to use confidence intervals to evaluate estimates from the sample data.
e. All of the above are true statements.

17. At the step when data are interpreted, a marketing manager should:
    a. leave it to the technical specialists to draw the correct conclusions.
    b. realize that statistical summaries from a sample may not be precise for the whole population.
    c. know that quantitative survey responses are valid, but qualitative research may not be valid.
    d. be satisfied with the sample used as long as it is large.
    e. All of the above are correct.

18. Which of the following statements about marketing research is *false*?
    a. A low response rate may affect the accuracy of results.
    b. Managers never get all the information they would like to have.
    c. Getting more or better information is not always worth the cost.
    d. Because of the risks involved, marketing managers should never base their decision on incomplete information.
    e. A marketing manager should evaluate *beforehand* whether research findings will be relevant.

Answers to Multiple-Choice Questions

1. b, p. 155
2. d, p. 157
3. d, p. 157
4. d, p. 160-161
5. d, p. 162
6. b, p. 163

7. c, p. 163
8. c, p. 165
9. c, p. 166
10. d, p. 166
11. e, p. 166-167
12. c, p. 168

13. d, p. 168
14. e, p. 172-173
15. c, p. 173-174
16. d, p. 174-175
17. b, p. 174-175
18. d, p. 177

Exercise 5-1

Problem definition in marketing research

Introduction

Perhaps the most important step in researching a marketing problem is defining the problem correctly. The marketing manager must clearly define the problem to be researched before the marketing researcher can develop an effective research design. This means that the marketing manager should direct the efforts of the researcher, rather than simply asking for some "marketing research" when a problem arises.

The strategic planning framework that is used throughout the text can be of great help in defining marketing problems. (See pages 48-50 of the text.) For instance, the problem may be caused by rapid changes in the uncontrollable variables—especially the economic, competitive, or legal environments—or the firm may have lost sight of its objectives. The problem could also be that the firm has neglected to select a target market, or that the needs and attitudes of its target market have changed. Finally, one or more of the "four Ps" may be inappropriate for the rest of the marketing mix.

Where more than one problem has been identified, it is generally desirable to start with the broadest or highest level problems. For example, a marketing manager should not be concerned with strategy planning until the firm's objectives have been made clear. Some marketing problems may require whole new strategies, while other problems may involve only one of the four Ps if all other elements of the firm's marketing strategy seem to fit together well. For example, changes in the economic environment may call for a whole new marketing strategy, while only some "minor" product change may be needed if the target market's needs have changed slightly or the product was not exactly what consumers wanted.

Assignment

This exercise will give you some practice in defining marketing problems which might require some research. Read the following cases and, for each one, clearly state the nature of the problem and explain why the problem might require some marketing research. If you feel there are several problems in the particular case, list them in the order of their importance and indicate which problems you would research first.

Note: Most managers would like to know more about "everything," but generally it is not practical to research every detail of a case. Therefore, in doing this exercise, it may be necessary for you to make some reasonable assumptions—based either on the facts of the case or your knowledge of the marketplace—in order to focus the problem and subsequent research on issues that really make a difference in the case.

The first case is presented with an answer, as an example.

1.   The Atlantic Hamburger shop opened on a lot adjoining a nationally-franchised hamburger shop which had been in operation about one year. During its grand opening, the Atlantic attracted large crowds of envious people wishing to try the products of this new business. However, after about ten days of operation, the number of customers coming into the Atlantic seemed to be declining.

     By the end of the first month, very few customers were coming in. At the same time, business next door at the franchised hamburger shop seemed to be prospering. The Atlantic offered all the items that the nationally-franchised shop offered, as well as several other items which were not on the menu of its franchised competitor. Prices were about the same at both shops.

     Sample Answer

     Since the Atlantic located its shop right next door to a nationally-franchised competitor, it apparently hopes to make a profit catering to the same target market (whatever that is!) as its competitor. Since the franchise operation is prospering, Place does not appear to be the problem. There are many shops of this type competing at, about the same price level with similar products, so Price is probably not the problem either. And the large crowds during the Atlantic's grand opening may rule out Promotion.

     Potential customers did "sample" the product, and apparently are not returning for more. Therefore, the problem may be in the *Product* area, and this possibility should be researched first. Target customers may not like the taste or appearance of the products, or they may not like the Atlantic's service (e.g., waiting time, cleanliness, appearance, the employees' attitudes, etc.). Marketing research can be used to determine if the Atlantic's product/service is really the problem and what changes are likely to be effective.

2.   The Torch Club, now a restaurant-dance floor-bar combination, is located about one mile from the edge of Eastern Provincial University and two miles from the downtown district of a city of about 150,000. The Club is large and could seat over 500 people comfortably. The business has been losing money for four years. In this period various things have been tried.

     First, the major emphasis was on indoor golfing with some food. After about six months, the emphasis was changed to a night club, emphasizing record playing, and go-go dancing—while at the same time retaining some of the golfing facilities. After several months of this, the emphasis was changed to family-style restaurant, featuring roasted chicken. Six months later, the business tried to become more attractive by featuring country and western, and sometimes rock'nroll music. About six months later, a number of billiard tables were installed in an effort to become a fancy billiard parlor.

     Currently, there is a small dance floor, and a band plays soft rock music on Wednesday, Friday, and Saturday nights. The record player has no special emphasis and the Club still has some of the golf facilities, billiard tables, a small sit-down bar, and a small restaurant area. At no time during its operation has it been profitable.

Answer

3. The Bronson Company, a leading manufacturer of breakfast cereals, has developed a new ready-to-eat breakfast cereal which is expected to become very popular among pre-school children. The cereal will be called "Kermits" and will be manufactured in frog-shaped pieces which look like the "Kermit the Frog" character that has become a big hit on children's television shows. The new cereal is also expected to appeal to health-conscious parents because it contains no sugar and tests conducted by an independent laboratory have shown it to be very nutritious.

Unfortunately, Bronson's new product is being introduced at a time when the government is trying to discourage the use of television advertising aimed at children under eight years old, and is also thinking of banning the use of cartoon characters such as "Tony the Tiger" to help sell products to children. Furthermore, many parent groups are in an uproar about commercial attempts to "manipulate" their children's minds. In particular, ready-to-eat breakfast cereals have received so much bad publicity from mass media sources that Bronson is not sure if parents will believe its claim about the nutritional benefits of "Kermits."

Answer

Questions for Discussion

What kinds of business problems are most apt to require marketing research? Why?

Learning aid for use with

Exercise 5-2

Evaluating marketing research

Introduction

Marketing managers need good information to develop effective marketing strategies. They need to know about the marketing environment variables, about possible target customers, and about the marketing mix decisions they can make.

Sometimes the only way to get needed information is with marketing research. When this is the case, the manager can sometimes get help--perhaps from marketing research specialists in the firm or from outside specialists. But, marketing managers must be able to explain what their problems are--and what kinds of information they need. They should also know about some of the basic decisions made during the research process--so they know the limitations of the research. They need to be able to see if the results of a research project will really solve the problem!

It is true that marketing research can involve many technical details--that is why specialists are often involved. But, often a marketing manager can use "common sense"--and knowledge of marketing strategy planning--to improve marketing research.

Assignment

In this exercise you are presented with short cases that involve marketing research. You are asked to identify and comment about the possible limitations of the research. The cases are accompanied by questions that will help to get your thinking started.

You will need to know about the marketing research ideas discussed in Chapter 5 to evaluate the cases. But, remember that the idea here is *not* just to memorize the points from the text. Rather, you should really think about the *problem*, and use common sense along with the information in the book to evaluate the case situation.

A sample answer is provided to the first case--to give you an example of the type of thinking that might be helpful. But--before you read the answer--think about how you would answer the question yourself.

1.   A marketing manager for a bank wants to survey potential customers to see if they know about the bank's new drive-in window services. An outside marketing research specialist tells the manager that for $5,000 the research firm can send out a mail survey to 500 people, tabulate the results, and present a report. He explains that the bank will need to provide a computer mailing list of people who have accounts at the bank--to save costs in developing the sample. He concludes by pointing out that the research will be quite inexpensive: "We will give you results

from a representative sample of 500 people, at only $10 per respondent. And you can be confident with a sample of 500 that the statistics are accurate."

a)   Is the proposed sample well-suited to the manager's problem? Why or why not?

Sample answer: No. The bank is interested in all potential customers and what they think about the bank's service. Using only customers in the sample might be convenient and inexpensive, but they might not be representative of noncustomers!

b)   Is the researcher's concluding statement misleading? (*Hint:* Think about the response rate issue.) Why or why not?

Sample answer: The statement is probably misleading. As noted above, the sample may not be representative. The estimated "$10 per customer" is unlikely because all of the questionnaires probably will not be returned. Total response will probably be much lower than 500, and the cost per actual respondent would therefore be higher. Finally, "confidence" in the results will depend on the response rate achieved--and how representative the results are of responses from noncustomers.

2.   Peter Belton is marketing manager for a financial services firm that offers consumers a wide choice of mutual funds. He is interested in developing ideas about new funds he should offer. One of the firm's financial planners suggested that they conduct a few focus group interviews with some current investor-customers to get ideas. So Belton hired an outside marketing research specialist to set up and videotape two focus group sessions.

After the sessions, the specialist presented a short summary report. Her main conclusion was that 40 percent of the participants would probably buy a fund that invested in biotechnology, and urged the company to develop such a fund quickly "since the market will be large." She added that, from watching the tapes, she was certain that the customers were unhappy with the performance of many of the firm's present funds. This left Belton quite concerned and wondering what to do.

a)   Is a focus group interview a good basis for drawing the type of conclusions offered by the outside researcher? Why or why not?

b)   Should Belton hire the marketing research firm to do a large survey to see if customers are really unhappy, as the specialist suggests based on the focus groups? Why or why not?

Learning aid for use with

3.　A marketing manager for an expensive men's clothing store is concerned that profits have dropped, and he has noticed that many customers who once were "regulars" are not coming back anymore. He decides to send out a questionnaire to a sample of old customers, using addresses from his mailing list. He wrote a letter asking customers to respond to his questionnaire. He also provided a postage paid envelope for return of the completed forms. The instructions on the short questionnaire were:

(1)　Please discuss the things you liked most about our store the last time you purchased clothing here?

(2)　Please explain what you liked least about our store. Please discuss anything that bothers you.

(3)　Please tell us what other men's clothing stores you may have patronized, and what is it about each store that you like?

(4)　Is a mail survey useful for questions like these? Why or why not?

(5)　What would you recommend if the manager asked you for ideas on how to get better information about his problem?

4.　A marketing manager for a wholesale supplier of industrial equipment is trying to decide how many machines to order during the coming year--to be sure to have enough on hand to meet demand. He decides that it would be useful to do a survey of customers to whom he has sold equipment in the last year. He wants to know how satisfied they are with their current equipment, and also how many want to buy another machine from him in the coming year. He would also like to know if his customers are in good enough financial shape to be able to afford additional equipment. He decides to have salesmen call the customers and ask the following questions:

(1)　How do you feel about the equipment you bought from us? Are you very satisfied, or only moderately satisfied?

(2)　Do you plan to buy another machine from us during the coming year? Yes, you plan to buy; or no, you don't plan to buy.

(3)　I have one final question, and your response will be strictly confidential and used only in statistical summaries with answers from other respondents. Would you please tell us how much money your firm earned during the last year?

Question for Discussion

How do the limitations of qualitative research differ from the limitations of quantitative research?

Chapter 6

Demographic dimensions of the Canadian consumer market

What This Chapter Is About

Chapter 6 is the first of a group of three chapters about customers and their buying behavior. Actually, we know a great deal about potential customers. Therefore, there is no reason for relying on common and *often erroneous stereotypes* and generalizations.

Here you will see that the Canadian population is growing and that disparities in income distribution are great. At the same time, however, expenditure patterns vary considerably by age, lifestage, and other dimensions. This data will provide background for our analysis of target markets. Try to get a "feel" for relationships. Don't just memorize a lot of "facts." Demographic relationships are enduring—and a good understanding of these relationships will help you avoid mistakes when decisions about the size of potential markets must be made quickly.

Important Terms

demographics, pp. 196-198
Census Metropolitan Area (CMA), p. 198
megalopolis, p. 200
mosaic, p. 201
birthrate, p. 207

age distribution, p. 207
income distribution, pp. 214-217
disposable income, p. 217
discretionary income, p. 217
lifestages, p. 219

True-False Questions

___ 1. The first and most basic question which must be answered about any potential market is: what are its relevant segmenting dimensions?

___ 2. The provinces of British Columbia and Alberta are each larger in population than the four Atlantic provinces combined.

___ 3. Of all the provinces, British Columbia had the highest percentage increase in population between 1982 and 1992.

___ 4. Quebec, of all the provinces, had the lowest percentage increase in population between 1982 and 1992.

___ 5. The fact that more people are moving from the country to the city has brought about an increase in the number of farms.

___ 6. A CMA is the "main labor market" of a continuous built up area having a population of at least 250,000.

_ 7. Just under half of Canada's total population resides in one of the country's 25 CMA's.

_ 8. It is predicted that the population will increase by over 200,000 each year due to immigration.

_ 9. Canada's population growth has slowed dramatically and ranks among the slow growth countries of the world.

_ 10. The median age of the Canadian population has remained unchanged since 1981.

_ 11. Lone parent families now account for about 5% of all Canadian families.

_ 12. In Canada, the top quintile of income earners usually receive at least 39% of total income.

_ 13. Just over 2/3rds of all Canadian women with children under 16 are now in the labour force.

_ 14. More than 50 percent of families have more than one wage earner.

_ 15. Since 1965, the poorest 20 percent of families have never received more than 6.5 percent of total family income.

_ 16. Those in the various income quintiles spend approximately the same percentage of income for food and shelter.

_ 17. Disposable income is the income remaining after taxes and savings have been subtracted.

_ 18. Most discretionary income is spent on necessities.

_ 19. While income has a direct bearing on spending patterns, other demographic dimensions—such as age and lifestage—may be just as important to marketers.

_ 20. The "new childless household" category of the lifestage approach likes to spend money but is also concerned about being ripped off.

_ 21. Other than English or French, Italian is the most frequently reported mother tonque among residents of both Vancouver and Montreal.

Answers to True-False Questions

1. T, p. 196	8. F, p. 201	15. T, p. 215
2. T, p. 197	9. T, p. 203	16. F, p. 218
3. T, p. 197	10. F, p. 207	17. F, p. 217
4. F, p. 197	11. F, p. 211	18. F, p. 217
5. F, p. 198	12. T, p. 215	19. T, p. 219
6. F, p. 198	13. T, p. 213	20. T, p. 226
7. F, p. 199	14. T, p. 213	21. F, pp. 204-205

Multiple-Choice Questions (Circle the correct response)

1. When analyzing a potential product-market, a marketing planner should decide:
   a. what its relevant segmenting dimensions are.
   b. where it is.
   c. how big it is.
   d. All of the above.

2. According to the text, which of the following provinces had the largest percentage increase in population between 1982 and 1992?
   a. Ontario
   b. New Brunswick
   c. Alberta
   d. Saskatchewan
   e. British Columbia

3. Which province registered the lowest percentage increase in population between 1982 and 1992?
   a. Prince Edward Island
   b. Quebec
   c. Manitoba
   d. Saskatchewan
   e. None of the above

4. The CMA with the largest number of individuals who report Chinese as their mother tongue is:
   a. Toronto
   b. Vancouver
   c. Montreal
   d. Victoria
   e. None of the above

5. The third most popular mother tongue in Vancouver is:
   a. French
   b. Italian
   c. Chinese
   d. German
   e. None of the above

6. Disposable income is defined as:
   a. total market value of goods and services produced.
   b. gross national product per capita.
   c. income available after taxes.
   d. income available before taxes.
   e. Income available after taxes and "necessities."

7. Which of the following lifestage groups is most receptive to trying new products and new brands?
    a. New childless households
    b. New parents
    c. Empty nesters
    d. Crowded nesters
    e. All are equally receptive

Answers to Multiple-Choice Questions

1. d, p. 196   4. a, pp. 204-205   6. c, p. 217
2. e, p. 197   5. e. pp. 204-205   7. a, p. 221
3. a, p. 197

Exercise 6-1

How demographic trends affect marketing strategy planning

Introductory Comments

Like Exercise 4-1, this exercise explores the strategic implications of changes and trends in marketing's uncontrollable environments—except that this exercise focuses exclusively on demographic trends within the cultural and social environment. It is critical that the students learn to anticipate and recognize such trends—as well as to constantly examine their marketing implications. Effective marketing strategy planners are—and must be—effective environmental scanners.

A common approach to identifying markets uses "demographic" characteristics of customers—such as age, sex, race, education, occupation, geographical location, income, marital status, and family size. The popularity of demographics is due to the fact that such characteristics are easily measured, easily understood, and readily available in published form. Demographic characteristics are very useful for identifying market segments, planning appropriate marketing mixes and estimating market potential.

This exercise will stress another major use of demographics—to monitor changes and trends in the uncontrollable cultural and social environments to help find new marketing opportunities.
We will focus on four major demographic trends:

1.   People in the "baby boom" generation are entering their peak earning—and saving—years.

2.   The increasing life spans of senior citizens.

3.   The "baby bust" of the 1970s means a smaller number of 18-25 year olds entering the work force.

4.   The trend toward smaller family units and a larger number of "single adult" households.

You will be asked to evaluate the likely positive or negative effects of these four trends on three major industries.

There are no "correct" answers to this exercise, of course, as the future effects of such trends are largely conjectural. However, the chart that follows suggests some possibilities for the three industries.

Assignment

Listed below are three major industries in Canada. In the space provided, discuss the likely positive and/or negative effects of the above-mentioned demographic trends on *each* of the three industries. Base your answers on the text discussion and your general knowledge—DO NOT DO ANY LIBRARY OR FIELD RESEARCH. Use your head instead—to apply what you already know!

Industries

Canadian Vacation Travel	Cosmetics	Pre-cooked Food

1. Industry: Canadian Vacation Travel

    a) Effects of baby boom generation's peak earnings and saving years.

    b) Effects of longer life span of senior citizens.

    c) Effects of the baby bust generation entering the work force.

    d) Effects of smaller family units and more "single adult" households.

2. Industry: Cosmetics

    a) Effects of baby boom generation's peak earnings and saving years.

    b) Effects of longer life span of senior citizens.

    c) Effects of the baby bust generation entering the work force.

    d) Effects of smaller family units and more "single adult" households.

3. Industry: Pre-cooked Food

   a) Effects of baby boom generation's peak earnings and saving years.

   b) Effects of longer life span of senior citizens.

   c) Effects of the baby bust generation entering the work force.

   d) Effects of smaller family units and more "single adult" households.

Question for Discussion

Name some other important demographic trends. How might these trends affect the three industries discussed in the exercise?

Name: _____   Course & Section: _____

Exercise 6-2

Strategy planning for consumer products: International markets

Introduction

Many brand names are recognized worldwide and firms with successful products in their domestic markets frequently turn to international markets for rapid growth and new profit opportunities. Marketing strategy planning is, in essence, no different for international markets than for domestic markets. The first should choose a target market and develop a marketing mix to satisfy the needs of the that target market.

But in practice, international marketing strategy planning can be much more difficult, however. Strategy planners often must deal with unfamiliar marketing environment variables. And there may be big differences in language, customs, beliefs, religion and race, and even income distribution from one country to another. Even identical products may differ in terms of which needs they satisfy, the conditions under which they are used, and people's ability to buy them. In addition, new and unfamiliar competitors are likely to be encountered.

Also, reliable data for market analysis may be harder to obtain when a firm moves into international markets. The wealth of published data which North American marketers tend to take for granted may not exist at all. And consumers in some countries are far less willing to take part in market research studies than most North Americans.

This exercise shows how some preliminary market analysis—i.e. forecasting of market size—might be done for international markets using demographic data (population figures and per capita expenditures) as a base.

Assignment

Read the following case and answer the questions which follow:

The Portable Potables Corporation recently developed a new beverage named "Mocha Magic," a chocolate-coffee flavored drink targeted to people who take their lunch to work. The flavorful combination is packaged in aseptic "drink boxes" which have a long shelf life and don't require refrigeration. Mocha Magic met with success when introduced for sale in the United States a year ago. Although the product had been formulated to be consumed cold, research showed a very large market for people who drink Mocha Magic warm, by microwaving it in its original carton. A majority of lunchrooms and cafeterias have one or more microwave ovens available.

PORTABLE POTABLES CORPORATION

When Portable Potables commissioned extensive survey data in the U.S., the company found that the new drink appealed to different groups of consumers, depending on their previous lunchtime drink habit. According to the survey, Mocha Magic had a favorable rating with 40 percent of the U.S. coffee drinkers, a 30 percent favorable rating with those who usually drank soft drinks, and a 10 percent favorable rating with those whose typical lunchtime drink was tea. Sales and survey data show that among those that like the taste, about 10 percent of purchasers actually switch to Mocha Magic. Little acceptance was achieved among wine, milk and water drinkers.

Encouraged by the success of Mocha Magic, Portable Potables Corporation decided to expand its market coverage overseas. The following four countries are being considered as potential new markets: United Kingdom, France, Spain, and Germany. Because limited funds for expansion are available, only *one* of these countries will be selected for the first international market for Mocha Magic. The marketing manager of Portable Potables was asked to decide which of the four countries would offer the highest dollar sales potential.

As a start, the manager obtained the market data shown in Table 6-1 by looking up the populations of the four countries in the *U.S. Statistical Abstract* and then asking a market research firm to estimate the average per capita expenditures in these countries for tea, coffee, and soft drinks.

TABLE 6-1
Estimated Average Annual per Capita Expenditures on
Selected Meal-Time Beverages in Four Countries

Country	Population	Per Capita Beverage Expenditures		
		Coffee	Soft Drink	Tea
United Kingdom	57,121,000	$40	$12	$80
France	56,184,000	$20	$40	$15
Spain	39,623,000	$15	$40	$30
Germany	79,070,000	$60	$80	$25

The manager got an initial estimate of dollar sales potential for Mocha Magic in each country based on the experience in the U.S. with each of the three segments identified by the present drink choice. For example, based on U.S. experience, 40 percent of the coffee drinkers in a country can be expected to like Mocha Magic, and of those, 10 percent are likely to switch their beverage purchases to Mocha Magic. So Mocha Magic can be expected to pick up 4 percent (that is, 40 percent times 10 percent) of coffee drinkers' per capita beverage purchases. Looking at Table 6-1, we see that in the U.K., per capita coffee purchases were $40, so Mocha Magic could expect $1.60 (that is 4 percent of $40) expenditure. This result is entered into the table which follows, and the calculations for the U.K. have been completed.

1. a. Determine the per capita dollar sales potential for Mocha Magic in France, Spain, and Germany by completing the table.

U.S. Experience				
Percent who like taste of Mocha Magic	**Former Drink Preference**			
	Coffee	Soft Drink	Tea	
	40	30	10	
Country	**Per Capita Potential Expenditure on Mocha Magic, by Segment**			**Total Potential per Capita Expenditure for Mocha Magic**
	Coffee	Soft Drink	Tea	
United Kingdom	$1.60	$0.36	$0.80	$2.76
France				
Spain				
Germany				

b. Now calculate the total sales potential by country. Again, the U.K. has been completed as an example.

Country	Population	Calculated per capita sales of Mocha Magic	Total Sales Potential
United Kingdom	57,121,000	$2.76	$157,653,960
France	56,184,000		
Spain	39,623,000		
Germany	79,070,000		

2. Based on your estimates in the table above, which one of the four countries would offer the highest dollar sales potential for Mocha Magic?

3.   What do the above calculations assume about the Portable Potables Corporation's potential target markets for Mocha Magic?

4.   Should Mocha Magic's market size forecasts be based solely on the data used above? What other demographic or psychographic data would be useful?

Question for Discussion

Will Portable Potables Corporation have to change it's marketing mix when it expands overseas?

Learning aid for use with

Chapter 7

● Behavioral dimensions of the consumer market

What This Chapter Is About

Chapter 7 focuses on the contribution of the behavioral sciences to our understanding of consumer behavior. As we saw in Chapter 6, demographic analysis does not fully explain *why* people buy or *what* they buy.

The importance of considering several behavioral dimensions at the same time is stressed. This is not easy because there are many psychological and sociological theories. Nevertheless, marketing managers must make decisions based on their knowledge of potential target markets. They must do their best to integrate the various theories and findings. This chapter is intended to get you started on this task.

At the beginning of the chapter, a buyer behavior model is presented to help organize your thinking. Then toward the end of the chapter, an expanded model of the consumer's problem solving process is presented. Try to find a way of integrating these models together for yourself. Behavioral science findings can be a great help, but you still must add your own judgment to apply the various findings in particular markets. These findings coupled with "market sense" can take you a long way in marketing strategy planning.

● **Important Terms**

economics—oriented, p. 227
economic needs, p. 227
buyer behavior, p. 227
needs, p. 228
wants, p. 228
drive, p. 228
physiological needs, p. 229
safety needs, p. 229
social needs, p. 229
personal needs, p. 229
perception, p. 230
selective exposure, p. 231
selective perception, p. 231
selective retention, p. 231
learning, p. 231
cues, p. 232
response, p. 232
reinforcement, p. 232
attitude, p. 232
belief, p. 233

psychographics, p. 234
lifestyle analysis, p. 234
social class, p. 236
reference group, p. 238
opinion leader, p. 238
culture, pp. 238-239
orientation, p. 241
horizon, p. 242
activity, p. 242
processing, p. 242
committed time, p. 243
obligated time, p. 243
problem-solving process, p. 252
extensive problem solving, p. 253
limited problem solving, p. 253
routinized response behavior, p. 253
low involvement purchases, p. 253
adoption process, p. 254
dissonance, p. 255

True-False Questions

___ 1. Because demographic analysis isn't of much value in predicting which specific products and brands will be purchased, many marketers have turned to the behavioral sciences for insight and help.

___ 2. Economic needs affect many buying decisions, but for some purchases the behavioral influences are more important.

___ 3. Economic needs include things such as convenience, efficiency in operation or use, dependability in use, and economy of purchase or use.

___ 4. A drive is a strong need that is learned during a person's life.

___ 5. Motivation theory suggests that people have hierarchies of needs, and that they never reach a state of complete satisfaction.

___ 6. The PSSP needs are power, security, social acceptance, and prestige.

___ 7. Consumers select varying ways to meet their needs because of differences in perception.

___ 8. Selective perception refers to a person's ability to screen out or modify ideas, messages, or information that conflict with previously learned attitudes and beliefs.

___ 9. Learning is a change in a person's thought processes caused by prior experience.

___ 10. Reinforcement of the learning process occurs when a cue follows a response and leads to a reduction in the drive tension.

___ 11. An attitude is a person's point of view towards something.

___ 12. Advertising is so powerful that changing consumers' negative attitudes is usually the easiest part of the marketing manager's job.

___ 13. Personality traits have been very useful to marketers in predicting which products or brands target customers will choose.

___ 14. Life-style analysis refers to the analysis of a person's day-to-day pattern of living--as expressed in his activities, interests, and opinions.

___ 15. Social influences are concerned with how an individual interacts with family, social class, and other groups who may have influence on the buying process.

___ 16. Buying responsibility and influence within a family vary greatly--depending on the product and the family.

___ 17. The social class system in Canada is usually measured in terms of income, race and occupation.

___ 18. A person normally has several reference groups.

___ 19. More than half of our society is *not* middle class.

Learning aid for use with

___ 20. Middle-class consumers tend to be more future-oriented and self-confident than lower-class consumers.

___ 21. The four major aspects of time that affect the buying process are orientation, horizon, activity, and procedural.

___ 22. The concept of horizon is an aspect of time that represents the degree of futurity that you are considering.

___ 23. There are four major processing variations that may describe an individual's progression through time: linear, segmented, cyclical, and procedural.

___ 24. The fact that some people consider themselves time short or overcommitted is unlikely to affect the kind of products they will consider.

___ 25. English Canadians are more willing than their French speaking counterparts to pay premium prices for convenience and premium brands.

___ 26. Whenever French Canadians consume less of a product than their English speaking counterparts it is obvious manufacturersshould pay more attention to the French market.

___ 27. Consumption patterns may differ markedly between French-language and English-language households of similar size, income level, and educational background.

___ 28. Dissonance might cause a consumer to pay more attention to automobile advertisements after a new car is purchased than before the purchase.

___ 29. Knowing how a target market handles the problem-solving process, the adoption process, and learning can aid marketing strategy planning.

Answers to True-False Questions

1. T, p. 227	11. T, p. 232	21. F, p. 241-242
2. T, p. 227-228	12. F, p. 232-233	22. T, p. 242
3. T, p. 227	13. F, p. 234	23. T, p. 242
4. F, p. 228	14. T, p. 234	24. F, p. 244
5. T, p. 229-230	15. T, p. 235-236	25. F, p. 245
6. F, p. 229	16. T, p. 236	26. F, p. 246
7. T, p. 230	17. F, p. 236	27. T, p. 247
8. T, p. 231	18. T, p. 238	28. T, p. 255
9. T, p. 231	19. T, p. 237	29. T, p. 255
10. T, p. 232	20. T, p. 237-238	

Multiple-Choice Questions (Circle the correct response)

1. According to the text, the "economics-oriented" model:
   a. says that the economic value of a purchase is the most important factor in a purchase decision.
   b. explains why people behave the way they do.
   c. includes psychological variables and social influences.
   d. is too simplistic to explain consumer behavior.
   e. assumes that consumers always buy the lowest price alternative.

2. Which of the following is *not* a psychological variable?
    a. Social class
    b. Motivation
    c. Perception
    d. Attitudes
    e. Learning

3. A good marketing manager
    a. knows that only a few basic needs explain almost all consumer product choices.
    b. doesn't have to understand consumer needs if his product has some design improvements over his competitor's product.
    c. should find ways to create internal drives in consumers.
    d. knows that consumer needs in product-markets are probably much more specific than those in a related generic market.
    e. will make fewer strategy planning mistakes if he uses the economic-man theory.

4. According to motivation theory, the *last* needs a family would usually seek to satisfy would be:
    a. safety needs.
    b. personal needs.
    c. physiological needs.
    d. social needs.

5. Motivation theory suggests that:
    a. lower-level needs must be completely satisfied before higher-level needs become important.
    b. a particular good or service might satisfy different levels of needs at the same time.
    c. all consumers satisfy needs in the same order.
    d. self-esteem is an example of a social need.
    e. All of the above are true statements.

6. When consumers screen out or modify ideas, messages, and information that conflict with previously learned attitudes and beliefs, this is called:
    a. selective retention.
    b. selective exposure.
    c. selective perception.
    d. selective dissonance.
    e. selective cognition.

7. A change in a person's thought processes caused by prior experience is called:
    a. learning
    b. attitude change
    c. belief change
    d. response
    e. reinforcement

8. Which of the following is not a major element in the learning process?
    a. Drive
    b. Cues
    c. Dissonance
    d. Reinforcement
    e. Response

9. An attitude:
   a. is easily changed.
   b. is a person's point of view toward something.
   c. is the same as opinion and belief.
   d. is a reliable indication of intention to buy.
   e. All of the above are true statements.

10. The AIO items used in life-style analysis include:
    a. activities, interests, and opinions.
    b. attitudes, interests, and opinions.
    c. activities, intentions, and opinions.
    d. attitudes, intentions, and opinions.
    e. attitudes, income, and opinions.

11. Which of the following is *not* a social influence?
    a. Culture
    b. Social class
    c. Family
    d. Reference group
    e. Personality

12. According to the text, social class is usually measured in terms of:
    a. income.
    b. occupation, education, and housing arrangements.
    c. income, occupation, and education.
    d. race, religion, and occupation.
    e. income, occupation, and religion.

13. Matt Kerr, now an account representative responsible for selling computer systems to some of ABC Corporation's major accounts—has been with ABC since graduating from the University of Toronto in 1965. Matt's father was a plumber, but Matt is a professional—one of ABC's top five salespeople—and earns about $70,000 a year in salary and commissions. Matt is a member of the _____ social class.
    a. upper
    b. upper-middle
    c. lower-middle
    d. upper-lower
    e. lower-lower

14. Which of the following statements about social class is NOT true?
    a. The various classes tend to shop in different stores.
    b. The upper class tends to avoid shopping at mass-merchandisers.
    c. Upper-middle class consumers tend to buy quality products which will serve as symbols of their success.
    d. Lower-class buyers often want guidance from a salesperson about what choice to make.
    e. Lower-class consumers are more likely to save and plan for the future than middle class consumers.

15. For which of the following products would reference group influence probably be *least important?*
    a. Clothing
    b. Cigarettes
    c. Furniture
    d. Canned peaches
    e. Wine

16. Opinion leaders are:
    a. usually better educated.
    b. usually reference group leaders.
    c. not necessarily opinion leaders on all subjects.
    d. usually wealthy, middle- or upper-class people.
    e. All of the above are true statements.

17. Which of the following is not a major aspect of time:
    a. Orientation
    b. Horizon
    c. Activity
    d. Processing
    e. Polychronics

18. Which one of the following terms is inappropriate when one considers an individual's progression through time:
    a. Linear
    b. Segmented
    c. Cyclical
    d. Procedural
    e. Monochronic

19. Which of the following pieces of Quebec legislation prohibits advertising directed toward children thirteen years of age or younger:
    a. Bill 101
    b. Bill 67
    c. Bill 34
    d. Bill 78
    e. None of the above

20. Behavioral scientists recognize different *levels* of consumer problem solving. Which of the following is *not* one of these levels?
    a. Routinized response behavior
    b. Limited problem solving
    c. Rational problem solving
    d. Extensive problem solving
    e. All of the above are recognized levels of problem solving.

21. Which of the following gives the proper *ordering* of the stages in the "adoption process"?
    a. Awareness, interest, trial, evaluation, decision, dissonance
    b. Awareness, interest, trial, decision, evaluation, confirmation
    c. Awareness, interest, evaluation, trial, decision, confirmation
    d. Interest, awareness, trial, decision, evaluation, dissonance
    e. Awareness, interest, evaluation, decision, trial, confirmation

22. Dissonance is:
    a. a type of cue.
    b. a form of laziness commonly observed among low-income consumers.
    c. a type of positive reinforcement.
    d. tension caused by uncertainty about the rightness of a decision.
    e. none of the above.

23. The present state of our knowledge about consumer behavior is such that:
    a. the behavioral sciences provide the marketing manager with a complete explanation of the "whys" of consumer behavior.
    b. we still must rely heavily on intuition and judgment to explain and predict consumer behavior.
    c. relevant market dimensions can be easily identified and measured using "psychographics."
    d. marketing research can't tell us much more about specific aspects of consumer behavior.
    e. All of the above are true statements.

Answers to Multiple-Choice Questions

1. d, p. 227	9. b, p. 232	17. e, pp. 241-243
2. a, p. 228	10. a, p. 234	18. e, p. 242
3. d, pp. 228-229	11. e, p. 235	19. c, p. 247
4. b, p. 229	12. b, p. 236	20. c, p. 253
5. b, p. 229	13. b, p. 237	21. c, p. 254
6. c, p. 231	14. e, p. 237	22. d, p. 255
7. a, p. 231	15. d, p. 238	23. b, p. 256
8. c, pp. 231-232	16. c, p. 238	

Exercise 7-1

Psychological variables and social influences affect consumer buying behavior

Introduction

To plan good marketing strategies, marketing managers must try to improve their understanding of buying behavior. Ideally, marketers would like to know *how* and *why* individual consumers buy the way they do. Then it might be possible to group individual consumers with similar needs and buying behavior into homogeneous market segments for which suitable marketing mixes could be developed.

This is easier said than done, however, because human behavior is very complex. Traditional demographic analysis, for example, can be used to study basic trends in consumer spending patterns, but it is of little use in explaining *why* people like, choose, buy, and use the products and brands they do.

For this reason, many marketers have turned to the behavioral sciences for help in understanding how and why consumers behave as they do. However, there is no "grand theory" available right now which ties together all the behavioral theories and concepts in a way which will explain and predict all aspects of human behavior. Therefore, marketers must try to understand the various behavioral theories and concepts. Then they can put them together into a model of consumer behavior which works in their own particular situation.

Hopefully, the complex decision-making processes which take place within the buyer behavior model are clearer to you after reading Chapter 7 of the text. Although the model presented in the text can't explain or predict consumer behavior, it does provide a useful framework which identifies the major variables that influence consumer behavior.

This exercise should improve your understanding of various psychological (*intra*personal) variables and social (*inter*personal) influences which may affect a consumer's behavior. You will recall from Chapter 7 that psychological variables focus on the individual while social influences involve relations with others.

Assignment

In the short cases which follow, a variety of psychological variables and social influences are operating to influence a consumer's response. For each case, identify the relevant psychological variables and social influences and briefly explain how each item is illustrated in the case. The first case has been completed for you as an example.

1.   Joan and Paul Davis and their two children are considering the purchase of a recreational vehicle. Paul is enthusiastic because, he argues, the RV would be perfect for family camping trips, as well

as fishing trips with his friends. Joan is less in favor of the purchase. She is nervous about camping in remote locations--and wonders how they would get help in emergencies. She also remembers a report that RVs get low gas mileage and are, therefore, expensive to run. Paul is quick to point out that the same report described the large potential savings of a week-long vacation in an RV compared to staying at a hotel or motel.

a. Psychological variables
   1) Motivation   Explanation: *Joan is afraid of being isolated--safety needs.*
   2) Perception   Explanation: *Joan only remembers the part of the report that supports her viewpoint.*

b. Social influences
   1) *Family*   Explanation: *Paul wants to take family camping vacations, but Joan is concerned about the family's safety.*
   2) *Reference Group*   Explanation: *Paul wants to take his friends on a fishing trip in "his" RV.*

2.   Graham Cardman has signed up for a two-week sailing adventure run by Outward Bound and has received instructions about special clothing to buy. He is shopping for a fleece sweater that will be warm when wet. His roommate comments: "The Gap is the best—it's what all the instructors use." But Graham comments: "I could never wear The Gap—that stuff looks too 'preppy'." Instead he orders a sweater from the Sears catalog which he uses for most of his school clothes. He likes Sears because they've always accepted returns without a hassle.

a. Psychological variables

   1) _____ Explanation: _____

   _____

   2) _____ Explanation: _____

   _____

   3) _____ Explanation: _____

   _____

b. Social Influences

   1) _____ Explanation: _____

   _____

   2) _____ Explanation: _____

   _____

3.   To reward himself for graduating from flight school, Denzell Darden has promised himself a new raincoat. He likes the look of the *Burberry* trench coat he sees in an advertisement in *GQ* magazine. Even though the new coat will cost more than $600, his mother encourages him: "You ought to feel

proud of yourself—go ahead and spend your whole paycheck on something that makes you feel good. Heaven knows, all your poor father could afford was a raincoat from Sears. Why, I don't suppose we ever spent more than $100 for a coat."

a. Psychological variables

1) _____ Explanation: _____

_____

2) _____ Explanation: _____

_____

3) _____ Explanation: _____

_____

b. Social Influences

1) _____ Explanation: _____

_____

2) _____ Explanation: _____

_____

4.   Debbie Shapiro has had a cold—and all of the typical symptoms that come with it—for almost a week. At first she didn't take any medicine—because when she was in the Navy she had learned that it was best just to "tough it out" when she got a cold. However, while she was at lunch with some friends they kidded her about her runny, red nose. When one of them offered Debbie a Contac cold capsule, she decided it wouldn't hurt to try it. To her surprise, she felt much better after taking the capsule. The next morning on her way to work, Debbie saw a large billboard for Contac which she had never noticed before—and with that reminder she stopped at a drugstore and bought a package of the medicine.

a. Psychological variables

1) _____ Explanation: _____

_____

2) _____ Explanation: _____

_____

3) _____ Explanation: _____

_____

b. Social Influences

    1) _____ Explanation: _____

_____

    2) _____ Explanation: _____

_____

5.   Robert Ezzell just returned from a year in France as an exchange student. To see his old friends, he is planning a dinner party with a French menu. As he is shopping for the necessary supplies, he recalls his first experience with escargot—a delicacy of broiled snails he plans to serve at his party. When Robert was told by his host family what he had been served, he was not sure he would be able to eat it. Nothing in his Canadian upbringing had prepared him to eat snails. However he did not want to offend his hosts, so he smiled bravely and downed the escargot. To his amazement it was delicious, and he now enjoys escargot frequently. He is sure he will have to be very persuasive to overcome his friends' initial reactions.

a. Psychological variables

    1) _____ Explanation: _____

_____

    2) _____ Explanation: _____

_____

    3) _____ Explanation: _____

_____

b. Social Influences

    1) _____ Explanation: _____

_____

    2) _____ Explanation: _____

_____

Question for Discussion

Which items—psychological variables or social influences—have more influence over consumer behavior and thus are more important for the marketing strategy planner?

Exercise 7-2

Consumer behavior is a problem-solving process

Introduction

While consumer behavior may often appear to be quite irrational to the casual observer, most behavioral scientists agree that consumers are *problem solvers* seeking to relieve tension caused by their unsatisfied needs. How an individual consumer goes about solving problems depends on the intrapersonal and interpersonal variables that affect that individual. In general, however, most consumers tend to follow a five-step problem-solving process:

1. Becoming aware of--or interested in--the problem.
2. Gathering information about possible solutions.
3. Evaluating alternative solutions--perhaps trying some out.
4. Deciding on the appropriate solution.
5. Evaluating the decision.

The length of time it takes to complete the problem-solving process and how much attention is given to each of the five steps depends, of course, on the nature of the problem and how much experience an individual has had in trying to solve this particular kind of problem. To understand the process better, it helps to recognize three levels of problem solving: *extensive problem solving, limited problem solving*, and *routinized response behavior*.

The purpose of this exercise is to illustrate the three levels of consumer problem solving by relating the problem-solving process to *your* problem-solving experiences in the marketplace.

Assignment

Think of *three* recent purchases that *you* made that involved extensive problem solving, limited problem solving, and routinized response behavior. For each of these purchases, outline the problem-solving process that you used. You may wish to follow the five-step process listed above, indicating how you went about performing each of the five steps.

1.	Routinized response behavior: Product _____

	Explanation:

2.	Limited problem-solving: Product _____

	Explanation:

3.	Extensive problem-solving: Product _____

	Explanation:

Question for Discussion

Which of the three levels of problem solving offers marketers the most opportunity? The least opportunity? Why?

Chapter 8

Business and organizational customers and their buying behavior

What This Chapter Is About

Chapter 8 discusses the buying behavior of the important business and organizational customers who buy for resale or for use in their own businesses. They buy more goods and services than final customers! There are many opportunities in marketing to producers, to middlemen, to government, and to nonprofit organizations--and it is important to understand how these organizational customers buy.

Organizations tend to be much more oriented towards economic factors in their buying behavior. Further, some must follow pre-set bidding and bargaining processes. Yet, they too have emotional needs. And sometimes a number of different people may influence the final purchase decision. Keep in mind that business and organizational customers are problem solvers too. Many of the ideas in Chapter 7 carry over—but with some adaptation.

This chapter deserves careful study because your past experience as a consumer is not as helpful here as it was in the last few chapters. Organizational customers are much less numerous. In some cases it is possible to create a separate marketing mix for each individual customer. Understanding these customers is necessary to plan marketing strategies for them. Try to see how they are both similar and different from final customers.

Important Terms

business and organizational customers, p. 260
new-task buying, p. 263
straight rebuy, p. 263
modified rebuy, p. 264
purchasing agents, p. 265
vendor analysis, p. 267
multiple buying influence, p. 268
buying centre, p. 269
inspection buying, p. 270
sampling buying, p. 270
description (specification) buying, p. 270
competitive bids, p. 270

negotiated contract buying, p. 271
requisition, p. 272
just-in-time delivery, p. 274
reciprocity, p. 274
Standard Industrial Classification
 (SIC) codes, p. 276
open to buy, p. 279
resident buyers, p. 280
contract farming, p. 281
agribusiness, p. 281
marketing boards, p. 282

True-False Questions

___ 1. Business and organizational customers are wholesalers or retailers, but not buyers who buy to produce other goods and services.

___ 2. Since sellers usually approach each business or organizational customer directly through a sales representative, it is possible that there can be a special marketing strategy for each individual customer.

___ 3. When the majority of a company's purchases involve straight rebuy buying, these purchases occupy most of an effective buyer's time.

___ 4. A salesperson usually must see the organizational buyer or purchasing agent first, before any other employee in the firm is contacted.

___ 5. "Vendor analysis" involves a formal rating of suppliers on all relevant areas of performance.

___ 6. Emotional needs are often quite relevant for the typical purchasing agent, and therefore a marketing mix should seek to satisfy both the buyer's company needs and the buyer's individual needs.

___ 7. Strong multiple buying influence is most likely to be involved when there is new-task buying.

___ 8. Multiple buying influence makes the promotion job easier.

___ 9. A buying centre consists of all the people who participate in or influence a purchase.

___ 10. Buying by inspection would probably be necessary for a firm that wanted to purchase a large supply of nuts and bolts.

___ 11. As products become more standardized, perhaps because of more careful grading and better quality control, sampling buying becomes possible.

___ 12. Services are usually purchased by description.

___ 13. Competitive bids are the terms of sale offered by different suppliers in response to the buyer's purchase specifications.

___ 14. Negotiated contracts commonly are used for products which can be described sufficiently well that suppliers know what is wanted and can submit definite prices or bids.

___ 15. Even if a firm has developed the best marketing mix possible, it probably will not get all of the business of its organizational customers.

___ 16. A requisition is a request to buy something.

___ 17. Organizational buyers typically do not even see a sales rep for straight rebuys.

___ 18. Buyers who delegate routine buying to a computer might be more favorably impressed by a new company's offer of an attractive marketing mix, perhaps for a whole line of products, rather than just a lower price for a particular order.

___ 19. "Just-in-time" delivery means reliably getting products there before or very soon after they are needed.

___ 20. Purchasing agents tend to resist reciprocity, but it may be forced on them by their sales departments.

___ 21. Manufacturers tend to be concentrated by geographic location and industry, and the majority of them are quite small.

___ 22. Two-digit SIC code breakdowns start with broad industry categories, but more detailed data may be available for three-digit and four-digit industries.

___ 23. Compared to manufacturers, services firms are more numerous, smaller, and more spread out.

___ 24. Most retail and wholesale buyers see themselves as selling agents for manufacturers.

___ 25. The large number of items bought and stocked by wholesalers and retailers makes it imperative that inventories be watched carefully.

___ 26. The retail buyer is "open-to-buy" whenever his cost of merchandise is less than his forecasted sales.

___ 27. Committee buying by retailers will probably force better strategy planning by wholesalers and manufacturers, instead of relying just on persuasive salespeople.

___ 28. Resident buyers are employees of retail stores whose job it is to reach the many small manufacturers in central markets who cannot afford large sales departments.

___ 29. All government customers are required by law to use a mandatory bidding procedure which is open to public reviews.

___ 30. Government buyers avoid the use of negotiated contracts whenever there are a lot of intangible factors.

1. F, p. 260	12. T, p. 270	23. T, p. 278
2. T, p. 262	13. T, p. 270	24. F, p. 279
3. F, pp. 263-264	14. F, p. 271	25. T, p. 279
4. T, p. 265	15. T, p. 272	26. F, pp. 279-280
5. T, p. 267	16. T, p. 272	27. T, p. 280
6. T, p. 267	17. T, p. 273	28. F, p. 280
7. T, p. 268	18. T, p. 274	29. T, p. 284
8. F, p. 268	19. F, p. 274	30. F, p. 284
9. T, p. 269	20. T, p. 274	
10. F, p. 270	21. T, p. 274	
11. T, p. 270	22. T, p. 276	

Multiple-Choice Questions (Circle the correct response)

1. The bulk of all buying done in Canada in not by final consumers—but rather by business and organizational customers. Which of the following is a business or organizational customer?
    a. a manufacturer.
    b. a retailer.
    c. a wholesaler.
    d. a government agency.
    e. All of the above are business and organizational customers.

2. A large manufacturer is about to purchase a large supply of an unfamiliar chemical that will be used in the production of an important new product. What kind of buying would the company be most likely to do?
    a. New-task buying
    b. Straight rebuy buying
    c. Modified rebuy buying

3. In comparison to the buying of final consumers, the purchasing of organizational buyers:
    a. is strictly economic and not at all emotional.
    b. is always based on bids from multiple suppliers.
    c. leans basically toward economy, quality, and dependability.
    d. is even less predictable.
    e. Both a and c are true statements.

4. Today, many agricultural commodities and manufactured items are subject to rigid control or grading. As a result, the buying and selling of these goods can be done at a low cost by:
    a. inspection.
    b. sampling.
    c. description.
    d. negotiated contracts.

5. An automobile manufacturer's practice of buying some of its raw materials from other manufacturers who in turn buy from it is an example of:
   a. tying contracts.
   b. vendor analysis.
   c. buying by description.
   d. being "open to buy."
   e. reciprocity.

6. A plastics manufacturer is selecting a new supplier. People from sales, production, quality control, and finance are working with the purchasing department on the decision. The sales manager wants to select a supplier that is also a customer for some of the firm's own products. The sales manager:
   a. is a gatekeeper.
   b. may not get his way because the government frowns on such deals.
   c. is trying to use vendor analysis to his advantage.
   d. is not a member of the buying center, so he can be ignored.
   e. none of the above.

7. Which of the following SIC codes would provide the most specific information about a sub-category of an industry?
   a. 3
   b. 31
   c. 314
   d. 3142
   e. Cannot be determined without additional information.

8. If you obtain a customer's three digit SIC code, you should know that:
   a. this firm might be manufacturing quite different products than other firms with the same number.
   b. the firm may also have a four digit code.
   c. a number of other firms probably have the same code.
   d. All of the above are true.
   e. None of the above is true.

9. As contrasted with manufacturers, producers of services are:
   a. more geographically spread out.
   b. more numerous.
   c. less well represented by SIC data.
   d. All of the above.
   e. None of the above.

10. Which of the following statements about retail buying is *false*?
    a. In most retail operations, a "resident buyer" runs his own department--and his decision is final.
    b. Retail buyers may be responsible for supervising the salesclerks who sell the merchandise they buy.
    c. Retail buyers make most purchases as straight rebuys.
    d. A retail buyer is usually "open to buy" only when he has not spent all of his budgeted funds.
    e. Resident buyers are independent buying agents who help producers and middlemen reach each other inexpensively.

11. Which of the following statements about bidding for government business is *true*?
   a. Government buying needs are hard to identify--and their primary concern is with finding the lowest price.
   b. Government buyers avoid using negotiated contracts since they must purchase at a pre-set price.
   c. A government buyer may be forced to accept the lowest bid whether he wants the goods or not.
   d. The biggest job of the government buyer is to locate enough potential suppliers so the bidding procedure works effectively.
   e. All of the above are false statements.

Answers to Multiple-Choice Questions

1. e, p. 261
2. a, p. 263
3. c, p. 265
4. c, p. 270

5. e, p. 274
6. e, p. 274
7. d, pp. 276-278
8. d, pp. 276-278

9. d, p. 278
10. a, p. 280
11. e, pp. 284-285

Exercise 8-1

Analyzing organizational buying behavior

Introduction

Some people see organizational buying and consumer buying as two very different processes. Organizational buying is thought of as "economic," while consumer buying is seen as "emotional." In fact, closer study of buying processes suggests that organizational and consumer buying may be quite similar in many ways. For example, like consumers, organizational buyers are *problem solvers*. And while their problems may be very different, both consumer and organizational buyers seem to use three levels of problem solving. In Chapter 7, we saw that consumer buyers do extended, limited, and routinized problem solving. Similarly, organizational buyers do *new-task, straight rebuy, and modified rebuy buying*.

Recognition of the three levels of problem solving by organizational buyers *and* the different problem solving steps they pass through has important implications for market analysis. It suggests that organizational markets can be segmented not only in terms of product-related needs, industry categories, and geographic location--but also in terms of similarities and differences in buying behavior. *Each level of problem solving may require a different marketing mix*--especially in regard to the promotion variable-- even when identical goods or services are involved. Knowing the nature of buying behavior at each level helps to determine the proper ingredients for a marketing mix.

This exercise shows how knowledge of organizational buying behavior can improve marketing strategy planning--in three "case" situations. You will be asked to identify the problem-solving level for a business product. Then you will discuss likely buying behavior and how this might affect a firm's marketing strategy planning.

Assignment

Assume the role of marketing manager for a large manufacturing firm. Your firm produces a variety of electrical components, including specialized electrical motors, for use as components in your customers' finished products. Very similar motors are typically available from several competing suppliers, including some larger and some smaller firms. While some slight differences in specifications may exist, all of the suppliers produce reliable motors that meet the quality and power standards set by customers' production and marketing departments. In fact, most of the competing suppliers use the same basic designs and materials for the motors they produce. And, with few exceptions, the prices charged by all suppliers tend to be almost identical.

Recently, you learned--from your sales force--of three potential customers whose needs might be satisfied by the motors you sell. Read each of the three buying situations described below, and then:

Learning aid for use with

a)   Determine which level of problem solving--new-task buying, straight rebuy, or modified rebuy--applies to each situation.

b)   Discuss in detail the probable nature of the firm's buying behavior in each situation. Which of the five problem solving steps in Chapter 7 (page 249) would be most important in each situation? Why? Which is the next most important? Why? How important would multiple buying influence be in each situation?

c)   Explain how your firm might vary its marketing mix to satisfy the potential customer's needs in each situation.

Situation 1:

The potential customer has been selling a very successful line of dishwashers for a number of years. The dishwasher uses the same motor (to pump hot water) that it has been using for years. But, appliance retailers have recently been complaining that the dishwasher makes too much noise, and that other producers have introduced new models that are not as loud. The potential customer thinks that your "low noise" motor could possibly be used instead of the motors it gets from its current supplier.

a)   Level of problem solving: _____

b)   Nature of buying behavior:

c)   Marketing mix:

Situation 2:

A potential customer has been purchasing a similar motor from one of your firm's competitors for several years, but is dissatisfied with its present supplier's delivery service and technical support.

a)   Level of problem solving: _____

b)   Nature of buying behavior:

c)   Marketing mix:

Learning aid for use with

Situation 3:

The prospect has been purchasing all of its motors from one of your competitors on a regular basis for several years. No change in this procedure is expected.

a) Level of problem solving: _____

b) Nature of buying behavior:

c) Marketing mix:

Question for Discussion

In which of the three buying situations would emotional needs be most important? Least important? To what extent does this depend on the overlap between individual buyer needs and company needs?

Exercise 8-2

Using SIC codes to analyze business markets

Introduction

Compared to the final consumer market, business markets have a smaller number of customers and much of the buying potential is concentrated among a relatively few large firms. Further, firms within the same industry tend to cluster together by geographic location. For these reasons, it may be less difficult to analyze business markets than consumer markets.

Much published data is available to help the marketing manager analyze business markets. The most important source of information is the federal government—which regularly collects data on the number of establishments, their sales volumes, and number of employees for a large number of industry groups. The data is reported for Standard Industrial Classifications (SIC) code industries—broken down by region, province, county, and Standard Metropolitan Statistical Area. As explained in Chapter 8 of the text, the SIC system combines and classifies business firms on the basis of product produced—or operation performed. Almost 100 major industry groups are identified by two-digit codes. Code 20, for example, identifies the "food and kindred products" industry. Each major industry is then subdivided into three-digit industries (e.g., code 202, "diary products") which in turn are subdivided further into four-digit industries (e.g., code 2021, "creamery butter"). However, four-digit detail is not available for all industries in every geographic area because Statistics Canada will not disclose an individual firm's data.

This exercise illustrates the usefulness of SIC-coded data for analyzing industrial markets. Note: You may find it helpful to read pages 276-278 in the text before doing this exercise.

Electricom Manufacturing Company produces a line of electrical products for business markets. Electricom's recently-appointed marketing manager is currently in the process of reevaluating the firm's marketing strategy for an important product, "electric widgets," which he suspects may not be realizing its full sales potential. In particular, he feels that Electricom has been following a "mass-marketing approach for this product and has neglected to identify which markets the product appeals to and their relative importance.

The marketing manager began his analysis by attempting to determine which four-digit SIC industries may have some need for electric widgets. First, he analyzed past sales records for the product and assigned SIC codes to previous and present customers. Next, he asked his sales manager to go through the SIC manual and check off the four-digit industries which he believed would be relevant for the product. Finally, to make sure that other potential customers were not being overlooked, he conducted a survey of companies falling under other SIC categories to find out whether they might have any possible use for the product. As a result of this analysis, a total of 12 industries were identified as potential target markets for electric widgets. These industries are listed in columns 1 and 2 of Table 8-1. Once an estimate of average purchase per production worker in each SIC is made, multiplying that figure by the number of production workers in any area reveals that area's market potential.

Table 8-1

Calculation of Market Potential for "Electric Widgets" Using Market Survey Approach for National and Saskatchewan Markets

SIC Code (1)	Effective Industries (2)	Market Survey Results — Product Purchases (3)	Market Survey Results — Number of Production Workers (4)	Market Survey Results — Average purchases Per Production Worker (5)	National Market Number of Production Workers (6)	Estimated National Market potential ($000's) (7)	Saskatchewan Market Number of Production Workers (8)	Estimated Saskatchewan Market Potential ($000's) (9)
3611	Electric measuring instruments	$ 6,400	3,200	$ 2.00	35,100	$ 70.3	2,800	$ 5.6
3612	Transformers	50,150	4,616	10.86	37,600	408.3	3,800	41.3
3621	Motors and generators	28,400	10,896	2.61	78,300	204.4	3,000	7.8
3622	Industrial controls	40,100	4,678	8.57	30,800	264.0	3,200	27.4
3631	Household cooking equipment	2,600	2,104	1.24	16,900	21.0	3,900	4.8
3632	Household refrigerators and freezers	149,600	5,215	28.69	40,100	1,153.3	—	—
3633	Household laundry equipment	35,200	3,497	10.07	17,800	179.2	—	—
3634	Electric housewares and fans	1,200	3,208	0.37	40,300	14.9	3,700	1.4
3635	Household vacuum cleaners	1,875	402	4.66	7,500	35.0	—	—
3636	Sewing machines	600	912	0.66	4,900	3.2	—	—
3661	Telephone and telegraph apparatus	65,500	6,451	10.15	101,600	1,031.2	—	—
3662	Radio and TV communication equipment	132,100	6,889	19.18	185,700	3,561.7	7,500	143.8
	Total	$508,925				$6,946.5		$232.1

Column:

(1), (2) Four-digit SIC industries making up the industrial market for "electric widgets."

(3) Dollar value, classified by industries, of purchases of "electric widges" as reported by those firms included in the survey.

(4) Number of production workers as reported by those firms included in the survey.

(5) Average dollar value of "electric widget" purchases per production worker for each SIC industry. Computed by dividing column 3 by column 4.

(6) Number of production workers for the entire Canadian market for the given SIC industries.

(7) The resultant estimated national market potential for the total market. Computed by multiplying column 6 by column 5.

(8) Number of production workers for Saskatchewan trading area for the given SIC industries. Note: Blanks in column 8 indicate either that there are no firms in Saskatchewan for a particular SIC industry, or that there are only a few firms and Saskatchewan has withheld the data in order to protect the confidentiality of the firms in question. Same source as column 6.

(9) The resultant estimated Saskatchewan area market potential. Computed by multiplying column 8 by column 5.

Source: Adapted with considerable modification from Francis E. Hummel, *Market and Sales Potentials* (New York: The Ronald Press Co., 1961), pp. 110, 112.

Having identified 12 potential target markets for electric widgets, the marketing manager then conducted another survey of a sample of firms belonging to each industry to determine the market potential for each industry. Included in the data he collected were the amount of each firm's annual dollar purchases for the product and the number of production workers employed. This data is summarized in columns 3 and 4 of Table 8-1. From the sample data for each SIC industry, the marketing manager then calculated the average dollar purchases per production worker. The results are shown in column 5.

1.   Complete column 5 of Table 8-1 by calculating the average dollar purchases per worker for SIC industry #3611--electric measuring instruments. Show your calculations below.

In order to project the sample data to the entire Canadian market, Electricom's marketing manager turned to *Statistics Canada* to find the national total of production workers employed by each industry. From this data, shown in column 6, he was then able to estimate the national market potential for each SIC industry by multiplying column 6 by column 5. These estimates are shown in column 7.

2.   Complete column 7 of Table 8-1 by calculating the national market potential for SIC industry #3611. Show your calculations below.

Finally, because Electricom's sales territories were aligned according to provinces, the marketing manager proceeded to estimate the market potential for each industry in each province. For example, he again turned to *Statistics Canada* to determine the number of production workers employed in the province of Saskatchewan. The results, computed by multiplying column 8 by column 5, are shown in column 9.

3.   Complete column 9 of Table 8-1 by calculating the market potential in Saskatchewan for SIC industry # 3611. Show your calculations below.

4.   a)   *For all industries combined,* what percentage of the total national market potential for electric widgets is represented by province of Saskatchewan? Show your work below.

     b)   *For SIC industry #3611 only,* what percentage of the national market potential for electric widgets is represented by the province of Saskatchewan? Show your work below.

Learning aid for use with

5. Suppose Electricom's marketing manager learned that his firm's electric widget sales to SIC industry #3612 amounted to about 20 percent of its national market potential for that industry--while sales to the other 11 industries ranged from 5-10 percent. Suppose further that he then decided that the firm should aim at achieving 20 percent of its national market potential in *each* of the 12 SIC industries--and set his sales quotas accordingly. Is it likely that Electricom could achieve these sales quotas? Why or why not? Comment on this approach to marketing strategy planning.

6. Which of the 12 SIC industries would you select as your target market(s) for the electric widgets if you were Electricom's marketing manager? Why?

   a) For the national market:

   b) For the Saskatchewan market:

Question for Discussion

After selecting its target market(s), how could Electricom then go about identifying and reaching those firms which make up the target market(s)? What other information would be needed and how could the information be obtained?

Chapter 9

Elements of product planning for goods and services

What This Chapter Is About

Chapter 9 introduces the idea of a "product"--which may be a physical good or a service or (often) a blend of both.

Then, the idea of product classes--and how they relate products to marketing mix planning is explained. Two sets of product classes--for consumer products and business products--are introduced. Notice that the same product might be classified in two or more ways at the same time--depending on the attitudes of potential customers.

These product classes should be studied carefully. They are an important thread linking our discussion of marketing strategy planning. In fact, these product classes can be a shorthand way of describing how customers look at Products--and this has a direct bearing on Place (how the Product will get to them) and Promotion (what the seller should tell them).

Chapter 9 also discusses other important aspects of Product--branding, packaging and warranties.

Branding is concerned with identifying the product. A good brand can help improve the product's image and reinforce the firm's effort to increase the product's degree of brand familiarity. A respected name builds brand equity.

The advantages and disadvantages of both dealer and manufacturer branding should be studied carefully. They will help you understand the "battle of the brands"--and why some markets are so competitive.

Packaging can actually improve a product--perhaps making it more appealing and/or protecting it from damage. Packaging can also complement promotion efforts by making the whole product more attractive or carrying a promotion message. A firm's commitment to recycling has become an important packaging issue.

Warranties are also important in strategy planning. Some consumers find strong warranties particularly attractive.

By the end of the chapter you should see that wise decisions on packaging and branding can improve any marketing mix--and may help a firm avoid extremely competitive--or even pure competition--situations.

Important Terms

product, p. 293
quality, p. 293
service, p. 295
product assortment, p. 296
product line, p. 296
individual product, p. 296
consumer products, p. 297
business products, p. 297
convenience products, p. 298
staples, p. 298
impulse products, p. 299
emergency products, p. 299
shopping products, p. 299
homogeneous shopping products, p. 299
heterogeneous shopping products, p. 300
specialty products, p. 300
unsought products, p. 300
new unsought products, p. 300
regularly unsought products, p. 300
derived demand, p. 302
capital item, p. 302
expense item, p. 303
installations, p. 304
accessories, p. 305
raw materials, p. 305
farm products, p. 305
natural products, p. 305
components, p. 306

supplies, p. 307
professional services, p. 308
branding, p. 308
brand name, p. 308
trademark, p. 308
service mark, p. 308
brand familiarity, p. 311
brand rejection, p. 311
brand nonrecognition, p. 312
brand recognition, p. 312
brand preference, p. 312
brand insistence, p. 312
brand equity, p. 313
family brand, p. 313
licensed brand, p. 314
individual brands, p. 314
generic products, p. 314
manufacturer brands, p. 315
dealer brands, p. 315
private brands, p. 315
battle of the brands, p. 315
packaging, p. 315
Trademark Act, p. 313
Hazardous Products Act, p. 317
Consumer Packaging and Labelling Act, p. 318
unit-pricing, p. 319
Universal Product Code (UPC), p. 319
warranty, p. 319

True-False Questions

___ 1. A "product" may not include a physical good at all.

___ 2. Quality refers to the ability of a product to satisfy a customer's need.

___ 3. The more features a product has the higher-quality product it is.

___ 4. It's usually harder to balance supply and demand for services than for physical goods.

___ 5. It is usually easier to achieve economies of scale when the product emphasis is on a service rather than a good.

___ 6. A product line should be thought of as a firm's product assortment.

___ 7. An individual product is a particular product within a product line and is usually differentiated by brand, level of service, size, price, or some other characteristic.

___ 8. Consumer product classes are based on how consumers think about and shop for a product.

— 9. Convenience products are products a consumer needs but isn't willing to spend much time or effort to shop for.

— 10. Because customers are not willing to spend much time or effort shopping for staples, branding is of little importance.

— 11. Impulse products are items that the customer decides to purchase on sight, may have bought the same way many times before, and wants "right now."

— 12. The distinctive aspect of emergency products is that they are only purchased when the consumer is in danger.

— 13. Shopping products are those products that a customer feels are worth the time and effort to compare with competing products.

— 14. If customers see a product as a homogeneous shopping product, they will base their purchase decisions on the one variable they feel is or can be different--price.

— 15. Price is considered irrelevant for products that the customer sees as heterogeneous shopping products.

— 16. Specialty products are expensive and unusual products that customers insist upon having and generally have to travel far to find.

— 17. Unsought products are those products that have no potential value for customers.

— 18. A consumer product must be either a convenience product, a shopping product, or a specialty product--it cannot be all three.

— 19. In times of recession, a good marketing mix aimed at business and organizational customers may not be very effective unless it has some impact on final consumer demand, because the demand for final consumer products derive from the demand for business products.

— 20. The fact that the demand for most business products is derived means that industry demand will be fairly elastic, although the demand facing individual firms may be extremely inelastic.

— 21. For tax purposes, the cost of a business expense item is spread over a number of years.

— 22. Since business products buyers do relatively little shopping compared to consumer products buyers, the business products classification system is determined by how buyers see the products and how they will be used.

— 23. Installations include only buildings and land rights--such as factories, farms, stores, office buildings, mining deposits, and timber rights.

— 24. If a customer purchases an installation, it is a capital item, but if it is leased the lease payments are an expense item.

— 25. Although accessories are capital items, purchasing agents usually have more say in buying accessory equipment than in buying installations.

___ 26. Raw materials become part of a physical good--and they are expense items.

___ 27. In contrast to farm products, natural products are produced by fewer and larger companies that are quite responsive to market demands and inclined to limit supply to maintain stable prices.

___ 28. Component parts and materials are capital items which have had more processing than raw materials.

___ 29. Unlike farm products that are bought by inspection or sampling, components are usually bought by description.

___ 30. A product originally considered a component part when it was sold in the OEM market might become a consumer product for the replacement market--and probably would require a different marketing mix.

___ 31. Supplies are commonly described as MRO items, meaning that "More Rational Ordering" procedures are normally followed for them.

___ 32. High-level executives may negotiate contracts for some important operating supplies that are needed regularly and cost a lot.

___ 33. Maintenance supplies are similar to consumers' convenience products--and branding may become important for such products.

___ 34. The market for repair supplies is more competitive than that for maintenance and operating supplies.

___ 35. Professional services are expense items, and often the cost of buying them outside the firm is compared with the cost of having company personnel do them.

___ 36. Branding is advantageous to producers--but not to customers.

___ 37. The terms branding, brand name, and trademark all mean about the same thing--and can be used interchangeably.

___ 38. Service mark is a legal term that refers to a service offering.

___ 39. Despite the many advantages of branding, a marketing manager would probably be wise to avoid spending large amounts on branding unless the quality can be easily maintained.

___ 40. A firm whose products have reached the brand insistence stage will enjoy a more inelastic demand curve than a firm whose products have achieved brand preference.

___ 41. A respected brand name lowers brand equity.

___ 42. Counterfeiting is illegal everywhere in the world.

___ 43. A licensed brand is a well-known brand that different sellers pay a fee to use.

—   44.   Generic products are products which have no brand at all other than identification of their contents and the manufacturer or middleman.

—   45.   The major disadvantage of manufacturer brands is that manufacturers normally offer lower gross margins than the middleman might be able to earn with his own brands.

—   46.   Eventually, dealer-branded products may win the "battle of the brands," perhaps because dealers are closer to customers and they can control shelf space.

—   47.   While packing is concerned with protecting the product, packaging refers only to promotion.

—   48.   Packaging plays no role when the product emphasis is on service.

—   49.   Better protective packaging is more important to final consumers than to manufacturers and middlemen.

—   50.   A firm should adopt a more expensive package only when the overall effect will be to reduce the total distribution cost for its product.

—   51.   Unit-pricing involves placing the price per ounce (or some other standard measure) on or near a product.

—   52.   Large supermarket chains have been eager to use the universal product code system--to speed the checkout process and eliminate the need for marking the price on every item.

—   53.   A warranty explains what a seller promises about its product.

1. T, p. 29	20. F, p. 302	39. T, pp. 310-311
2. T, p. 293	21. F, p. 303	40. T, p. 312
3. F, pp. 293-294	22. T, p. 303	41. F, p. 312
4. T, p. 295	23. F, p. 304	42. F, p. 313
5. F, p. 296	24. T, p. 304	43. T, p. 314
6. F, p. 296	25. T, p. 305	44. T, p. 314
7. T, pp. 296-297	26. T, p. 305	45. T, p. 315
8. T, pp. 297-298	27. T, pp. 306-307	46. T, p. 315
9. T, p. 298	28. F, pp. 306-307	47. F, p. 315
10. F, pp. 298-299	29. T, p. 307	48. F, p. 316
11. T, p. 299	30. T, p. 307	49. F, p. 317
12. F, p. 299	31. F, p. 307	50. F, p. 317
13. T, p. 299	32. T, p. 307	51. T, p. 319
14. T, p. 299	33. T, p. 308	52. T, p. 319
15. F, p. 300	34. F, p. 308	53. T, p. 319
16. F, p. 300	35. T, p. 308	
17. F, p. 300	36. F, p. 310	
18. F, p. 301	37. F, p. 308	
19. F, p. 302	38. T, p. 308	

Multiple-Choice Questions (Circle the correct response)

1. According to the text, the term "product" means:
   a. any tangible item that satisfies needs.
   b. goods but not services.
   c. the need-satisfying offering of a firm.
   d. any item that is mass produced by a firm.
   e. all of the above.

2. Regarding quality:
   a. the best credit card may not be the one with the highest credit limit.
   b. the best clothing may not be a pair of slacks, but a pair of jeans.
   c. the best computer may not be the most powerful one.
   d. All of the above are true.
   e. None of the above is true.

3. Marketing mix planning for services
   a. is easier than for physical goods because services don't need to be stored.
   b. is more likely to be influenced by economies of scale.
   c. must consider where the service is produced.
   d. All of the above are true.
   e. None of the above is true.

4. The set of all products a firm sells is called its:
   a. product line.
   b. individual products.
   c. product assortment.
   d. tangible products.

5. The text's consumer product classes are based upon:
    a. methods of distribution.
    b. SIC codes.
    c. the nature of the products.
    d. the way people think about and shop for products.
    e. the way firms view their products.

6. Which of the following is *not* included as a product class in the classification system for consumer products given in the text?
    a. Convenience products
    b. Staple products
    c. Specialty products
    d. Shopping products
    e. Durable products

7. As Carla Tomas was doing her weekly supermarket shopping, she walked down the cat food aisle to pick up her usual six cans of brand "X." However, she came upon a special display of a new, highly advertised brand and decided to try it instead. In this case, the cat food she bought is:
    a. an impulse product.
    b. a specialty product.
    c. an unsought product.
    d. a homogeneous shopping product.
    e. a staple product.

8. You are stranded in your automobile during a snowstorm. You decide to walk to the closest service station for tire chains. In this case you would consider the tire chains as:
    a. emergency products.
    b. staple products.
    c. impulse products.
    d. shopping products.
    e. specialty products.

9. Mr. Beza feels that most people are too emotional and status-minded concerning their automobile purchases. "An automobile's only function is transportation," he says, "and those high-priced 'chrome-wagons' can't do anything that most lower priced cars won't do." Beza only considers Fords, Chevrolets, and Plymouths when he looks around for a new car and he feels all these cars are alike. For him automobiles are:
    a. a specialty product.
    b. a homogeneous shopping product.
    c. a convenience staple product.
    d. a heterogeneous shopping product.
    e. a staple product.

10. Specialty products would be best described as having:
    a. brand insistence and inelastic demand.
    b. brand preference and inelastic demand.
    c. brand insistence and elastic demand.
    d. brand preference and elastic demand.
    e. a relatively high price and durability.

11. Which of the following statements about consumer products is *true*?
    a. Convenience products are those that customers want to buy at the lowest possible price.
    b. Shopping products are those products for which customers usually want to use routinized buying behavior.
    c. Specialty products are those that customers usually are least willing to search for.
    d. Unsought products are not shopped for at all.
    e. None of the above statements are true.

12. Motels are a good example of:
    a. convenience products.
    b. shopping products.
    c. specialty products.
    d. unsought products.
    e. Could be any of the above.

13. Which of the following is *not* a general characteristic of most business products?
    a. Buyers tend to buy from only one supplier.
    b. Their demand is derived from the demand for final consumer products.
    c. Industry demand may be inelastic while each company's demand may be elastic.
    d. Buying is basically concerned with economic factors.
    e. All of the above are characteristics for most business products.

14. Tax regulations affect business buying decisions because:
    a. expense items are depreciated.
    b. capital items are written off over several years.
    c. installations are expensed in one year.
    d. capital items are expensed in one year.

15. The business product classes discussed in the text are based on:
    a. how sellers think about products.
    b. how buyers see products.
    c. how the products are to be used.
    d. all of the above.
    e. both b and c.

16. Which of the following is *not* one of the business product classes discussed in the text?
    a. Professional services
    b. Farm products
    c. Component parts
    d. Accessory equipment
    e. Fabrications

17. Which of the following business products to be purchased by a firm is *most* likely to involve top management in the buying decision?
    a. Raw materials
    b. Accessory equipment
    c. Operating supplies
    d. Installations
    e. Component parts

18. Which of the following would *not* be classified as accessory equipment?
    a. Office typewriters
    b. Filing cases
    c. Portable drills
    d. All of the above might be accessory equipment.
    e. None of the above is likely to be accessory equipment.

19. Raw materials are usually broken down into two broad categories which are:
    a. domestic animals and crops.
    b. farm products and natural products.
    c. forest products and mineral products.
    d. maintenance materials and operating materials.
    e. farm products and chemicals.

20. Which of the following would *not* be considered a component part by an auto manufacturer?
    a. Automobile batteries
    b. Steel sheets
    c. Automobile jacks
    d. Tires
    e. All of the above can be considered component parts, except when they are sold in the replacement market.

21. A marketing manager for a firm which produces component parts should keep in mind that:
    a. most component buyers prefer to rely on one reliable source of supply.
    b. the replacement market for component parts generally requires the same marketing mix as the one used to serve the original equipment market.
    c. any product originally sold as a component part becomes a consumer product when sold in the replacement market.
    d. the original equipment market and the replacement market for component parts should be viewed as separate target markets.
    e. All of the above are true statements.

22. Supplies may be divided into three main categories. Lubricating oils and greases for machines on the production line would be classified as:
    a. maintenance items.
    b. production items.
    c. operating supplies.
    d. repair supplies.
    e. accessories.

23. A "brand name" is:
    a. any means of product identification.
    b. a word used to identify a seller's products.
    c. the same thing as "branding."
    d. the same thing as a "trademark."
    e. All of the above.

Learning aid for use with

24. Which of the following conditions would *not* be favorable to branding?
    a. Dependable and widespread availability is possible
    b. Economies of scale in production
    c. Fluctuations in product quality due to inevitable variations in raw materials
    d. Product easy to identify by brand name or trademark
    e. Large market with a variety of needs and preferences

25. What degree of brand familiarity has a manufacturer achieved when the firm's particular brand is chosen out of habit or past experience, even though various "name" brands are available?
    a. Brand rejection
    b. Brand preference
    c. Brand recognition
    d. Brand insistence
    e. Nonrecognition of brand

26. A firm that has decided to brand all its products under one label is following a policy of:
    a. dealer branding.
    b. generic branding.
    c. family branding.
    d. manufacturer branding.
    e. None of the above.

27. Which of the following statements about manufacturer or dealer brands is *true*?
    a. Dealer brands are distributed only by chain-store retailers.
    b. Dealer brands may be distributed as widely or more widely than many manufacturer brands.
    c. Dealer brands are the same as "licensed brands."
    d. Manufacturer brands are sometimes called private brands.
    e. All of the above are true.

28. A wholesaler might develop a dealer brand because it:
    a. permits the wholesaler to raise prices.
    b. usually leads to faster turnover of products.
    c. usually leads to less inventory carrying costs.
    d. usually cuts his promotion costs.
    e. protects against channel changes by manufacturers.

29. Which of the following statements regarding the "battle of the brands" is *true*?
    a. It is pretty well over as the dealers now control the marketplace.
    b. Middlemen have no real advantages in the battle of the brands.
    c. If the present trend continues, manufacturers will control all middlemen.
    d. Manufacturer brands may be losing ground to dealer brands.
    e. The battle of the brands has increased the differences in price between manufacturer brands and dealer brands.

30. Which of the following statements about the strategic importance of packaging is *false*?
    a. A package may have more promotional impact than a firm's advertising efforts.
    b. A new package can become the major factor in a new marketing strategy by significantly improving the product.
    c. Packaging is concerned with both protection and promotion.
    d. Better packaging always raises total distribution costs.
    e. A package should satisfy not only the needs of consumers but also those of business and organizational customers.

1. c, p. 293	11. d, p. 300	21. d, p. 307
2. d, p. 293	12. e, p. 301	22. c, p. 307
3. c, p. 296	13. a, p. 302	23. b, p. 308
4. c, p. 296	14. b, p. 302	24. c, p. 310
5. d, p. 297	15. e, p. 303	25. b, p. 312
6. e, p. 297	16. e, p. 303	26. c, p. 313
7. e, p. 298	17. d, p. 304	27. b, p. 315
8. a, p. 299	18. d, p. 305	28. e, p. 315
9. b, p. 299	19. b, p. 305	29. d, p. 315
10. a, p. 300	20. b, pp. 306-307	30. d, p. 317

Exercise 9-1

Classifying consumer products

Introduction

Consumer product classes are based on *the way people think about and buy products*. However, different groups of potential customers may have different needs and buying behavior for the same product. Thus, the same product could be placed in two or more product classes--depending on the needs and behavior of target customers. Therefore, product planners should focus on specific groups of customers (i.e., market segments) whose needs and buying behavior are relatively homogeneous.

This exercise will give you some practice in using consumer product classes. As you do the exercise, you will see that the product classes have very little meaning unless they are related to specific target markets.

Assignment

The buying behavior of several customers or potential customers is described below for Kodak disposable cameras. (A disposable camera is basically a "box" of film with a built in lens; after the roll of film in the camera is used up, the customer turns in the whole camera to have the prints processed). Assume in each situation that the customer being described is representative of a particular group of customers--all possessing the same needs and exhibiting similar buying behavior. Then: (a) indicate in which consumer product class the product should be placed based on the characteristics of each group of customers and (b) state *why* you placed the product in this class. Use the following classes, which are described on pages 297-300 in the text.

Staple convenience product	Heterogeneous shopping product
Impulse convenience product	Specialty product
Emergency convenience product	New unsought product
Homogeneous shopping product	Regularly unsought product

The first situation has been answered for you as an example.

1.   Lynne Baker is attending her niece's wedding and knows that the family will give her copies of the photographs taken by the professional photographer hired to cover the event. On the way to the wedding, she notices Kodak disposable cameras on display in the gift shop of the hotel where she is staying--and immediately decides to buy one to take "candid" photographs at the reception, even though she knows that the prices in the hotel may not be a good "bargain."

Product Class: *Impulse convenience product.*

Reason: *Mrs. Baker clearly bought the camera "on impulse" and knows that the hotel store offers convenience--at a price. She doesn't want to go shopping for alternative products or cheaper prices.*

2. John Hodges is a salesman for a producer of automotive paints. While calling on one of his large customers, an automobile paint and body shop, a lady drove up in a car with a dull-looking paint. She wanted to get an estimate to have it repainted. She explained that the car had recently been painted at another body shop, but that the whole job turned out poorly because the body shop had painted the car while it was raining--and had used an inferior brand of paint that offered no guarantee. It occurred to Hodges that it might be really useful to have a picture of the car, to "remind" his customers of the hazards of shifting to some unknown brand of paint. So, he rushed into the Phar-Mor Discount Store across the street and quickly bought a Kodak disposable camera. With the camera, he was able to get a picture before the lady drove away.

    Product Class: _____

    Reason:

3. Jill Davis drives a truck for a package delivery service. When she stopped at a truck stop to get a snack, the checkout clerk pointed at a display of Kodak disposable cameras and asked her if she had bought one yet. Jill said, "No, and I can't imagine why I would want one." The clerk explained that many truck drivers were carrying these cheap cameras to document accidents--and the clerk pointed to a hand lettered sign near the camera display that said: "Will your boss believe your side of the story?" Jill decided that maybe a camera wasn't such a bad idea after all, so she bought one of the Kodak disposables.

    Product Class: _____

    Reason:

4. Margaret Meany is an insurance adjuster for Allrisk Insurance Company. She has found the new disposable cameras really handy for her work. Whenever she has to check out a car that has been damaged in an accident, she uses a disposable camera to take as many pictures as she needs. Until recently she used an expensive 35mm camera, but it was a hassle to carry. Further, she has found that it's easy to run into any nearby convenience store, drugstore, or grocery store to pick up a Kodak disposable.

Product Class: _____

Reason:

5. Paul Romeo has decided to take a vacation from his financial job in Vancouver by enrolling in a two-week ice climbing expedition in Washington state. He wants to bring back pictures of his exploits, but he is worried that his expensive Hasselblad camera might be damaged during the climb. On his lunch hour, he goes to a nearby camera store to find a lightweight disposable camera. The salesman shows him both Fuji and Kodak disposable cameras, but he chooses the Kodak brand because it has a wide-angle lens that will be better for taking panoramic picture of the mountains.

    Product Class: _____

    Reason:

6. Victoria Whestone is taking her fifth trip to Maui. She wants to photograph coral reefs while she takes scuba lessons. On previous trips she has seen other vacationers using disposable underwater cameras—but they always seem to be out-of-stock at the beach. When she asked for the water-proof Kodak disposable camera at her local drugstore, the clerk explained that they carried a different brand that is "just as good." After thinking about it for a moment, Victoria decided she didn't want to risk it with a camera different from what she'd seen being used—so she decided to drive to a camera store to find the Kodak.

    Product Class: _____

    Reason:

7.   Yves Berger, who fancies himself quite a photographer, is planning a picture-taking vacation in France. When he goes to the camera store to pick up a dozen rolls of Kodak Ektar high speed film for his Nikon Pro 35mm camera, the sales rep suggests that Yves take along a Kodak disposable camera. "You'll be surprised," said the salesperson, "how good the pictures really are." Yves said "I know they're good, but all I need is the Ektar--perhaps I'll buy a disposable some other time."

    Product Class: _____

    Reason:

8.   Anne Petrie has been reading an article in the newspaper about twenty fun things to do with a Kodak disposable camera.   When she went to her local Kmart to buy one of the Kodak disposables, she noticed that another brand of disposable camera was on display right next to the Kodaks. After looking at the package, she decided to buy the other brand because "the Kodak brand is more expensive and probably not any better."

    Product Class: _____

    Reason:

Question for Discussion

What implications do your answers to the above exercises have for Kodak when planning its marketing strategies? Be specific?

Learning aid for use with

Exercise 9-2

Classifying business products

Introduction

Compared to consumer products buyers, business products buyers do relatively little shopping. The accepted practice is for the seller to come to the buyer. This means that business product classes based on shopping behavior are *not* useful. The business product classes are determined by *how buyers see products* and *how the products will be used*.

The business product classes may be easier to use than consumer product classes, because business and organizational buyers tend to have similar views of the same products. Another reason is that the way a purchase is treated for tax purposes affects its classification. The treatment is determined by Revenue Canada rather than the buyer—so little variation is possible.

However, it is possible that a product may be placed in different classes by two buyers because of how they view the purchase. A "small" truck might be classified as an "accessory" by a large manufacturer, while a small manufacturer would view the same truck as an important "installation." Thus, how the customer sees the product is the determining factor--and it will affect marketing mix planning!

Assignment

This exercise focuses on the essential differences between business product classes. After carefully reading the following cases, indicate which type of business product each case is *primarily* concerned with. Use the following classes:

Installations	Component materials
Accessories	Supplies
Raw materials	Professional services
Component parts	

Then explain your answers, taking into consideration the various characteristics of each type of product as explained in the text on pages 303-308. The first case is answered for you as an example.

1. Delray Washington manages airplane maintenance for a major airline. As chief mechanic she knows which parts often need replacing and orders seals, O-rings and gasket kits in large quantities so she will always have them on hand.

    a) Product Class: *Supplies (repair items)*

    b) Reason: *Although the engine parts are components parts when a plan is manufactured, Washington keeps those replacement parts on hand so they are supplies—just like oil and grease—to the major airlines, i.e. the purchasers of the planes.*

2. Tom Mattern is the foreman for Shadyoak Vineyard in BC's Okanagan Lake area. Shadyoak doesn't make any wines itself. Each year the best grapes are sold to local wineries to make expensive varietal wines and the remainder of the crop is sold at wholesale to makers of table wines who buy grapes by the railcar load.

    a) Product Class: _____

    b) Reason:

3. The office staff for *Kemler's Old Car Buying Guide* are debating whether to add a computerized voice-mail system. One advocate of the idea argues that "all the other car magazines are using voice-mail to take classified ads. The customer can leave the ad--along with a credit card number--whenever it's convenient. Clearly, it's the wave of the future." Tom Kemler, who inherited the business from his grandfather has a different opinion: "These systems cost too much. And they won't bring in any more ads--they'll just encourage people to call in ads at the last minute right at our deadline."

    a) Product Class: _____

    b) Reason:

4. MARKIT is a marketing research company that helps clients improve their management and marketing decision making—through data collection and evaluation. The firm employs specialists in consumer, industrial, transportation, medical, and government research. It offers clients national field

4. surveys, consumer mail panels, test marketing facilities, shopping center interviews, group interviewing facilities, and a telephone interviewing center—in addition to sophisticated computer and data analysis programs.

a) Product Class: _____

b) Reason:

5. Juanita Martinez is the marketing manager for Protection Products, a company that makes expensive rigid camera cases and equipment like tripods for independent film production companies. She is currently planning to introduce a lightweight, flexible tripod for use with professional video cameras.

a) Product Class: _____

b) Reason:

6. David Harris runs a company which makes electronic connectors. Manufacturers use them in computers and a wide range of electronic equipment to join groups of wires to internal components. Some manufacturers contract for purchase directly with Harris, but because these connectors must all conform to worldwide standards, they are also sold "off the shelf" by many wholesale distributors.

a) Product Class: _____

b) Reason:

7.   Kim Ito's company makes rechargeable power supplies for use with portable computers. The power supplies are designed to make it fast and easy for manufacturers of notebook size computers to install them as the computer is moving down an assembly line.

a) Product Class: _____

b) Reason:

Question for Discussion

Which types of products would most likely be associated with the following kinds of buying: (a) new-task buying, (b) straight rebuy, (c) modified rebuy? Why? Illustrate with examples from Exercise 9-2.

Learning aid for use with

Exercise 9-3

Achieving brand familiarity

Introduction

In hopes of developing a strong "customer franchise," Canadian firms spend billions of dollars annually to promote brands for their products. Nevertheless, many brands are, for practical purposes, valueless because of their *nonrecognition* among potential customers. And while obtaining *brand recognition* may be a significant achievement—given the many nondescript brands on the market—this level of brand familiarity does not guarantee sales for the firm. To win favorable position in monopolistic competition, a firm may need to develop *brand preference* or even *brand insistence* for its products.

Why are some firms more successful than others in their branding efforts? The reasons are not always clear. Unfortunately, brand loyalty, like many aspects of buying behavior, remains a rather mysterious phenomenon. In general, a firm probably must produce a good product and continually promote it, but this alone may not ensure a high level of brand familiarity--particularly if the firm does not direct its efforts toward some specific target market.

This exercise gets at some important problems in branding--such as conditions favorable to branding--and the difficulty of achieving brand familiarity for certain types of products. As you do the exercise, you may begin to wonder if brands are really relevant for some product classes. You may also wish to speculate about how much effort is spent promoting brands to consumers who have no use for the product in question--or for whom brand names are meaningless.

Assignment

1.   List *from memory* (DO NOT DO ANY "RESEARCH") up to five brand names for each of the following product types. List the first brands that come to mind. If you cannot think of *any* brands for a particular product type, write "none" in the Brand 1 column.

Product	Brand 1	Brand 2	Brand 3	Brand 4	Brand 5
Bottled Water					
Ice Cream					
Fiberglass insulation					
Mattresses					
Crayons					
Dishwashers					

2. What level of brand familiarity do you think exists among the majority of consumers for each of the following products?

Product Types	Level of Brand Familiarity
a) Bottled Water:	_____
b) Ice Cream:	_____
c) Fiberglass Insulation:	_____
d) Mattresses:	_____
e) Crayons:	_____
f) Dishwashers:	_____

3. From the product types listed in Questions 1 and 2, indicate for which one branding would be *most appropriate* and explain what conditions make branding so favorable for that product type.

Product type: _____

Conditions:

4. From the product types listed in Questions 1 and 2, indicate for which one branding would be *least appropriate* and explain what conditions make branding so unfavorable for that product type.

Product type: _____

Conditions:

Question for Discussion

Why would a firm want to "license" the use of another firm's brand name?

Learning aid for use with

Exercise 9-4

Comparing branded product offerings

Introduction

Most manufacturers of consumer products use *manufacturer brands* (often called "national brands") to try to develop a loyal group of customers for their products. At the same time, more and more wholesalers and retailers are offering consumers *dealer brands* (sometimes called "private brands") to try to develop channel and store loyalty. As a result, millions of dollars are spent each year for promotion in a "battle of the brands."

The "battle of the brands" takes many forms--and attitudes toward brands vary a lot both among consumers and marketers. Some retailers tend to stock mainly manufacturer brands. Meanwhile, some manufacturers--particularly in the shoe industry--have opened up their own retail outlets to promote their own brands.

To add to the "battle of the brands," some food retailers also carry *generic products*--unbranded products in plain packages (or unpackaged!)--to appeal to price-conscious consumers. This gives consumers even more products to choose from--but may make it more difficult and confusing to determine the "best buy."

This exercise is designed to give you additional insight into the "battle of the brands." You are asked to make price comparisons between manufacturer brands and dealer brands--and then decide which is the "better buy."

Assignment

1. Visit a large chain supermarket and record the prices of the items listed on the next page. For each item, select the same size of one manufacturer brand and one dealer brand. Record the name of the manufacturer brand and then its price. If no dealer brand is available, rewrite the price of the generic product in the dealer column.

2. Which do you think is the "better buy"--manufacturer brands or dealer brands? Why? What factors did you take into consideration in deciding which is the better buy?

PRICE COMPARISON CHART				
Store Visited:				Date:
Item	Size	Name of Manufacturer Brand	Price of Manufacturer Brand	Price of Dealer Brand
Spaghetti Sauce				
Ketchup				
Mayonnaise				
White Vinegar				
Ground Coffee				
Coffee Creamer				
Peanut Butter				
Bran Flakes				
Sliced Peaches, can				
Vegetable Oil				
White Flour				
Bathroom Tissue				
Liquid Dish Detergent				
Liquid Bleach				
Orange Juice				
Milk				
Bologna, Sliced				
Margarine, Stick				
Canned Sweet Corn				
Trash Bags, kitchen				
Baby Powder				
Disposable Razors				
Dandruff Shampoo				

Question for Discussion

Why would a manufacturer be willing to produce dealer brands for a supermarket if it already is producing and advertising a similar product with its own brand name?

Learning aid for use with

Chapter 10

Product management and new-product development

What This Chapter Is About

Chapter 10 introduces product life cycles--and shows the need for managing products and developing new products.

Modern markets are dynamic--and the concepts introduced in this chapter should deepen your understanding of how and why markets evolve. Product life cycles should be studied carefully--to see how marketing strategies must be adjusted over time. In later chapters you will get more detail about how the marketing mix typically changes at different stages of the life cycle. So now is the time to build a good base for what is to come.

This chapter is one of the most important in the text, because new products are vital for the continued success of a business. Yet, a large share of new products fail. Such failures can be avoided by using the new-product development process discussed in the text. Think about this process carefully, and try to see how you could help develop more satisfying and profitable products. Creativity in product planning--perhaps seeing unsatisfied market needs--could lead to breakthrough opportunities!

Important Terms

product life cycle, p. 326
market introduction, p. 327
market growth, p. 327
market maturity, p. 327
sales decline, p. 328
fashion, p. 331
fad, p. 332

new product, p. 339
The Hazardous Products Act, p. 344
product liability, p. 344
concept testing, p. 345
product managers, p. 349
brand managers, p. 349

True-False Questions

___ 1. The product life cycle is divided into four major stages: market introduction, market growth, market maturity, and market saturation.

___ 2. A firm's marketing mix usually must change--and different target markets may be appealed to--as a product moves through the different stages of its life cycle.

___ 3. Industry sales and profits tend to rise and fall together as a product moves through its life cycle.

___ 4. The market introduction stage is usually extremely profitable due to the lack of competitors.

— 5. Industry profits tend to reach their peak and start to decline during the market growth stage-- even though industry sales may be growing rapidly.

— 6. Industry profits decline throughout the market maturity stage because aggressive competition leads to price cutting and increased expenditures on persuasive promotion.

— 7. During the sales decline stage, new products replace the old--and all firms remaining in the industry find themselves operating at a loss.

— 8. In general, product life cycles appear to be getting longer due to a decline in product innovation.

— 9. A fashion is the currently accepted or popular style.

— 10. A fad is an idea that is fashionable only to certain groups who are enthusiastic about it--but these groups are so fickle that a fad is even more short-lived than a regular fashion.

— 11. Once a firm introduces a product to a market, it has no other choice but to watch its product move through the remaining stages of the product life cycle.

— 12. Strategy planning can sometimes extend product life cycles, delaying the move from market maturity to sales decline.

— 13. The same product may be in different life cycle stages in different markets.

— 14. While a lot of strategy planning is necessary to introduce a new product, no strategy is required to get rid of a dying product.

— 15. According to the text, a new product is one that is new in any way for the company concerned.

— 16. Twelve months is the longest time that any product may be called "new" according to Consumer and Corporate Affairs Canada.

— 17. Since new products are vital to the survival of most firms, the objective of the new-product development process should be to approve as many new-product ideas as possible.

— 18. Product planners should consider long-term welfare in addition to immediate satisfaction-- and therefore should offer "pleasing products" instead of "desirable products."

— 19. Product liability means the legal obligation of sellers to pay damages to individuals who are injured by defective or unsafe products.

— 20. Concept testing is done before any tangible product has been developed--and involves marketing research to determine potential customers' attitudes towards the new-product idea.

— 21. The development step (in new-product development) involves the testing of physical products as well as test marketing--something that must be done for all products prior to commercialization.

— 22. The specific organization arrangement for new-product development may not be too important--as long as there is top-level support.

___ 23. Product managers sometimes have profit responsibilities and much power, but often they are "product champions" who are mainly involved in planning and getting promotion done.

Answers to True-False Questions

1. F, p. 326	9. T, p. 331	17. F, p. 339
2. T, p. 327	10. T, p. 332	18. F, p. 343
3. F, p. 327	11. F, p. 336	19. T, p. 344
4. F, p. 327	12. T, p. 335	20. T, p. 345
5. T, p. 327	13. T, p. 337	21. F, p. 346
6. T, p. 327	14. F, pp. 337-338	22. F, p. 346
7. F, p. 328	15. T, p. 339	23. T, p. 349
8. F, p. 330	16. T, p. 339	

Multiple-Choice Questions (Circle the correct response)

1. The product life cycle has four stages. Which of the following is *not* one of these?
   a. Market introduction
   b. Market growth
   c. Market maturity
   d. Economic competition
   e. Sales decline

2. During the *market introduction* stage of the product life cycle:
   a. considerable money is spent on promotion while place development is left until later stages.
   b. products usually show large profits if marketers have successfully carved out new markets.
   c. most potential customers are quite anxious to try out the new-product concept.
   d. funds are being invested in marketing with the expectation of *future* profits.
   e. product and promotion are more important than place and price.

3. Which of the following statements regarding the *market growth* stage of the product life cycle is *false*?
   a. Innovators still earn profits--but this stage is less profitable for them than the previous stage.
   b. This is the time of peak profitability for the industry.
   c. The sales of the total industry are rising fairly rapidly as more and more customers buy.
   d. Monopolistic competition is common during this stage.

4. Regarding product life cycles, good marketing managers know that:
   a. all competitors lose money during the sales decline stage.
   b. they are getting longer.
   c. industry sales reach their maximum during the market growth stage.
   d. firms earn their biggest profits during the market introduction stage.
   e. industry profits reach their maximum during the market growth stage.

5. A particular industry is experiencing no real sales growth and declining profits in the face of oligopolistic competition. Demand has become quite elastic--as consumers see competing products as almost homogeneous. Several firms have dropped out of the industry, and there has been only one recent new entry. Firms in the industry are attempting to avoid price-cutting by budgeting huge amounts for persuasive advertising. In which stage of the product life cycle are firms in this industry competing?
    a. Market maturity
    b. Sales decline
    c. Market growth
    d. Market introduction

6. Marketing managers should recognize that:
    a. product life cycles appear to be getting longer.
    b. every segment within a market has the same product life cycle.
    c. the product life cycle describes the sales and profits of individual products, not industry sales and profits.
    d. firms that enter mature markets have to compete with established firms for declining industry profits.
    e. None of the above is a true statement.

7. In planning for different stages of the product life cycle, strategy planners must be aware that:
    a. losses can be expected during the market introduction stage.
    b. the life cycles of mature product-markets can be extended through strategic product adjustments.
    c. offering the product to a new market segment may start a whole new life cycle.
    d. products can be withdrawn from the market before the sales decline stage--but even here a phase-out strategy is usually required.
    e. All of the above are true statements.

8. Which of the following statements about "new products" is *false*?
    a. In order for it to be considered new, there should be a functionally significant change in the product—according to the CCAC.
    b. A product should be considered "new" by a particular firm if it is new in any way for that company.
    c. The CCAC considers 12 months as the maximum time that a product should be called "new."
    d. A product may be called "new" any time a package change or modification is made, according to the CCAC.
    e. A product should be considered "new" by a firm if it is aimed at new markets.

9. Regarding the new-product development process,
    a. screening criteria should be mainly quantitative--because qualitative criteria require too much judgment.
    b. concept testing tries to see how the new product works in the hands of potential customers.
    c. it tries to "kill" new ideas that are not likely to be profitable.
    d. market tests should be conducted for all new product ideas before commercialization.
    e. All of the above are true.

10. Which of the following types of products provides low immediate satisfaction but high long-run consumer welfare?
    a. Salutary products
    b. Pleasing products
    c. Desirable products
    d. Deficient products

11. Product or brand managers are commonly used when a firm:
    a. has several different kinds of products or brands.
    b. wants to eliminate the job of the advertising manager.
    c. has one or a few products--all of which are important to its success.
    d. wants to eliminate the job of sales manager.
    e. wants one person to have authority over all the functional areas that affect the profitability of a particular product.

Answers to Multiple-Choice Questions

1. d, p. 326
2. d, p. 327
3. a, p. 327
4. e, pp. 327-328

5. a, pp. 327-328
6. d, pp. 327-328
7. e, pp. 327-328
8. d p. 339

9. c, p. 341
10. a, p. 343
11. a, pp. 349-350

Exercise 11-2

Determining market exposure policies

Introduction

Once a producer decides to use middlemen (wholesalers and retailers) to help distribute its products, it must decide what degree of market exposure will be best: *exclusive distribution, selective distribution*, or *intensive distribution*. Contrary to popular opinion, maximum exposure is not always desirable. The ideal market exposure should meet--but not exceed--the needs of target customers. As one moves from exclusive distribution to intensive distribution, the total marketing cost may increase--and the quality of service provided by middlemen may actually decline.

When deciding about the desired market exposure, a marketing manager should consider the functions which middlemen will be asked to perform and the product class for his product. The product classes summarize some of what is known about the product--including what the target customers think of it, their willingness to shop for it, and the amount of personal attention and service they want. The product class often determines the "ideal" market exposure.

Of course, there sometimes is a difference between a product's *ideal* market exposure and the exposure which it can achieve. Middlemen are not always willing to carry a new product, especially when several similar products are already on the market. Similarly, middlemen who are interested in carrying a product may not have the opportunity, unless the producer wants them as a channel partner.

Assignment

This exercise will give you some practice in determining the "ideal" degree of market exposure for a company. Six cases are presented below--with the first serving as an example. Read each case carefully and then indicate (a) the product class which is involved, and (b) the degree of market exposure (intensive, selective, or exclusive) which you think would be "ideal." Then in part (c), explain *why* you think the indicated degree of market exposure would be ideal. State any assumptions which you have made. *Note:* "Ideal" here means the degree of market exposure which will satisfy the target customers' needs (but not exceed them) *and also* will be achievable by the producer. For example, a new producer of "homogeneous" cookies might desire intensive distribution, but agree to sell to only a few food chains because it knows it will not be able to obtain intensive distribution with its undifferentiated cookies. So its "ideal" is selective distribution, and it will adjust the rest of its marketing mix accordingly.

Note: Exhibits 9-4 and 9-5 on pages 298 and 303 of the text may be helpful in completing this exercise.

1. Boger Mfg., Inc. manufactures a wide line of kitchen dinette sets for sale throughout Canada. The products are distributed through retail outlets. Retailers are supposed to stock a large assortment of dinette sets, along with a large inventory of replacement parts. The tables and chairs are usually shipped to the retailers unassembled. According to a recent cost study, 30 percent of Boger's retailers account for about 80 percent of the company's sales.

   a)   Product class: *Heterogeneous shopping products*

   b)   "Ideal" market exposure: *Selective distribution*

   c)   Why?   *The recent cost study shows that a small percentage of retailers are producing most of the business. These middlemen might do an even better job if given more assistance and less direct competition from retailers carrying the same products. Since customers are willing to shop around, reducing the number of outlets would be possible--and might benefit consumers through larger retail inventories and increased customer service.*

2. SteelCo, Inc., makes and sells a low-priced line of file cabinets for use in offices. One style of cabinet is designed to store standard size business papers, and another style is designed for computer output. The files are sold directly to universities and other institutions--and indirectly through wholesalers to office equipment dealers. SteelCo's files sell to final customers (not the middlemen) at prices ranging from about $90 to $300. Most dealers handle several competing brands of file cabinets, including some "high-quality" brands that sell for as much as $1,000.

   a)   Product class: _____

   b)   "Ideal" market exposure: _____

   c)   Why? _____

   _____

   _____

   _____

   _____

3. Sokaki, Ltd. is a Japanese manufacturer of a full line of power construction equipment—including portable cement mixers, ditch-digging machines, cranes, and the like. Sokaki products are distributed through over 800 independent dealers scattered throughout Canada, the United States, and Europe. In some large cities with an active construction industry, there may be several dealers who sell competing equipment, but typically there is only one or two Sokaki dealers in a given city. Many of Sokaki's dealerships are quite small, and the company lacks adequate dealers in several key market areas. To further complicate matters, price wars between dealerships are becoming common as construction has been depressed and demand for the equipment is weak. In fact, some Sokaki dealers often find themselves competing directly with other Sokaki dealers—since many of the customers are finding it worthwhile to travel hundreds of miles to purchase new equipment at a discounted price.

Learning aid for use with

a) Product class: _____

b) "Ideal" market exposure: _____

c) Why? _____

_____

_____

_____

_____

4. National Meat Co. (NMC) is a large, well-known producer of pre-packaged, sliced cold cuts and luncheon meats that are distributed through supermarkets and other food retailers. NMC is about to launch a new product, Lunch Chums, which packages a luncheon meat, crackers, and a fruit snack together. The proposed marketing mix includes heavy national TV advertising directed to families with children. The ads--which show a busy family getting ready to leave the house for work and school--note that Lunch Chums combined with a carton of milk provide more nutrition that most school cafeteria lunches, at a lower price, and with no preparation time.

a) Product class: _____

b) "Ideal" market exposure: _____

c) Why? _____

_____

_____

_____

_____

5. Deco Products, Ltd., manufactures decorative items for the home. It recently added a line of blown glass oil lamps to its product line. The attractively styled oil lamps provide a nice decorating touch on a dining room table or sideboard, and they burn for hours and give off the warm light of candles but without the mess of dripping wax. The oil lamps are available in several traditional and contemporary styles so they will match any type of furnishings. They are priced at $40 each and are usually sold in pairs. Like most of the company's products, the oil lamps are sold in gift shops, department stores, and specialty shops such as Pier 1 franchise outlets. Initial sales for the oil lamps have been quite promising. The product seems to have good "eye appeal," according to one shop owner. Apparently, the early customers hadn't planned to buy anything like an oil lamp, but once they saw them displayed in the store, they couldn't resist buying them.

a) Product class: _____

b) "Ideal" market exposure: _____

c) Why? _____

_____

_____

_____

_____

6. Italio, Inc. designs and manufactures a high-quality line of fashionable shoes that are popular among young professional women. The line is quite expensive--and it is sold through specialty shops which handle only this type of fashion shoe (including competing brands). Italio will only work with retailers who agree to stock a large variety of sizes and colors of Italio shoes. They also must agree to promote the Italio line very aggressively. In return, Italio agrees not to distribute its line to other retailers within the specialty shop's immediate trading area. Since continuing promotion seems to be necessary in this highly competitive market, advertisements for Italio shoes appear regularly in fashion magazines targeted at professional women and on select cable TV broadcasts, including broadcasts of women's tennis tournaments.

a) Product class: _____

b) "Ideal" market exposure: _____

c) Why? _____

_____

_____

_____

_____

Question for Discussion

How do you think each firm should try to achieve the "ideal" degree of market exposure you discussed above? Are there any legal constraints they should consider?

Chapter 12

Logistics and distribution customer service

What This Chapter Is About

Chapter 12 is concerned with what is often the "invisible" part of marketing--the physical movement and storing of products--and its not so invisible outcome, the customer service level customers get. Decisions in the logistics area may also have a very significant impact on the cost of a marketing strategy.

This chapter covers some important details concerning logistics and distribution customer service. But the major focus is on integrating transporting and storing into one coordinated effort--not only within an individual firm but also *among firms* in the channel--to provide customers with the appropriate physical distribution customer service level at the lowest total cost. You'll see how and why many firms are adopting approaches such as just-in-time delivery and electronic data interchange (EDI) to improve coordination of logistics in the channel.

The total cost approach to physical distribution, the physical distribution concept, and customer service levels are all important ideas which have significantly improved some companies' marketing strategy planning. But they are not yet well accepted. Try to see why. Helping to apply these ideas may offer a breakthrough opportunity for you.

Important Terms

physical distribution (PD), p. 378
logistics, p. 378
customer service level, p. 378
physical distribution (PD) concept, p. 379
total cost approach, p. 380
transporting, p. 382
pool car service, p. 385
diversion in transit, p. 385
containerization, p. 388

piggyback service, p. 388
freight forwarders, p. 389
storing, p. 390
inventory, p. 390
private warehouses, p. 391
public warehouses, p. 392
distribution centre, p. 393
electronic data interchange (EDI), p. 396

True-False Questions

___ 1. Physical distribution--which is the transporting and storing of goods within individual firms and along channel systems--accounts for nearly half the cost of marketing.

___ 2. Logistics is just another word for physical distribution.

___ 3. Customer service level is a measure of how rapidly and dependably a firm can deliver what customers want.

____ 4. Marketing managers should be careful to avoid offering customers a level of physical distribution service that might increase storing or transporting costs.

____ 5. According to the physical distribution concept, a firm might lower its total cost of physical distribution by selecting a higher cost transportation alternative.

____ 6. The total cost approach to PD involves evaluating each possible PD system--and identifying all of the costs of each alternative.

____ 7. When a firm decides to minimize total costs of physical distribution, it may also be settling for a lower customer service level and lower sales and profits.

____ 8. A higher physical distribution service level may mean both higher costs and higher profits.

____ 9. Transporting--which is the marketing function of moving goods--provides time, place, and possession utilities.

____ 10. The value added to products by moving them should be greater than the cost of the transporting, or there is little reason to ship in the first place.

____ 11. Since 1980, there has been much more government regulation over transporting.

____ 12. Railroad pool car service appeals mainly to very large shippers who are transporting to only a few locations.

____ 13. Railroads offering "diversion-in-transit" enable shippers to ship commodities away from the source, stop them along the way for processing, and then start them moving again, as long as the final destination stays the same.

____ 14. In contrast to railroads which are best suited for moving heavy and bulky freight over long distances, the flexibility of trucks make them especially suitable for moving small quantities of goods short distances.

____ 15. Trucking rates are roughly one-half of airfreight rates.

____ 16. Water transportation is very important to international trade, but it plays a small role within the Canadian market.

____ 17. An important advantage of using airfreight is that the cost of packing and unpacking goods for sale may be reduced or eliminated.

____ 18. The fact that rates on less-than-full carloads or truckloads are often much higher than those on full carloads or truckloads is one reason for the development of wholesalers.

____ 19. Even though freight forwarders usually do not own their own transporting facilities, they can obtain low transporting rates by combining small shipments into more economical quantities.

____ 20. When a firm's small shipments have to be moved by varied transporters, it probably should consider employing the services of freight forwarders.

____ 21. While transporting provides time utility, the storing function provides place utility.

___ 22. Inventory means the amount of goods being stored.

___ 23. The storing function offers several ways to vary a firm's marketing mix--and its channel system--by: (1) adjusting the time goods are held, (2) sharing the storing costs, and (3) delegating the job to a specialized storing facility.

___ 24. Unless a large volume of goods must be stored regularly, a firm should probably choose public warehouses over private warehouses--even though public warehouses do not provide all the services that could be obtained in the company's own branch warehouses.

___ 25. The distribution center concept is based on the assumption that--unless storage creates time utility--reducing storage and increasing turnover will lead to bigger profits.

___ 26. Just-in-time shifts more responsibility for PD activities to the supplier.

___ 27. Electronic data interchange sets a standard for communication between different firms' computer systems.

___ 28. Improved order processing can sometimes have the same effect on customer service levels as faster, more expensive transportation.

Answers to True-False Questions

1. T, p. 378
2. T, p. 378
3. T, p. 378
4. F, pp. 378-9
5. T, p. 380
6. T, pp. 380-1
7. T, p. 381
8. T, p. 381
9. F, p. 382
10. T, p. 382

11. F, p. 383
12. F, p. 385
13. F, p. 385
14. T, p. 385
15. T, p. 387
16. F, p. 386
17. T, p. 387
18. T, p. 389
19. T, p. 389
20. T, p. 389

21. F, p. 390
22. T, p. 390
23. T, p. 391
24. F, p. 392
25. T, p. 393
26. T, pp. 394-5
27. T, p. 396
28. T, p. 396

Multiple-Choice Questions (Circle the correct response)

1. Performance of the physical distribution functions provides:
   a. time utility.
   b. place utility.
   c. possession utility.
   d. All of the above.
   e. Only a and b above.

2. The physical distribution customer service level is important because:
   a. it is a measure of how rapidly and dependably a firm delivers what its customers want.
   b. it may result in lost sales if it is too low.
   c. it may result in lower profits if it is too high.
   d. All of the above.
   e. None of the above.

3. According to the "physical distribution concept":
   a. transporting and storing are independent activities.
   b. all transporting and storing activities of a business and a channel system should be thought of as part of one system.
   c. inventories should be based on production requirements.
   d. the production department should be responsible for warehousing and shipping.
   e. the lowest-cost distribution system is the best alternative.

4. The "total cost approach" to physical distribution management:
   a. emphasizes faster delivery service and thus favors the use of airfreight over railroads.
   b. often ignores inventory carrying costs.
   c. might favor a high-cost transportation mode if storage costs are reduced enough to lower total distribution costs.
   d. seeks to reduce the cost of transportation to its minimum.
   e. All of the above are true.

5. Which of the following statements reflects a marketing-oriented approach to physical distribution?
   a. "We should create a position of physical distribution manager and give him authority to integrate all physical distribution activities to minimize the total cost of distribution."
   b. "We should aim to keep our customers fully satisfied 100 percent of the time as this will increase our sales and give us a competitive advantage."
   c. "We should replace our warehouses with distribution centers to speed the flow of products and eliminate all storage."
   d. "We should choose the physical distribution alternative that will minimize the total cost of achieving the level of customer service our target market requires."
   e. All are equally "marketing-oriented."

6. A marketing-oriented physical distribution manager would *insist* that:
   a. the storage function be eliminated to reduce inventory costs.
   b. efficiency in physical distribution can be best achieved by minimizing costs.
   c. emphasis must be on maximizing the customer service level.
   d. both customer service level and total distribution costs be considered.
   e. none of the above.

7. Transporting costs
   a. are usually more than the value added by shipping, but the products are shipped anyway as there is no choice.
   b. do not vary much as a percentage of the final price of products, since big items are shipped by inexpensive means and small items are shipped by more expensive approaches.
   c. usually do not add much to the final cost of products which are already valuable relative to their size and weight.
   d. usually are not large enough to limit the target market that a marketing manager can serve.
   e. None of the above is true.

8. Which of the following transportation modes is "best" regarding "number of locations served"?
   a. Rail
   b. Water
   c. Truck
   d. Pipeline
   e. Air

9. A railroad shipping process which allows redirection of carloads already in transit is called:
   a. diversion in transit
   b. freight forwarding
   c. transloading privileges
   d. pool car shipping
   e. piggyback service

10. Berry Bros. wants to ship a somewhat bulky, high-valued commodity a short distance--and it is seeking low-cost and extremely fast service. Berry should use:
    a. airfreight.
    b. railroads.
    c. inland waterways.
    d. trucks.
    e. None of the above.

11. Compared to other forms of transportation, airfreight may result in:
    a. a lower total cost of distribution.
    b. less damage in transit.
    c. higher transportation rates.
    d. lower packing costs.
    e. All of the above.

12. Grouping individual items into an economical shipping quantity and sealing them in protective containers for transit to the final destination is called:
    a. containerization
    b. pool car service
    c. freight forwarding
    d. piggyback service
    e. all of the above

13. Freight forwarders:
    a. are not very active in international shipping because they are unwilling to handle all the paperwork necessary in overseas shipments.
    b. generally own their own transportation facilities--including pickup and delivery trucks.
    c. can be especially helpful to the marketing manager who ships in large quantities.
    d. accumulate small shipments from shippers and then reship them in larger quantities to obtain lower transportation rates.
    e. All of the above are true statements.

14. Storing:
    a. is related to Place--but has no effect on Price.
    b. is necessary because production does not always match consumption.
    c. must be performed by all members of a channel system.
    d. decreases the value of products.
    e. All of the above are true statements.

15. A manufacturer having irregular need for regional storage of bicycles should use which one of the following?
    a. A private warehouse to be sure of adequate space
    b. Public warehouses to provide flexibility and low unit cost
    c. Merchant wholesalers
    d. Agent middlemen
    e. Commission houses

16. A distribution centre is designed to:
    a. stockpile goods for long periods and avoid rising prices.
    b. buy low and sell high.
    c. reduce inventory turnover.
    d. speed the flow of goods and avoid unnecessary storing.
    e. all of the above.

17. Just-in-time systems:
    a. reduce PD costs for business customers.
    b. increase PD costs for suppliers.
    c. shift less responsibility for PD to business customers.
    d. shift more responsibility for PD to suppliers.
    e. All of the above.

18. Electronic data interchange:
    a. puts information in a standardized format.
    b. makes inventory reports more accessible.
    c. is common in domestic and international communication.
    d. both a and b.
    e. all of the above.

Answers to Multiple-Choice Questions

1. e, p. 378
2. d, p. 378
3. b, p. 379
4. c, p. 380
5. d, pp. 378-82
6. d, pp. 379-82

7. c, p. 382
8. c, pp. 385-6
9. a, p. 385
10. d, p. 385
11. e, p. 387
12. a, p. 388

13. d, p. 389
14. b, p. 390
15. b, p. 392
16. d, p. 393
17. e, pp. 394-5
18. e, p. 396

Learning aid for use with

Exercise 12-1

Evaluating physical distribution alternatives

Introduction

Within the framework of marketing strategy planning, physical distribution managers seek to provide the level of customer service that satisfies the needs of the firm's target market. Given some specified level of customer service, it is also the physical distribution manager's job to provide that service at the lowest cost possible. This total cost approach is based on the idea of "tradeoffs" among parts of the distribution system.

For example, a physical distribution manager may be making a tradeoff when he or she decides to lower transportation costs, because such a move usually results in larger inventory costs. Following the total cost approach, you would not try to minimize with transportation *or* inventory costs. Instead, you would design and operate the physical distribution system in a way that would *minimize the total cost of offering the desired customer service level*. The following exercise will illustrate this idea in greater detail.

Assignment

Read the following case and answer the questions that follow.

TOUSSAINT RESTAURANT EQUIPMENT COMPANY

The Toussaint Restaurant Equipment Company is studying its physical distribution system to see if the system needs to be revised. At present, all of Toussaint's products are manufactured at the firm's plant in Montreal and are then shipped by train to several branch warehouses across Canada. When an order is received at the Quebec head office, the order is faxed to the branch warehouse closest to the customer. The products are then shipped directly to the customer by truck. Toussaint tries to maintain a "80 percent/three-day" customer service level—that is, it tries to deliver 80 percent of its orders to the customer within three days after the orders are received.

But some of the company managers have expressed dissatisfaction with the present distribution system. Toussaint's sales manager feels that the 80 percent service level compares poorly with the service customers have come to expect from other suppliers--and that a goal of at least 90 percent delivered within 3 days can be achieved by adding more warehouses. The production manager notes that restaurant equipment isn't perishable and because customers want Toussaint's unique features they don't mind waiting for new equipment to be delivered. She proposes a target delivery time of four weeks which will even out the production schedule and amount to a 10 percent/three-day customer service level; the traffic manager claims this will increase transportation costs too much. Finally, the finance manager has suggested that the firm try to minimize its total distribution costs by providing whatever level of customer service it can while operating at the lowest possible total cost.

To help resolve this conflicting advice from his top managers, Toussaint's president, Henri Grosfacile, has asked his assistant to analyze the relationship between alternative customer service levels and physical distribution costs. The results of this analysis are shown in Figure 12-1.

FIGURE 12-1
Distribution Costs at Different Customer Service Levels

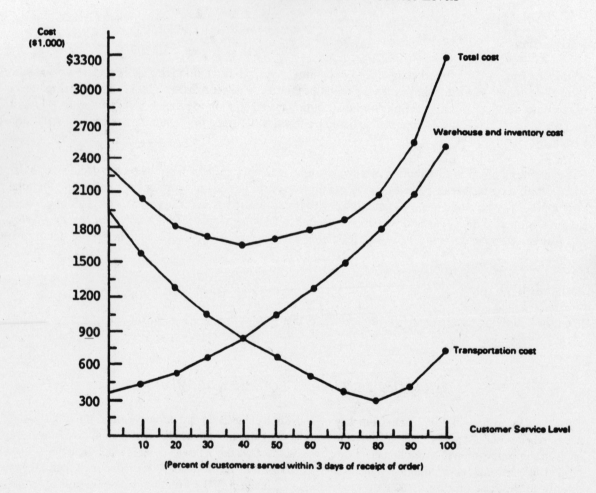

1. At what customer service level would the total cost of distribution be *minimized* as the finance manager suggests? What would the minimum total cost be?

    Customer service level _____ % Total cost $_____

Learning aid for use with

2. According to Figure 12-1, what is Toussaint's total cost of physical distribution at its present 80 percent customer service level? $_____

3. What would the total cost be if a 90 percent service level were adopted, as the sales manager desires?
$_____

4. What would the total cost be if a 10 percent service level were adopted, as the production manager has suggested?
$_____

5. What would the *total cost* be if Toussaint attempted to *minimize* its:

   a) warehouse and inventory costs $_____

   b) transportation costs $_____

6. What would the total cost be if Toussaint were to *maximize* its customer service level?

   $_____

7. Based on the information in Figure 12-1, what is the optimal level of customer service?

8. As marketing manager for the Toussaint Company, what advice would you give the president concerning the customer service level decision?

Question for Discussion

What determines the level of service that customers expect?

Exercise 12-2

Integrating physical distribution

Introduction

Successful marketers must pay attention to the distribution customer service they provide their customers. They also must worry about the cost of the service they provide--because ultimately the price of a product should cover the cost. Deciding on the right balance between the distribution customer service level and the costs of transporting and storing is sometimes difficult--and identifying how best to achieve that balance can be even more of a challenge. The job of integrating all of the logistics activities is even more complicated when it requires coordination among different firms in a channel. But the job must be done and done well. One firm can't just reduce its own PD costs if that raises costs somewhere else in the channel--or reduces the service level. For example some business customers may demand just-in-time delivery or expect the convenience and speed of electronic data interchange (EDI)--because that is what is required to make the whole channel more competitive.

Many marketing managers know about the physical distribution concept, but it's easy to fall into the trap of just accepting a firm's PD system as "the way it's always been"--never even bothering to think about how to improve it. This exercise gives you practice in analyzing different PD situations--and in applying the concepts discussed in Chapter 12 to improve a marketing strategy.

Assignment

Read each of the following situations carefully. Identify the major PD problem(s) and then make specific suggestions about how you might improve the strategy. State any assumptions that you think are important to your recommendation. In your answer, be sure to show that you understand the various concepts--including the different storing and transporting alternatives--discussed in the text. The first problem is answered for you as an example of the approach to take. But keep in mind that there may be more than one "correct" answer in each situation. The solution will depend, in part, on your creativity!

1. The Orthopedics Group is a partnership of surgeons who treat broken bones for patients who live in a medium-size U.S. town. Most patients need to be in a cast for four to six weeks, and after that many must wear a removable brace for a few more weeks—until the bone is strong. Recently, the Orthopedics Group contacted to provide care to members of a local Health Maintenance Organization, and they agreed that the HMO could do a survey to evaluate patient satisfaction. The doctors were surprised to find that many patients gave them a low rating—primarily because of the inconvenience involved in being fitted for braces. Hospitals in a large city keep a complete assortment of braces on hand, but that is not feasible for a small clinic with limited space. So the Orthopedics Group orders

braces from a wholesaler by phone the day a patient's cast is removed, and then the patient schedules another appointment to come back the next day—after the wholesaler delivers the brace—to have it fitted.

Problem: *Fitting of the braces may not be the most important part of what the doctors do, but the unavailability of braces when patients (customers) expect them results in a breakdown in satisfaction with the service. The anxiety of a day without the brace probably doesn't help.*

Recommendation: *Although it may not be possible to stock all of the different types and sizes of braces, the clinic might try to stock one each of the most frequently used braces. Even a "less-than-complete" inventory might avoid many of the problems. Further, and perhaps more important, the timing of the "demand" for a particular size and type of brace does not arise as a surprise. Most patients have had a cast on for a number of weeks before they come in for the appointment to have it removed. It should be a simple matter for the clinic to order needed braces several days before each patient's cast-removal appointment. Earlier ordering could solve the problem--and increase satisfaction.*

2. Prescient Furniture Company makes a wide variety of stylish upholstered sofas and chairs. Over time, an increasing share of the company's business has come from special orders which consumers place through furniture stores, most of which handle a number of competing lines. As special orders increased, Prescient slowly increased the choices among upholstery fabrice--and the firm now offers more than 250 colors and patterns. Some customers seem to be delighted with this unique array of choices. Even so, sales have slowly tapered off--and at a recent dealer meeting, several retailers complained that not many customers where willing to wait eight to twelve weeks for Prescient to produce and deliver a custom order. Prescient's sales manager urged the retailers to carry more chairs and sofa in stock, so that they could sell more Prescient furniture "off the display floor."

    a) Problem:

    b) Recommendation:

3. Awnings Away is the second largest producer of high quality coated fabrics used for outdoor awnings for fine homes, restaurants, and hotels, and in other applications--including boat covers. Awnings Away sells fabric directly to the thousands of awning fabricators who serve customers in their local markets. Once a consumer selects a fabric from a sample and tells a fabricator what to make, the fabricator calls the regional Awnings Away sales rep and places an order. Each week's orders are then processed through the home office and the bulky fabric is shipped by truck to the fabricator from either the company's east coast or west coast warehouse. This approach reduces transportation costs and makes it easier to manage the inventory in the

warehouse. Although many fabricators are loyal to Awnings Away fabric, a new competitor from Europe has been taking a share of the market, apparently in large part because it is able to fill orders within a week rather than the three weeks it takes, on average, for Awnings Away. The Awnings Away marketing manager does not expect the new competitor to be able to survive, however, because its delivered prices are about 10 percent higher.

a) Problem:

b) Recommendation:

4.   Nordic Motors is a manufacturer of family automobiles and has enjoyed real success in serving a small, but profitable, segment of the Canadian market. Nordic's vehicles are renown for safety and durability. But this success brings problems. Nordic must provide dealers with repair parts for five different models, many of which have changed significantly over the years. Yet, the success of Nordic's strategy depends on strong service from dealers—to keep customers happy, word-of-mouth favorable, and repeat sales strong. The company operates 4 Canadian parts warehouses and ships to dealers by common carrier truck. As the number of older models still in service has increased, dealers have begun to complain about the long re-stock time *and* the large number of parts they must keep in stock to handle the discontinued models. Some customers face a long wait for parts before the dealer can fix a car.

a) Problem:

b) Recommendation:

5.   CookieLight makes a variety of sugar-free cookies that are sold by several large supermarket chains in the midwest. Data from the stores' checkout computers is automatically linked to the CookieLight bakeries in Toronto so that each day's production run, and the shipments to each store, can exactly match the assortment needed to refill each store's display. This reduces inventory costs and also results in fresh cookies. While studying sales figures, the CookieLight marketing manager noticed that during the previous two months there had been no sales of Almond cookies at one store. On investigation, the manager discovered that a case of Almond cookies were crushed in transit. The shattered cookies—clearly visible through their plastic bags—had been placed on the rack by a stock clerk. Because no customers were buying the damaged cookies, none passed through the checkout scanners, and no replacements were ordered.

a) Problem:

b) Recommendation:

Question for Discussion

Given the difficulties of coordinating physical distribution activities in a channel, wouldn't it be easier and cheaper for most manufacturers to make all the important PD decisions--and then deal only with middlemen who will accept those decisions.

Chapter 13

Retailers and their strategy planning

What This Chapter Is About

Chapter 13 looks at the many changes that have been taking place in retailing.

Try to understand why and how retailers behave--because retailing probably will continue to change in the future. In particular, try to see why there are so many different types of retailers--and why some seem to be doing well while others have serious problems. Note the differences in retailing in different nations.

Don't just memorize the definitions of the various types of retailers. Instead, study what each is doing for some group of target customers. A diagram is presented later in the chapter to help organize your thinking.

It is useful to think of retailers from their point of view--rather than only as outlets for manufacturers' products. Most retailers see themselves as buyers for their customers, rather than selling arms of manufacturers. Try to look at retailing the way they do. This should increase your understanding of this vital part of our marketing system.

Important Terms

retailing, p. 402
convenience store, p. 404
shopping stores, p. 404
specialty stores, p. 404
general stores, p. 406
single-line stores, p. 406
limited-line stores, p. 406
specialty shop, p. 407
department stores, p. 408
supermarkets, p. 408
catalog showroom retailers, p. 409
discount houses, p. 409
mass-merchandisers, p. 409
superstores (hypermarkets), p. 410

convenience (food) stores, p. 411
automatic vending, p. 411
telephone and mail-order, retailing, p. 412
door-to-door selling, p. 414
scrambled merchandising, p. 414
wheel of retailing theory, p. 416
(corporate) chain store, p. 420
cooperative chains, p. 420
voluntary chains, p. 420
franchise operation, p. 421
planned shopping centre, p. 422
neighborhood shopping centres, p. 423
community shopping centres, p. 423
regional shopping centres, p. 423

True-False Questions

___ 1. Retailing covers all of the activities involved in the sale of products to final consumers.

___ 2. More than three fourths of all new retailing ventures fail during the first year.

___ 3. A consumer's choice of a retail store appears to be based almost entirely on emotional needs--economic needs have almost no influence.

___ 4. By definition, a convenience store would not stock shopping products or specialty products.

___ 5. The major attraction of a shopping store would be the width and depth of its merchandise assortment.

___ 6. A specialty store is one that handles an assortment of unusual or exotic merchandise.

___ 7. A hundred and fifty years ago, general stores--that carried anything they could sell in reasonable volume--were the main retailers in the United States.

___ 8. A limited-line store will typically carry a broader assortment than a single-line store.

___ 9. Limited-line stores may carry several lines of merchandise--but with a very limited assortment of products within each line.

___ 10. A specialty shop is a type of limited-line store that usually is small, has a distinct personality, and aims at a carefully defined market segment by offering knowledgeable salespeople, better service, and a unique product assortment.

___ 11. A specialty shop would probably be viewed by most customers as a specialty store that stocks primarily specialty products.

___ 12. Department stores are becoming less important and they now account for only about 1 percent of retail sales.

___ 13. The mass-merchandising concept says that retailers should offer low prices to get faster turnover and greater sales volumes—by appealing to larger markets.

___ 14. A well-managed supermarket can generally count on a net profit level of only about 1 percent of sales.

___ 15. Catalog showroom retailers have become quite successful using their strategy of stocking little inventory and delivering by mail.

___ 16. While discount selling generally involves price cutting on a limited assortment of products, many modern discount houses are fast-turnover, price-cutting operations that offer full assortments, better locations, and more services and guarantees.

___ 17. The average mass-merchandiser has a store that is about the same size as an average supermarket.

___ 18. Superstores are simply large mass-merchandisers that carry more shopping products.

— 19. Single-line mass merchandisers attract large numbers of customers with their convenient assortment and low prices in a single product category.

— 20. Convenience food stores limit their assortment to those "pickup" or "fill-in" items that are needed between major shopping trips to a supermarket, and thus earn smaller profits as a percent of sales.

— 21. Automatic vending has low operating costs because labor costs are very low.

— 22. Telephone and mail-order retailing grew for a while but now seems to have leveled off at less than 2 percent of retail sales.

— 23. Although it's an expensive method of selling—door-to-door retailers may be especially useful for the sale of unsought products.

— 24. "Scrambled merchandising" is a way of describing the activities of modern retailers who are willing to carry "unconventional" assortments of products—anything they can sell profitably.

— 25. All major retailing developments can be explained by the "Wheel of Retailing" theory—which describes a recurring retail cycle from low cost and low prices to higher cost and higher prices.

— 26. While only 8.4 percent of retail chains have sales volume over $100,000,000 this group accounts for over 75 percent of sales.

— 27. One of the incentives to chain store development is the availability of economies of scale.

— 28. Voluntary chains are formed by independent retailers in their efforts to compete with corporate chains—while cooperative chains operate similarly except that they are sponsored by wholesalers.

— 29. The very high failure rate among franchise operations explains why franchises are becoming less popular.

— 30. By the year 2000 franchise holders will account for one-half of all retail sales.

— 31. A good example of a planned shopping center is the central business district found in most large cities.

— 32. Neighborhood shopping centers consist primarily of convenience stores.

— 33. Although community shopping centers may provide a variety of convenience products—their major emphasis is on shopping products.

— 34. Regional shopping centers typically serve 40,000 to 150,000 people within a radius of 3-4 miles.

— 35. Around the world, mass-merchandising is more popular in less-developed nations because they need the lower prices more.

___ 36. In the future, in-home shopping and electronic retailing are both expected to become more popular.

Answers to True-False Questions

1. T, p. 402	13. T, p. 409	25. F, p. 417
2. T, p. 403	14. T, p. 409	26. T, p. 420
3. F, pp. 403-4	15. F, p. 409	27. T, p. 420
4. F, p. 404	16. T, p. 409	28. F, p. 420
5. T, p. 404	17. F, p. 410	29. F, p. 421
6. F, p. 404	18. F, p. 410	30. T, p. 421
7. T, p. 406	19. T, p. 410	31. F, p. 422
8. F, p. 406	20. F, p. 411	32. T, p. 423
9. F, p. 406	21. F, p. 412	33. F, p. 423
10. T, p. 407	22. F, p. 412	34. F, p. 423
11. F, p. 407	23. T, p. 414	35. F, p. 424
12. F, p. 408	24. T, p. 414	36. T, p. 426

Multiple-Choice Questions (Circle the correct response)

1. Which of the following best describes what "retailing" involves?
   a. The sale of consumer products to wholesalers, retailers, or final consumers.
   b. The performance of all merchandising activities except promotion and pricing.
   c. The sale of both business and consumer products.
   d. The sale of products to final consumers.
   e. All of the above describe what retailing involves.

2. Retail stores can be classified as convenience stores, shopping stores, and specialty stores. This classification is based on:
   a. the size of the store.
   b. the way customers think about the store.
   c. the location of the store.
   d. the salesclerks in the store.
   e. All of the above.

3. Tom Trotter regularly reads local newspaper ads to compare supermarket prices and featured products--and seldom shops at the same supermarket two weeks in a row. Tom seems to think of these supermarkets as:
   a. convenience stores selling convenience products.
   b. specialty stores selling shopping products.
   c. convenience stores selling shopping products.
   d. shopping stores selling convenience products.
   e. convenience stores selling specialty products.

4. A small privately owned men's clothing store in a university town has stressed personal services (e.g., free 90-day credit) and first-name relationships with student customers. The store carries only expensive, well-known brands of clothing and offers the largest selection of such merchandise in the area. Which of the following classifications is this retailer attempting to achieve?
   a. Specialty store--shopping products
   b. Shopping store--specialty products
   c. Specialty store--convenience products
   d. Shopping store--shopping products
   e. Convenience store--convenience products

5. Which of the following are *not* "conventional retailers" according to the text?
   a. General stores
   b. Single-line stores
   c. Supermarkets
   d. Limited-line retailers
   e. All of the above

6. Which of the following would be considered a *limited-line* retailer?
   a. Supermarket
   b. Gas station
   c. Mass-merchandiser
   d. Drugstore
   e. Bakery shop

7. Specialty shops:
   a. generally try to become well known for the distinctiveness of their line and the special services offered.
   b. generally carry complete lines--like department stores.
   c. carry specialty products almost exclusively.
   d. generally achieve specialty store status.
   e. All of the above are true.

8. Department stores:
   a. are often frowned upon by the retailing community because they provide too many customer services.
   b. normally are large stores which emphasize depth and distinctiveness rather than variety in the lines they carry.
   c. achieve specialty store status with some consumers--and thus may be the only way to reach these market segments.
   d. account for less than 1 percent of the total number of retail stores--but over half of total retail sales.
   e. All of the above are true statements.

9. Which of the following statements about supermarkets is *true*?
   a. Supermarkets should be classified as "conventional retailers."
   b. Net profits after taxes in supermarkets usually run about 1 percent of sales--or less.
   c. The minimum annual sales volume for a store to be classified as a supermarket is $500,000.
   d. They typically carry 15,000 product items.
   e. All of the above are true statements.

10. Catalog showroom retailers:
    a. are essentially mail-order sellers.
    b. must charge above-average prices to cover the costs of printing and distributing catalogs to consumers.
    c. stress convenience as their most distinguishing feature.
    d. minimize handling costs by keeping their inventories in backroom warehouses until customer orders are placed.
    e. All of the above are true statements.

11. Large departmentalized retail stores that are larger than supermarkets and follow the discount house's philosophy of emphasizing lower margins to achieve faster turnover are called:
    a. department stores.
    b. mass-merchandisers.
    c. planned shopping centers.
    d. specialty shops.
    e. box stores.

12. The "superstore concept":
    a. is just another name for the mass-merchandising concept.
    b. essentially refers to large department stores which have adopted supermarket-style operating procedures and methods.
    c. is concerned with providing all of the customer's routine needs at a low price.
    d. probably will not be accepted by mass-merchandisers.
    e. All of the above are true.

13. The modern convenience (food) stores are successful because they offer:
    a. wide assortments.
    b. low prices.
    c. expanded customer service.
    d. the right assortment of "fill-in" items.
    e. All of the above.

14. Which of the following statements about telephone and mail-order retailing is *true*?
    a. It is hard to target customers using mail-order retailing.
    b. Mail-order houses tend to have lower operating costs than conventional retailers.
    c. All mail-order houses offer both convenience products and shopping products.
    d. Although mail-order houses have declined in number in North America, they have achieved more than 15 percent of total Canadian retail sales.
    e. Mail-order retailers place their primary emphasis on low-price merchandise.

15. Which of the following concepts is best illustrated by a retail bakery that sells wristwatches?
    a. The "superstore"
    b. Scrambled merchandising
    c. Time-sharing
    d. The "wheel of retailing" theory
    e. Mass-merchandising

16. The "Wheel of Retailing" theory suggests that:
    a. retail stores do not have life cycles.
    b. retailing profits tend to be cyclical.
    c. only the largest retailers have a chance to survive in a fast-moving economy.
    d. new types of retailers enter as low-price operators and eventually begin to offer more services and charge higher prices.
    e. only discounters can survive in the long run.

17. A group of retailers banding together to establish their own wholesaling organization would be known as a:
    a. cooperative chain.
    b. voluntary chain.
    c. consumer cooperative.
    d. corporate chain.
    e. franchise.

18. Franchisors:
    a. are similar to voluntary chain operators.
    b. often provide franchise holders with training.
    c. usually receive fees and commissions from the franchise holder.
    d. reduce their risk of starting a new retailing business.
    e. All of the above are true statements.

19. A new shopping center has been built in an area which allows it to serve about 80,000 people with a five- to six-mile radius. It is composed of a supermarket, drugstore, hardware store, beauty shop, laundry and dry-cleaning store, a gas station, and a small department store. This center would be considered:
    a. a community shopping center.
    b. a neighborhood shopping center.
    c. a central business district.
    d. a regional shopping center.

20. The development of new, more efficient retailers around the world is dependent upon:
    a. the political and legal environment.
    b. the technological environment.
    c. the social and cultural environment.
    d. the economic environment.
    e. all of the above.

21. Which of the following is *least likely* to occur in retailing in the future?
    a. Conventional retailers will continue to feel a profit squeeze.
    b. Scrambled merchandising will decline.
    c. There will be more vertical arrangements between producers and retailers.
    d. There may be an increase in in-home shopping.
    e. Stores will continue to make shopping more convenient.

1. d, p. 402
2. b, p. 404
3. d, pp. 404-5
4. a, p. 404
5. c, p. 408
6. e, p. 406
7. a, p. 407

8. c, p. 408
9. b, p. 409
10. d, p. 409
11. b,, pp. 409-410
12. c, p. 410
13. d, p. 411
14. b, p. 413

15. b, p. 414
16. d, pp. 416-17
17. a, p. 420
18. e, p. 421
19. a, p. 423
20. e, pp. 424-5
21. b, p. 426

Exercise 13-1

Analyzing store-product combinations

Introduction

In Chapter 9, consumer products were classified--as convenience products, shopping products, specialty products, and unsought products--based on how different consumers think about and buy products. But just as the same *product* can mean different things to different people, the same *retail store* may also be seen differently by different target customers. Thus, in Chapter 13--building on the earlier discussion of consumer behavior and product classes--retail stores are classified as convenience stores, shopping stores, and specialty stores.

Because marketing planners should consider both product- and store-related needs, it is helpful to put the products and store classes together to form store-product combinations. (See Exhibit 13-2 on page 405 of the text.)

This exercise illustrates how different customer needs and shopping behavior for basically the same product--in this case, men's shirts--can result in different target customers seeking different store-product combinations. As you do the exercise, try to think about the strategy implications of store-product combinations--both for retailers as well as for manufacturers and wholesalers.

Assignment

The needs and shopping behavior of potential customers for men's shirts are described in the following cases. Assume in each case that the customer being described is representative of a group of customers having similar needs and shopping behavior. Read each case carefully and then: (a) indicate which of the following store-product combinations is most relevant and (b) briefly explain your answer in the space provided. The first case is answered for you as an example.

1. Convenience store selling convenience products
2. Convenience store selling shopping products
3. Convenience store selling specialty products
4. Shopping store selling convenience products
5. Shopping store selling shopping products
6. Shopping store selling specialty products
7. Specialty store selling convenience products
8. Specialty store selling shopping products
9. Specialty store selling specialty products

1. After spilling his morning cup of coffee all over his white shirt, bank executive Hodding Roberts telephoned all the nearby clothing stores to find one that was willing to deliver a new shirt in time for him to attend an important luncheon meeting. Eaton's Department Store told him they would send a clerk right over with a shirt.

    a) Store-product combination: *Shopping store, convenience product.*

    b) Explanation: *Hodding didn't insist on one store but did choose one that was prepared to make a delivery. The product itself is a matter of convenience—he would have accepted any style.*

2. While waiting at the mall for photos of his camping trip to be developed at the one-hour photo store, Chris Van Dyke remembered that he needed a new shirt to attend a wedding the following weekend. He wanted a white shirt with French cuffs and walked into Eaton's to see if he could find one, because it is next-door to the photo store.

    a) Store-product combination: _____

    b) Explanation: _____

    _____

    _____

3. Bill Bigg was very happy with the Yves St. Laurent double breasted navy-blue blazer that he purchased on a business trip to Paris and had been looking for a new shirt to complete his "look". While waiting for an appointment at his dentist's office, he saw an ad in an *Esquire* for a Van Heusen tab-collar shirt that was just right. So on his way home Bill stopped at the downtown Eaton's store—which carried a variety of dress shirts—and found the Van Heusen shirt he wanted.

    a) Store-product combination: _____

    b) Explanation: _____

    _____

    _____

4. Arlo Taylor borrowed a plain white shirt from one of his fraternity brothers to go on an important job interview. To his dismay, on his way back to the frat house, he saw that his pen had leaked on the pocket of the shirt. He remembered that the shirt had an Eaton's label. He was too embarrassed to return a ruined shirt so he borrowed some money from a friend and a car from one of the other brothers and drove three hours to the nearest branch of Eaton's and told the clerk: "You've got to find me a plain white shirt with a 15" collar and a 33" sleeve in Eaton's own brand."

    a) Store-product combination: _____

b) Explanation: _____

_____

_____

5. Returning to his hotel from a late meeting on an out-of-town business trip. Brent Dunn walked through Eaton's Department Store. He noticed that white shirts were on sale and decided to buy one in his size because he remembered that his shampoo had leaked over part of his clean shirt for the next day's sales presentation. Although he'd washed out the stain, he wasn't sure that it would be dry in time.

a) Store-product combination: _____

b) Explanation: _____

_____

_____

6. As a new graduate, Dave French was about to start a new job and needed about a dozen new dress shirts. His employer requires him to wear a plain white shirt and Dave needs a store with a good selection because he needs shirts with extra-long sleeves that not all stores carry. He decided to buy all of the shirts at Eaton's Department Store because Eaton's was the only store in town where Dave had a charge account.

a) Store-product combination: _____

b) Explanation: _____

_____

_____

7. Maria Vera made a "battle-plan" for her Christmas shopping. She allocated a whole day to the endeavor and went to two regional malls accompanied by her best friend Meghan Anders. They enjoy shopping together and comparing selection, pricing and the displays at different department stores. Finding that Eaton's has a large menswear department, Maria looked there for a shirt for her brother. After considering several alternatives she and Meghan agree on a Ralph Lauren Polo Oxford because the style and workmanship make it a good value.

a) Store-product combination: _____

b) Explanation: _____

_____

_____

8.   As lunch-break "treat" Patty Leath had a routine of stopping at the Tysons Corner Eaton's for a cappuccino in their coffee bar. On her way back to her car she noticed that the men's department was featuring Gant shirts so she bought one for her boyfriend, Dudley. Dudley wore Gant shirts in boarding school and insisted that they made the only Oxfords that fit him correctly.

   a)   Store-product combination: _____

   b)   Explanation: _____

   _____

   _____

9.   Aki Iwatani always bought his business suits at Eaton's because they carry good-quality merchandise and because the store's tailors are the only ones he has found who know how to fit him. A former collegiate wrestler, he is powerfully built, though short. When he returned for the final fitting of his most recent summer-weight suit, he decided to pick up a dozen plain white shirts.

   a)   Store-product combination: _____

   b)   Explanation: _____

   _____

   _____

Question for Discussion

How might a retailer such as Eaton's Department Store use the above store-product combinations in planning its marketing strategies? Are these combinations also relevant for wholesalers and manufacturers?

Exercise 13-2

Identifying and analyzing retail stores

Introduction

Retailing involves the sale of products to final consumers. There are approximately 180,000 retail stores in Canada. However, as discussed in the text, there are many different types of retailers and they vary both in size and method of operation. Marketing managers of consumer products at all channel levels must understand retailing—for if the retailing effort is not effective, the products may not be sold and *all* members of the channel will suffer. Likewise, consumers must be concerned with retailing—because their standard of living is partly dependent on how well retailing is done.

The purpose of this exercise is to focus your attention on the retailers who serve *your* community. What types of stores are there? How do they operate? Who are their target customers? Why might there be different types of retailers selling *basically* the same kinds of products?

Assignment

Listed below are several types of retail stores which were discussed in the text. For each type:

a)   Give the name and address of a store in your community that illustrates this type.

b)   Briefly describe the store in terms of its *width* and *depth* of assortment. Is it a single-line or limited-line store or a "scrambled merchandiser"? Does the store stress high turnover or low turnover products?

c)   Briefly describe the store in terms of its price/service blend (is the store price-oriented or service-oriented) and estimate whether the store's gross margin is in the *low range* (below 20 percent), *medium range* (20-35 percent), or *high range* (over 35 percent).

Note: If your community does not have a particular store type, write "none" under part (a) and then answer parts (b) and (c) in terms of how you *think* that type of store would operate.

                                                                                  Learning aid for use with

1. *Limited-Line "Conventional" Retailer*

   a) Store name and address: _____

   b) Assortment: _____

   c) Price/Service blend: _____

   Gross margin range: _____

2. *Department Store*

   a) Store name and address: _____

   b) Assortment: _____

   c) Price/Service blend: _____

   Gross margin range: _____

3. *Supermarket*

   a) Store name and address: _____

   b) Assortment: _____

   c) Price/Service blend: _____

   Gross margin range: _____

4. *Convenience (Food) Store*

   a) Store name and address: _____

   b) Assortment: _____

   c) Price/Service blend: _____

   Gross margin range: _____

5. *Catalog Showroom*

   a) Store name and address: _____

   b) Assortment: _____

   c) Price/Service blend: _____

   Gross margin range: _____

6. *Mass-Merchandiser*

    a) Store name and address: _____

    b) Assortment: _____

    c) Price/Service blend: _____

        Gross margin range: _____

7. *Single-line Mass-Merchandiser*

    a) Store name and address: _____

    b) Assortment: _____

    c) Price/Service blend: _____

        Gross margin range: _____

Question for Discussion

Why are there so many different types of retailers in Canada? What implications does this have for marketing strategy planning?

Learning aid for use with

Chapter 14

Wholesalers and their strategy planning

What This Chapter Is About

Chapter 14 discusses various kinds of specialized wholesalers who have developed to provide "wholesaling functions"--really just variations of the basic marketing functions. You should become familiar with the various types: what they do, and roughly what they cost.

Wholesalers are not guaranteed a place in channel systems. Some have been eliminated. Others probably will be. And other wholesalers have been making a "comeback" in some lines. Try to understand why.

Like other firms, wholesalers must develop market-oriented strategies. But wholesalers are channel specialists--so think of them as members of channel systems--rather than as isolated firms. This will help you see why wholesalers are very important members of *some* channel systems--while they are not used at all in other channels.

Important Terms

wholesalers, p. 432
merchant wholesalers, p. 436
service wholesalers, p. 436
general merchandise wholesalers, p. 436
single-line (or general-line) wholesalers, p. 436
limited-function wholesalers, p. 436
cash-and-carry wholesalers, p. 437
specialty wholesalers, p. 438
drop-shippers, p. 439
truck wholesalers, p. 439
mail-order wholesalers, p. 440
producers' cooperatives, p. 440
rack jobbers, p. 441
agent middlemen, p. 442
manufacturers' agent, p. 443
export agents, p. 444

import agents, p. 444
brokers, p. 444
export brokers, p. 444
import brokers, p. 444
selling agents, p. 444
combination export manager, p. 445
commission merchants, p. 445
export commission houses, p. 445
import commission houses, p. 445
auction companies, p. 445
manufacturers' sales branches, p. 446
factors, p. 446
field warehouser, p. 446
sales finance companies, p. 447
floor planning, p. 447

True-False Questions

___ 1. A producer who uses a direct channel system normally is also considered a wholesaler--because he must take over the wholesaling functions that an independent wholesaler might provide.

___ 2. All wholesalers perform the following functions for their customers: anticipate needs, regroup products, carry stocks, deliver products, grant credit, provide information and advisory service, provide part of buying function, and own and transfer title to products.

___ 3. A wholesaler might help a producer by reducing the producer's need for working capital.

___ 4. The typical merchant wholesaler's operating expenses amount to about 20 percent of sales.

___ 5. Merchant wholesalers don't necessarily provide all of the wholesaling functions, but they do take title to the products they sell.

___ 6. Service wholesalers provide all of the wholesaling functions--while limited-function wholesalers provide only certain functions.

___ 7. A general merchandise service wholesaler may represent many different kinds of manufacturers and supply many different kinds of retailers.

___ 8. Even though cash-and-carry wholesalers are limited-function wholesalers, they operate like service wholesalers, except that the customer must pay cash.

___ 9. Drop-shippers own the products they sell--but do not actually handle, stock, or deliver them.

___ 10. Truck wholesalers' operating costs are relatively high because they provide a lot of service relative to how much they sell.

___ 11. Mail-order wholesalers should probably be classified as retailers--since they sell out of catalogs.

___ 12. Producers' cooperatives are limited-function wholesalers that specialize in supplying consumer cooperatives at the retail level.

___ 13. Rack jobbers are limited-function wholesalers, with relatively high operating costs, who help retailers offer a more attractive assortment of products--especially nonfood items.

___ 14. A manufacturer who has the capability of operating its own distribution facilities but lacks customer contacts should consider the use of agent middlemen to facilitate the buying and selling functions.

___ 15. Agent middlemen are less common in international trade than in North American markets because merchant wholesalers can both sell products and handle the financing.

___ 16. The key role of manufacturers' agents is to provide well-established customer contacts for new products--while assuming all the risks of taking title to the products they handle.

___ 17. A broker's "product" is information about what buyers need--and what supplies are available.

___ 18. A small manufacturer with limited financial resources whose only skills are in production should probably consider contracting with a selling agent to act, in effect, as the firm's marketing manager.

_ 19. Probably the most important function of a commission merchant is anticipating the needs of its customers.

_ 20. The primary advantage of auction companies is that they facilitate buying by description.

_ 21. The fact that many manufacturers have set up their own sales branches suggests that the use of wholesalers usually makes distribution costs unnecessarily high.

_ 22. A small manufacturer of textiles with limited financial resources should probably consider selling its accounts receivable to a factor.

_ 23. A manufacturer who wants to maintain an inventory of goods in a sparsely populated rural area should seek the services of a field warehousing organization.

_ 24. Many appliance dealers do not own outright any of the appliances on their display floor-- instead the inventories are financed by sales finance companies as part of an arrangement called "floor planning."

_ 25. Many manufacturers and retailers have realized that wholesaling functions are not always necessary, so wholesalers have been eliminated at an increasing rate in recent years.

_ 26. Most modern wholesalers have become more streamlined in their operations, more computerized in controlling their inventories, and more selective in their distribution policies.

_ 27. Recent trends in wholesaling indicate that wholesaling will survive, even though some wholesalers may disappear.

Answers to True-False Questions

1. F, p. 432	10. T, p. 440	19. F, p. 445
2. F, p. 433	11. F, p. 440	20. F, pp. 445-46
3. T, p. 434	12. F, p. 440	21. F, p. 446
4. F, p. 434	13. T, p. 441	22. T, p. 446
5. T, p. 436	14. T, p. 442	23. F, p. 446
6. T, p. 436	15. F, p. 442	24. T, p. 447
7. T, p. 436	16. F, p. 443	25. F, pp. 447-48
8. T, p. 437	17. T, p. 444	26. T, p. 449
9. T, p. 439	18. T, p. 444	27. T, pp. 450-51

Multiple-Choice Questions (Circle the correct response)

1. Which of the following is *not* a typical wholesaling function?
   a. provide market information to a producer.
   b. grant credit to customers.
   c. supply capital to pay the cost of carrying inventory.
   d. all of the above are typical wholesaling functions.
   e. none of the above is a typical wholesaling function.

2. Which of the following types of wholesalers has the *highest* operating expenses as a percent of sales?
   a. Manufacturers' agents
   b. Manufacturers' sales branches
   c. Brokers
   d. Commission merchants
   e. Merchant wholesalers

3. The two basic types of merchant wholesalers are:
   a. single-line and specialty.
   b. service and limited-function.
   c. service and general merchandise.
   d. single-line and limited-function.
   e. agents and brokers.

4. Regarding merchant wholesalers, which of the following statements is TRUE?
   a. They own (take title to) the products they sell.
   b. Merchant wholesalers are the most numerous wholesalers and handle over half of all wholesale sales.
   c. General merchandise wholesalers of consumer products handle a broad variety of nonperishable items, including both convenience and shopping products.
   d. A specialty wholesaler generally would offer a narrower range of products than a single-line wholesaler.
   e. All of the above are true.

5. Which of the following types of wholesalers do *not* carry stocks for their customers?
   a. Cash-and-carry wholesalers.
   b. Rack jobbers.
   c. Truck wholesalers.
   d. Drop-shippers.
   e. Mail-order wholesalers.

6. Which of the following statements about rack jobbers is *true*?
   a. Rack jobbing is a relatively high-cost operation--costing more than the average for merchant wholesaling.
   b. Rack jobbers provide retailers with specialized information about consumer preferences.
   c. Rack jobbers are practically full-service wholesalers--except they usually do not grant credit.
   d. Rack jobbers developed because many grocers did not wish to bother with reordering and maintaining displays of nonfood items.
   e. All of the above are true statements.

7. A type of middleman that does *not* take title to the products is known as:
   a. an agent middleman.
   b. a limited-function wholesaler.
   c. a rack jobber.
   d. a merchant wholesaler.
   e. a drop-shipper.

8. Which of the following statements is *false*?
   a. Agent middlemen generally do not take title to products they sell.
   b. Manufacturers' agents usually do not represent competing manufacturers.
   c. Brokers are often used because of the seasonal nature of production or demand.
   d. Manufacturers' agents generally have more authority over prices and terms of sale than do selling agents.
   e. Agent middlemen are very common is international trade.

9. Turgo, Inc. has just developed a new convenience product for which it wants intensive distribution nationally. It expects a low initial demand and wants to keep selling costs as low as possible while keeping control of marketing. This is Turgo's first product and working capital is small. Which of the following channels would be best?
   a. Turgo's own sales force direct to retailers.
   b. Manufacturers' agents to merchant wholesalers to retailers.
   c. Commission merchants to retailers.
   d. Turgo's own sales force direct to merchant wholesalers to retailers.
   e. Selling agents to merchant wholesalers to retailers.

10. The principal function of a broker is to:
    a. transport acquired products.
    b. facilitate inspection of products.
    c. establish a central market.
    d. bring buyers and sellers together.
    e. distribute grocery products.

11. The Jory Co. handles the entire output of several small clothing manufacturers on a national basis. The firm has almost complete control of pricing, selling, and advertising. In addition, Jory often provides working capital to the producers, who have very limited financial resources. In return, Jory is paid a substantial commission on all sales. The Jory Co. is a:
    a. selling agent.
    b. commission merchant.
    c. full-service wholesaler.
    d. manufacturers' agent.
    e. broker.

12. Manufacturers' sales branches:
    a. have very low sales per branch.
    b. are mainly used in weak market areas, where there is not enough business for other types of wholesalers.
    c. operating costs would be even lower than they are now if manufacturers didn't "charge" them with extra expenses.
    d. handle about a third of all wholesale sales.
    e. serve the same basic needs as do brokers.

13. The Perlman Corp. manufactures and distributes a specialized line of textile products. An opportunity has arisen for Perlman to expand its product line. However, most of Perlman's working capital is tied up due to slow payment of accounts receivable--and management does not wish to take on any additional debt at this time. Perlman should consider employing the services of a:
    a. sales finance company.
    b. field warehouser.
    c. factor.
    d. floor planner.
    e. any of the above.

14. Which of the following statements is *least relevant* in explaining the "Comeback of the Wholesaler"?
    a. It is due to a natural rise in the need for wholesaling services.
    b. It is caused in part by the fact that wholesalers are now more "retailer-minded."
    c. It has been aided by more selective choice of customers--as many small retailers were clearly unprofitable.
    d. Many wholesalers no longer require each customer to pay for all of the services they provide *some* customers.
    e. Greater emphasis has been placed on training and advising retailer-customers.

Answers to Multiple-Choice Questions

1. d, pp. 432-34
2. e, p. 434
3. b, p. 436
4. e, p. 436
5. d, p. 439

6. e, p. 441
7. a, p. 442
8. d, pp. 443-4
9. b, pp. 443-4
10. d, p. 444

11. a, p. 444
12. d, p. 446
13. c, p. 446
14. a, pp. 447-52

Learning aid for use with

Exercise 14-1

Choosing the right kind of wholesaler

Introduction

Wholesalers are less dominant than they once were, but they are still a very important part of our economy. Wholesalers have become more specialized, so a marketing manager who must select a wholesaler must be concerned not only with finding a "good one," but also finding the right *type* of wholesaler.

There are two important types of wholesalers--*merchant wholesalers* and *agent middlemen*. The most important difference between the two types is that merchant wholesalers take title to (own) the products they handle, while agent middlemen do not. There are several types of merchant wholesalers and agent middlemen--and each performs different tasks. A marketing manager should select the type best suited to his marketing strategy. The various types of wholesalers are:

A.   *Merchant Wholesalers*

    1.   *Service Wholesalers*--including general merchandise, single-line and specialty wholesalers.
    2.   *Limited-function Wholesalers*--including cash and carry, drop-shippers, truck wholesalers, mail-order wholesalers, producers' cooperatives, and rack jobbers.

B.   *Agent Middlemen*--including auction companies, brokers, commission merchants, manufacturers' agents, and selling agents.

Assignment

This exercise will give you some practice in choosing the right type of wholesaler. Each of the following cases describes a situation in which a buyer or seller *might* want to use one or more types of merchant wholesalers or agent middlemen. Read each case carefully and then indicate which type(s) of wholesaler(s) would be most appropriate for each situation. Then explain your answer.

The first case is answered for you as an example.

1.   Jack Miller, a farmer in Manitoba has six truckloads of pumpkins that he wants to sell before Halloween. Local auction prices have been low, however, and Miller hopes that selling the pumpkins in Toronto may bring higher prices. Unfortunately, he is too busy with the rest of his fall harvest to bring the pumpkins to Toronto's central market and search for the best price.

a) Type of Wholesaler: *Agent middleman--commission merchant*

b) Explanation: *The farmer needs a low-cost wholesaler on a temporary basis to represent him in a distant market--providing market contacts, aggressive selling including price negotiation, and transporting. [Note: in the long run, the farmer might be better off joining a producers' cooperative--if one is operating.]*

2. Sol Feferman recently developed a patented recycling process for diseased trees. Officials from nearby cities--lacking any ecologically acceptable alternatives for disposing of trees that have been cut down--have agreed to deliver their trees free of charge to Feferman's plant. There, the trees are processed and converted into products such as wood chips for landscaping, bark mulch, railroad ties, and patio blocks. However, Feferman has little marketing experience and know-how. Usually buyers come to him by word of mouth--and then he is not sure how to price his products. The firm is in trouble financially and may have to declare bankruptcy unless Feferman can locate a steady and sizable market for his products. But, he has no funds to hire a sales rep or to promote his products.

a) Type of Wholesaler: _____

b) Explanation: _____

_____

_____

3. Bob Miles and his wife Jane have been managing an oyster bar at the beach. That seemed like an interesting thing to do when they graduated from college, but now they want to start their own business. They thought that the growing interest in health food would open up some interesting opportunities. So using money from the sale of their house, they made a down payment on a bakery which formerly belonged to a local cookie manufacturer. As their first product, they decided to produce a unique sesame seed and honey snack bar. They "discovered" the recipe for this unusual product while traveling in Greece, and they are certain that it will be a profitable item if they can distribute it through health food stores and nutrition centers. A number of the health food stores in their area have already expressed interest in carrying the bars. But the Miles know that they will need to obtain wider distribution--i.e., outside their present area--to be successful. One of the problems with expanding distribution, however, is that the bars use no preservatives--so they are perishable.

a) Type of Wholesaler: _____

b) Explanation: _____

_____

_____

4. Chemco Corporation--a large manufacturer of chemical products for paper manufacturing--has decided to produce and sell a new line of automobile tires. The company deliberately avoided the highly competitive tire market in the past--but now feels that it has a product that is much

safer than any tires currently on the market. Chemco plans to distribute its new tires through gasoline service stations, automotive stores, hardware stores, department stores, mass merchandisers, and perhaps even supermarkets. At the present time, the company has very limited financial resources--due to the cost of expanding its manufacturing facilities to produce the new line of tires.

a)   Type of Wholesaler: _____

b)   Explanation: _____

_____

_____

5.   Nortex, Inc. is an established company that sells a full line of grinding equipment, sandpapers, and polishing compounds to a variety of industrial accounts. Recently Nortex developed a special compound for an auto producer to use to polish out small scratches in the paint of new cars. The new polish proved to be very effective and easy to use. Nortex decided that the polish might do well in the consumer market. The polish was test marketed in Toronto recently—and met with considerable success. Now Nortex has decided to sell the polish in other large cities—including Montreal, Calgary, Edmonton and Vancouver. Nortex has adequate resources to finance the manufacturing and physical distribution of the product to these areas. However, the company does not have any established contacts with auto supply retailers in the new markets. Further, Nortex is reluctant to hire and train new sales reps to promote its only consumer product.

a)   Type of Wholesaler: _____

b)   Explanation: _____

_____

_____

6.   Collins Packing Company of Penticton, B.C. recently bought several small fruit packers. This greatly expanded its processing capacity beyond the quantity of fruit it has been selling under its own brand. It was successful in buying the packers at a very low price because they had not been able to find enough business at profitable prices and were near bankruptcy. Collins Packing hopes to expand sales of its own brand over the next few years, but does not expect sales to increase much this year. Therefore, it is looking for some way to quickly "get rid of" fairly large quantities of canned sweet cherries, pears, plums, and several kinds of berries.

a)   Type of Wholesaler: _____

b)   Explanation: _____

_____

_____

7.   Goodco, Inc. makes "Made-Rite" potato chips—the best selling brand of potato chips in the metropolitan Toronto area. The company has grown considerably since it was stated during the 1930s. In fact, Made-Rite potato chips have become so popular among customers that the company is now planning to expand its market coverage to the west. New plants will be opened in Calgary and Vancouver. However, company officials doubt that Goodco can afford to operate its own plant-to-retailer delivery service in the new market areas—as it now does in the Toronto area.

a)   Type of Wholesaler: _____

b)   Explanation: _____

_____

_____

8.   Koppers Fiberglass Works produces a line of fiberglass shingles that are used for residential and commercial roofing. It supplies home builders, large roofing contractors, and lumber yards throughout a three-state area. Koppers uses its own trucks for deliveries within a hundred miles-- and ships carload quantities by railroad. Currently, four sales reps call directly on its present customers. The company is faced with large swings in demand, however, and has had difficulty finding new customers.

a)   Type of Wholesaler: _____

b)   Explanation: _____

_____

_____

Question for Discussion

Why are there so many different types of wholesalers?

Learning aid for use with

Exercise 14-2

Analyzing channels of distribution

Introduction

A channel of distribution consists of different people performing different functions. They are linked together by a common interest in marketing products that someone needs and wants. At one end of the channel are producers and at the other end are customers, and often there are "middlemen" in between.

Most products are *not* distributed directly from the manufacturer to the consumer or final user. In fact, the variety of middlemen has actually increased over the years. Middlemen exist because they perform some necessary functions--often more efficiently and economically than could either manufacturers or consumers.

This exercise focuses on several important types of middlemen. The objective is to determine what specific functions and activities each middleman performs--and to understand the role each plays in the distribution channel. Further, the exercise illustrates that while one type of middleman can sometimes be substituted for another--in other situations different types of middlemen perform complementary functions. Thus, while one channel may be longer than some others, it may also be faster, more economical, or more effective.

Assignment

The activities of several types of middlemen are described below in five cases. For each middleman described:

A.   Identify the *general type* of middleman (a full-service merchant wholesaler, a limited-function merchant wholesaler, or an agent middleman) *and* the *specific type* of middleman (rack jobber, broker, etc.).

B.   Diagram the channel or *channels* of distribution that are described in the case, using the following letters.

(M)   for Manufacturers   [A]   for Agent Middlemen

⟨R⟩   for Retailers   [W]   for Full-Service Wholesalers

(C)   for Consumers or   [L]   for Limited-Function Middlemen
       Final Users

The first case has been completed as an example.

1. Ralph Brown sells carload quantities of chemicals to industrial users--for several chemical manufacturers. Brown takes title to the products he sells. But he does not take physical possession of them, although he often arranges for transporting the products. One part of his business that is costly is the frequent need to provide credit to small customers.

   a) General Type: *Brown is a limited-function merchant wholesaler.*

   Specific Type: *drop-shipper*

   b) Diagram of the Channel:

2. Dura Textiles, Inc., is the manufacturer of Durabright brand acrylic fabrics. Durabright is the leading brand of fabric used in manufacturing waterproof awnings for stores, hotels, and homes. There are about 5,000 "fabricators" around the country who use Durabright to produce custom awnings for their clients. The fabricators order Durabright from distributors. The distributors maintain inventories (usually at a number of different branch locations) so that they can provide fast delivery of Durabright. The distributors also offer the fabricators credit, and they carry a complete assortment of grommets, zippers, snaps, metal poles, and other items the fabricators need to make awnings. Dura Textiles has six salespeople who call on the distributors.

   a) General Type: _____

   Specific Type: _____

   b) Diagram of the Channel:

Learning aid for use with

3.   Recently, Dura Textiles has developed new fabric designs for use in making cushions for outdoor furniture. However, Dura's traditional distributors have not done a very good job of seeking out orders from the hundreds of small manufacturers who produce outdoor furniture. As a result, Dura has turned to people like Nat Lane for additional help in reaching this market. Lane, who also represents producers of a number of other noncompeting lines, aggressively promotes Durabright to manufacturers of outdoor furniture in his region. Lane earns a commission of 6 percent on all of the sales he generates. When Lane calls in an order, Dura ships the fabric directly to the furniture manufacturer.

a)   General Type: _____

Specific Type: _____

b)   Diagram of the Channel:

4.   Red Star is a hardware wholesaler who sponsors a voluntary chain of independent hardware retailers. In addition to the usual wholesaling functions, Red Star provides special services for its affiliated stores: its own "dealer brand" products at very competitive prices, free-standing advertising inserts for distribution in the retailer's local newspaper, other merchandising assistance, employee training programs, store location and design assistance, and accounting aid. Merchandise economies are achieved through group buying, and a modern distribution center is used to lower operating costs.

Some retailers who handle only small assortments of hardware items are too small to benefit from membership in the chain. Red Star operates a subsidiary to provide a smaller assortment of household items (such as extension cords, spray paint, screw drivers) for these "unaffiliated" customers. Retailers must provide their own transportation. The products are priced attractively--considering the small order quantities--but no credit is offered.

a)   General Type: _____

Specific Type: _____

b)   Diagram of the Channel:

5. Kole Pottery, a small company on Saltspring Island, British Columbia, produces handcrafted pottery plates, cups, bowls, and vases. The owners of Kole Pottery want to focus on designing and producing pottery, not on the administrative and financial responsibilities of the business. As a result, they have worked out an arrangement with Craftware, Inc., a wholesaler that basically operates as a "marketing manager" for Kole Pottery. Craftware finds retail gift shops to carry the pottery—and handles pricing, selling, advertising, and all paperwork on orders, including billing and collections. Craftware earns a large commission on all sales, but Kole's owners like the arrangement because all they need to do is arrange transportation to get the pottery to the retailers.

    a) General Type: _____

        Specific Type: _____

    b) Diagram of the Channel:

6. A number of different food processors, supermarket and restaurant chains, and full-service and limited-function wholesalers turn to West Coast Produce Company when they want to find a supply of seasonal fruits and vegetables. West Coast Produce doesn't grow fruits or vegetables itself, nor does it work with any particular farmer on a continuous basis. Instead, farmers who want to find buyers for large quantities of produce that need to be sold quickly turn to West Coast Produce for help. West Coast handles the products, negotiates prices, and completes the sale for the producers. Farmers pay West Coast a commission for its work.

    a) General Type: _____

        Specific Type: _____

    b) Diagram of the Channel:

Question for Discussion

Are salespeople middlemen? Where are salespeople shown in channel diagrams?

Learning aid for use with

Chapter 15

Promotion--Introduction

What This Chapter Is About

Chapter 15 introduces Promotion--the topic of Chapters 15-17. Be sure to see that Promotion is only one of the four Ps--*not* the whole of marketing. Promotion tries to carry out promotion objectives--just as the other Ps have their own specific objectives.

This chapter looks at promotion objectives and methods from a strategic viewpoint--with emphasis on developing a good promotion blend. Early in the chapter, much attention is given to the communication process and the adoption of new ideas. These theoretical concepts should be studied carefully. They provide a solid base for strategy planning of personal selling (Chapter 16) and advertising (Chapter 17). The concepts of pushing and pulling are also discussed.

Although some of the material appears theoretical, it is important because not all promotion decisions are "just common sense." Poor decisions here could lead to "mass marketing" and the use of a "shotgun" rather than a "rifle" approach to Promotion. This chapter should help you bring a rifle to promotion planning--to practice "target marketing."

Important Terms

promotion, p. 457
personal selling, p. 458
mass selling, p. 458
advertising, p. 458
publicity, p. 458
sales promotion, p. 459
communication process, p. 463
source, p. 463
receiver, p. 463
noise, p. 463
encoding, p. 464
decoding, p. 464
message channel, p. 464
AIDA model, p. 466
adoption curve, p. 467

innovators, p. 468
early adopters, p. 468
early majority, p. 469
late majority, p. 469
laggards, p. 469
nonadopters, p. 469
pushing, p. 470
pulling, p. 471
primary demand, p. 474
selective demand, p. 475
sales managers, p. 477
advertising managers, p. 477
public relations, p. 477
sales promotion managers, p. 477

True-False Questions

___ 1. Promotion is communicating information between seller and potential buyer--to influence attitudes and behavior.

___ 2. Advertising is any form of nonpersonal presentation of ideas, goods, or services.

___ 3. Sales promotion refers to activities such as personal selling, advertising and publicity.

___ 4. All sales promotion is aimed at final consumers or users.

___ 5. In total, personal selling is several times more expensive than advertising.

___ 6. The overall objective of promotion is to affect behavior.

___ 7. The three basic objectives of promotion are to inform, persuade, and/or remind.

___ 8. Much of what we call promotion is really wasted effort because it does not really communicate.

___ 9. A major advantage of personal selling is that the source can get immediate feedback to help direct subsequent communication efforts.

___ 10. The term "noise" refers only to distorting influences within the message channel which reduce the effectiveness of the communication process.

___ 11. If the right message channel is selected, problems related to encoding and decoding in the communication process will be avoided.

___ 12. The communication process is complicated by the fact that receivers are usually influenced not only by the message but also by the source and the message channel.

___ 13. The AIDA model consists of four promotion jobs: attention, information, desire, and action.

___ 14. The adoption curve focuses on the process by which an individual accepts new ideas.

___ 15. Publicity in technical journals is likely to be a more effective method of promotion than personal selling for reaching extremely innovative business firms.

___ 16. The late majority are influenced more by other late adopters--rather than by advertising.

___ 17. Salespeople should usually be expected to do all the promotion to middlemen.

___ 18. One reason personal selling is important in promotion to middlemen is that marketing mixes often have to be adjusted from one geographic territory to another.

___ 19. Promotion to employees is especially important in service-oriented industries where the quality of the employees' efforts is a big part of the product.

___ 20. "Pulling a product through the channel" means using normal promotion effort to help sell the whole marketing mix to possible channel members.

___ 21. The large number of potential customers practically forces producers of consumer products and retailers to emphasize mass selling and sales promotion.

___ 22. Business customers are much less numerous than final consumers--and therefore it becomes more practical to emphasize mass selling in the promotion blends aimed at these markets.

___ 23. Situations that may affect the promotion blend are the size of the promotion budget, the nature of the product and its stage in the product life cycle, and the nature of competition.

___ 24. During the market introduction stage of product life cycles, promotion must pioneer acceptance of the product idea--not just the company's own brand--to stimulate primary demand.

___ 25. In the market growth stage of the product life cycle, promotion emphasis must begin to shift from stimulating selective demand to stimulating primary demand for the company's own brand.

___ 26. In the market maturity stage, the promotion blend of consumer products firms rely almost exclusively on advertising to consumers.

___ 27. Firms in monopolistic competition may favor mass selling because they have differentiated their marketing mixes somewhat--and have something to talk about.

___ 28. Planning of promotion blends can be best accomplished by placing specialists in charge of each promotion method; for example, the firm might appoint a sales manager, an advertising manager, and a sales promotion manager to weigh the pros and cons of the various approaches and come up with an effective blend.

___ 29. To avoid conflicts, it is usually best for sales promotion to be handled by a firm's advertising manager and sales manager--not by a sales promotion specialist.

___ 30. Spending on sales promotion is growing, but never at the expense of advertising and personal selling.

___ 31. Sales promotion aimed at final consumers usually is trying to increase demand and speed up the time of purchase.

___ 32. Sales promotion aimed at middlemen--sometimes called trade promotion--stresses price-related matters.

1. T, p. 457
2. F, p. 458
3. F, p. 459
4. F, pp. 459-51
5. T, p. 459
6. T, p. 461
7. T, pp. 461-2
8. T, p. 463
9. T, p. 463
10. F, p. 463
11. F, p. 464

12. T, p. 464
13. F, p. 466
14. F, p. 467
15. T, p. 468
16. T, p. 469
17. F, p. 470
18. T, pp. 470-71
19. T, p. 471
20. F, p. 471
21. T, p. 472
22. F, p. 472

23. T, p. 474
24. T, p. 474
25. F, pp. 475-6
26. F, p. 476
27. T, p. 476
28. F, p. 477
29. F, p. 477
30. F, p. 478
31. T, p. 478
32. T, p. 479

Multiple-Choice Questions (Circle the correct response)

1. Promotion does *not* include:
   a. personal selling.
   b. advertising.
   c. publicity.
   d. sales promotion.
   e. Promotion includes all of the above.

2. Personal selling is more appropriate than mass selling when:
   a. the target market is large and scattered.
   b. there are many potential customers and a desire to keep promotion costs low.
   c. flexibility is not important.
   d. immediate feedback is desirable.
   e. All of the above are true.

3. Sales promotion activities:
   a. try to stimulate interest, trial or purchase.
   b. always involve direct face-to-face communication between sellers and potential customers.
   c. usually take a long time to implement.
   d. are usually a good substitute for personal selling and advertising.
   e. All of the above.

4. Sales promotion can be aimed at:
   a. final consumers or users.
   b. middlemen.
   c. the company's own sales force.
   d. all of the above.
   e. only a and b above.

5. Promotion is intended to make a firm's demand curve:
   a. become more elastic--while shifting it to the right.
   b. become more inelastic--while shifting it to the left.
   c. become more elastic--while shifting it to the left.
   d. become more inelastic--while shifting it to the right.

6.   Which basic promotion objective should be emphasized by a firm whose product is very similar to those offered by many competitors?
     a. Communicating
     b. Persuading
     c. Reminding
     d. Informing

7.   Which of the following is *not* one of the basic elements in the communication process?
     a. Feedback
     b. Receiver
     c. Encoding
     d. Dissonance
     e. Message channel

8.   Communication is *most difficult* to achieve when:
     a. the source and the receiver are not in face-to-face contact with each other.
     b. immediate feedback is not provided.
     c. any trace of "noise" remains in the message channel.
     d. the source and the receiver do not have a common frame of reference.
     e. the encoder does not do the decoding.

9.   The AIDA model's four promotion jobs are getting:
     a. awareness, interest, demand, action.
     b. attention, interest, desire, action.
     c. action, interest, desire, acceptance.
     d. awareness, interest, decision, acceptance.

10. Jaime Garriss is strongly influenced by her peer group--and she often adopts a new product only after they have pressured her to try it. She makes little use of mass media and salespeople as sources of information. In terms of the adoption curve, she would be in what category?
     a. Laggard
     b. Late majority
     c. Early adopter
     d. Innovator
     e. Early majority

11. The Calmar Corporation is introducing a new product next month. To prepare for the introduction, the marketing manager is having his sales force call on distributors to explain the unique features of the new product, how the distributors can best promote it, and what sales volume and profit margins they can reasonably expect. In addition, Calmar is budgeting 2 percent of its estimated sales for magazine advertising aimed at distributors. This is an example of:
     a.   selective distribution.
     b.   a "pulling" policy.
     c.   exclusive distribution.
     d.   a "pushing" policy.
     e.   intensive distribution.

12. Which of the following statements about the *target of promotion* and promotion blends is *true*?
    a. There is no one right promotion blend for all situations.
    b. Promotion to middlemen emphasizes personal selling.
    c. Promotion to employees involves pushing.
    d. Promotion to final consumers is usually a combination of pushing and pulling.
    e. All of the above are true.

13. Regarding planning a promotion blend, a good marketing manager knows that:
    a. the job of reaching all the people in a "buying center" is made easier by their low turnover.
    b. there is not much chance of economies of scale in promotion.
    c. it is seldom practical for salespeople to carry the whole promotion load.
    d. salespeople can be very economical since they devote almost all of their time to actual selling activities.
    e. None of the above is true.

14. During the market introduction stage of the product life cycle, the basic objective of promotion is to:
    a. spend more money on promotion than competitors.
    b. remind customers about the firm and its products.
    c. inform the potential customers of the product.
    d. stimulate selective demand.
    e. persuade the early majority to buy the product.

15. Deciding on the appropriate promotion blend is a job for the firm's:
    a. advertising agency.
    b. marketing manager.
    c. advertising manager.
    d. sales manager.
    e. sales promotion manager.

16. Sales promotion:
    a. is often a weak spot in many firms' marketing strategies.
    b. spending is growing rapidly.
    c. involves a wide variety of activities which often require the use of specialists.
    d. can make the personal selling job easier.
    e. All of the above are true statements.

17. Sales promotion:
    a. to consumers usually is trying to increase demand or speed up the time of purchase.
    b. aimed at middlemen is sometimes called trade promotion.
    c. might include free samples of a product.
    d. aimed at employees is common in service firms.
    e. all of the above.

Answers to Multiple-Choice Questions

1. e, pp. 457-8
2. d, p. 458
3. a, p. 459
4. d, p. 459
5. d, p. 461
6. b, p. 462

7. d, p. 463
8. d, p. 464
9. b, p. 466
10. b, p. 469
11. d, p. 470
12. e, pp. 470-473

13. c, pp. 470-474
14. c, p. 474
15. b, p. 477
16. e, pp. 477-481
17. e, pp. 477-481

Exercise 15-1

The communication process in promotion

Introduction

Promotion must communicate effectively--or it's wasted effort. Yet it is often difficult to achieve effective communication. The communication process can break down in many different ways.

Understanding the whole communication process can improve promotion. As discussed in more detail in the text (see pages 463-65 and Exhibit 15-4), the major elements of the communication process include:

> a source,
> encoding,
> a message channel,
> decoding,
> a receiver,
> feedback, and
> noise.

Each of these different elements can influence the effectiveness of a firm's promotion effort--so marketing managers need to consider each element when planning or modifying their promotion. The whole promotion effort may fail because of a failure in just one element.

This exercise is designed to enhance your understanding of the communication process in promotion planning. The focus here is on specific elements of the process.

Assignment

Listed below are several descriptions of different promotion situations. In each case, there is a problem with the promotion effort. For some reason, communication has not been effective. You may see different elements of the promotion process that may be related to the problem. But, the focus of each situation is on a specific element of the process. So, for each situation, write down *one* element (from the list above) that you think is the major problem. Then, briefly explain why you think that element is a problem, and how the communication process might need to be changed to correct the problem. (Note: your recommendation may include changing one or more elements of the communication process other than the one that you noted as the major problem.)

Learning aid for use with

1. A weekly magazine that wanted to increase subscriptions among "news hounds" placed ads on a cable news channel. The ads dramatized stories in the magazine and its in-depth news coverage and thorough reporting. However, the cable channel scheduled the ads to play during the sports portion of the news broadcast—and by then many of the hardcore "news hounds" in the audience weren't paying much attention.

   a) Problem element of the communication process: _____

   b) Explanation:

2. Home-Based Life Insurance Company has equipped its sales agents with notebook computers so they can quickly do a detailed, personalized analysis of a prospect's needs and present the results with on-screen graphs--while working with the prospect. The company thought that the computers would be especially helpful for presentations about its combined insurance and retirement-savings products--which are targeted at retired professionals who are interested in leaving a "nest-egg" for their grandchildren. However, since the agents started using the on screen presentations, their ratio of "closes" (signed contracts) to sales calls has dropped for the retiree market segment. One of the retirees commented to the salespeople that "we old people don't want all this razzle-dazzle, we just want to hear what you have to say about the plan." But most of the agents continue to use the notebook computers anyway--because of its powerful presentation graphics.

   a) Problem element of the communication process: _____

   b) Explanation:

3.   A company that produces expensive leather briefcases for business executives wants to expand its sales in overseas markets. In Canada, the company's ads—placed in business magazines—show a group of well-dressed men and women executives preparing for a meeting. Each executive has a briefcase, and the headline for the ad says "If you want respect, it's as important to look professional as it is to act professional." The company adapted this same copy thrust to a Japanese ad that featured Japanese models. But, the effort was a failure. In Japan, there are still very few women in high executive positions, and for many target customers the ad did not help to create a "prestige" image for the company's products.

    a) Problem element of the communication process: _____

    b) Explanation:

4.   A carpet manufacturer developed a series of newspaper ads that showed a picture of a small boy tracking across carpet, under a headline that promoted the carpet as "wear-dated." The copy in the ad went on in some detail to describe the fibers used to produce the carpet as especially tough and able to withstand long use. Yet, marketing research showed that potential customers did not have a favorable impression of the carpet. Apparently many readers associated the expression "wear-dated" with phrases such as "It will wear out" and "Looks dated and unfashionable."

    a) Problem element of the communication process: _____

    b) Explanation:

5.   An automobile insurance company hired sales reps to telephone customers whose policies are about to expire and ask them if they would like to renew their policies. Research shows that most drivers appreciate this service--since it means that there will not be a lapse in their policy. The company has screened and hired sales reps carefully. Each salesperson has been trained concerning the prices for different policies. The company leaves it to each sales rep to decide what to say--so that the presentation will be as natural as possible. But, the inexperienced salespeople have trouble getting the conversation started--and often the customer hangs up before the point of the call is clear.

a) Problem element of the communication process: _____

b) Explanation:

6.   A company has been doing advertising for its line of weight-loss diet supplements. The supplements are targeted to overweight, middle-aged men and women. The company's ads appear on TV exercise programs that are viewed by the same target market. In the ad, a trim professional model explains the product and how safely and effectively it works. But the ads do not seem to be effective. Apparently the overweight viewers don't believe that a trim model really knows about the difficulties of losing weight.

Problem element of the communication process: _____

Explanation:

Question for Discussion

Does market segmentation make it easier--or more difficult--to develop effective promotion communications? Why?

Exercise 15-2

Using the adoption curve to develop
promotion blends

Introduction

We have continually stressed that each of the "four Ps" should be matched with the needs and characteristics of target markets. But marketing mix planning can get more complicated in the promotion area. Even though a target market may have fairly homogeneous needs--*groups of people within this market may differ considerably in their sources of information and how quickly they adopt new products.* Therefore, marketing managers may need to use several promotion blends--over time--to communicate effectively with this target market.

Promotion blend planning should use the adoption curve--which shows when different groups accept ideas. Five adopter groups are commonly used: innovators, early adopters, the early majority, the late majority, and laggards.

As outlined in the text (see pages 466-69), a unique pattern of communication exists within and between each of these adopter groups. Therefore, each may require its own promotion blend.

Assignment

This exercise is designed to show how an understanding of the adoption curve can be helpful when planning promotion blends. Read the following case and then *develop a promotion blend for each adopter group* within the firm's target market. Outline in detail what kind of mass selling, personal selling, and sales promotion you would use, if any, to reach each adopter group. Be specific. For example, if you decide to advertise in magazines, give examples of the magazines you would use. Above all, be creative--it's expected of you!

After you outline your promotion blend for each adopter group, explain *why* you chose that particular blend in the space marked "Comments." Here, you should consider some of the important characteristics of each adopter group--as discussed in the text.

Note that you are only being asked to focus on *promotion to final consumers*. The firm would also have to do some promotion work in the channels--just to obtain distribution--and adoption curve thinking should be applied to middleman adoption too. But all of this promotion activity should be ignored here--because we want to focus on the way that final consumers would accept the product and its impact on promotion planning.

ELECTECH, LTD.

Electech, Ltd.--one of the world's largest manufacturers of electronic equipment--has just announced the introduction of a revolutionary new "personal information system" called the Mediamax. Aimed primarily at the "serious consumer" market, the Mediamax features a fascinating combination of features and capabilities. It can play and record sound, perform calculations, and display text, numbers, pictures and other images on a small (4" diameter) high resolution display screen. It also has built-in software for jotting down notes, maintaining an appointment calendar, and performing calculations. One electronics magazine described the Mediamax as "like a personal CD player, a programmable calculator, a personal organizer, and a dictating machine all rolled into one exquisite, hand-held design." The sound quality of the Mediamax is exceptional. In fact, in the past this quality of sound could only be achieved with prerecorded compact discs. But, rather than relying on CDs to store music the Mediamax uses a new optical disk technology. An optical disk looks like a standard 3.5" computer floppy disk, but it can store as much information as a CD. Further, information (music, software, data) is stored on these optical disks in a digital format. Digital recording has been standard on computers for years, but the development of the optical storage disk has made it possible to incorporate a "*digital enhancement*" system that reduces static and distortion when recording or playing music. This means that the user can record collections of tapes or CDs--and get a higher quality sound than was possible with the original. Further, the Mediamax has *automatic indexing*--so the Mediamax electronically "marks" the beginning of any material stored on the disk--whether it is music or dictation. This allows the user to easily and quickly skip over a selection and "search" for a particular song or message. While such features can be found on some CD players and multimedia computers, the Mediamax is the first system to offer high quality digital recording on a high capacity removable media that can handle music as well as standard "computer-type" files. Further, one optical disk can store many more songs than a standard CD.

The Mediamax also offers several other important benefits. With its built-in rechargeable lithium battery, small case, light weight (about the same as a Sony DiscMan), and stereo headset, the unit is truly portable and can be used anywhere--at home, school or office, on trips, while taking a walk, or at the beach. In addition, it features an innovative system of "user friendly" instructions (the user selects either on-screen or audio instructions) and controls so that is so simple even a child can automatically "program" any of the Mediamax's functions. For example, it will play back a selection of songs in any order, any number of times, while the user is at the same time updating calendar entries or doing calculations.

The Mediamax also has a unique "digital dubbing" feature and built in microphone. This allows the user to simultaneously listen to and record (or "edit") a selection on the optical disk. For example, users can listen to and then modify previously recorded reminders (such as a daily "to do" list). This may be used for dictation, or the user can even play an instrumental selection and add in his or her own voice track. In combination, all of these features make the Mediamax one of the world's most sophisticated consumer audio recorders.

The Mediamax has a manufacturer's suggested list price of $1,095--but it is expected to retail for about $695. This price is not out of line when one considers the unique capabilities of the Mediamax--but the price is much higher than consumers are used to paying for a CD player, a dictating machine, a personal organizer, or a programmable calculator. Further, some of the possible uses of the unit will never have occurred to potential customers. For example, the dictation and "edit" feature of the Mediamax makes it easy for the user to create and update an "audio" appointment calendar, address book, phone list, or even diary. Therefore, promotion may be critical for the new unit--which will be distributed through electronics retailers, some computer and stereo dealers, and selected electronics equipment mass-merchandisers.

Electech, Ltd. managers are not sure what promotion blend to use to introduce this new recorder. One manager has noted that some customers will adopt the Mediamax faster than others--and therefore the promotion blend may have to vary over time. So, they are asking you to advise them.

Suggested Promotion Blends for Communicating with Potential Consumers in Each Adopter Group

1. Innovators

    a) Market characteristics: _____

    _____

    _____

    _____

    b) Promotion blend: _____

    _____

    _____

    _____

    c) Comments: _____

    _____

    _____

    _____

2. Early adopters

    a) Market characteristics: _____

    _____

    _____

    _____

    b) Promotion blend: _____

    _____

    _____

    _____

c) Comments: _____
_____
_____
_____

3.   Early majority

   a)   Market characteristics: _____
   _____
   _____
   _____

   b)   Promotion blend: _____
   _____
   _____

   c)   Comments: _____
   _____
   _____
   _____

4.   Late majority

   a)   Market characteristics: _____
   _____
   _____
   _____

   b)   Promotion blend: _____
   _____
   _____
   _____

c) Comments: _____

_____

_____

_____

5.   Laggards

   a)   Market characteristics: _____

_____

_____

_____

   b)   Promotion blend: _____

_____

_____

_____

   c)   Comments: _____

_____

_____

_____

Question for Discussion

Which of the adopter categories is probably the most important from the viewpoint of the marketing strategy planner? That is, which is most crucial in launching a successful new product? Why?

Chapter 16

Personal selling

What This Chapter Is About

Chapter 16 is concerned with the strategy decisions in the personal selling area.

It is important to see that not all sales jobs are alike. This is why a good understanding of the three basic sales tasks--order getting, order taking, and supporting--is important. The blend of these tasks in a particular sales job has a direct bearing on the selection, training, and compensation of salespeople.

Making an effective sales presentation is an important part of personal selling. Three approaches are explained. Each can be useful--depending on the target market and the products being sold.

Try to see that the strategy personal selling decisions are a part of the whole marketing strategy planning effort. Our earlier discussion of buyer behavior and communication theory is applied here. Be sure to see how materials are being tied together. This chapter continues the strategy planning emphasis which has been running throughout the text.

Important Terms

basic sales tasks, p. 489
order getters, p. 489
order getting, p. 489
order takers, p. 492
order taking, p. 492
supporting salespeople, p. 495
missionary salespeople, p. 495
technical specialists, p. 495
team selling, p. 496
major accounts sales force, p. 497

telemarketing, p. 497
sales territory, p. 498
job description, p. 499
sales quota, p. 503
prospecting, p. 505
sales presentation, p. 506
prepared sales presentation, p. 507
close, p. 507
consultative selling approach, p. 507
selling formula approach, p. 508

True-False Questions

___ 1. It should be the responsibility of the sales manager--not the marketing manager--to make final decisions about how many and what kind of salespeople are needed.

___ 2. Personal selling has declined in importance to the point that there are now more Canadians employed in advertising than in personal selling.

___ 3. Professional salespeople don't just try to sell the customer--they try to help him buy.

___ 4. Some salespeople are expected to act as marketing managers for their own geographic territories and develop their own marketing mixes and strategies.

___ 5. Three basic sales tasks are found in most sales organizations--although in some situations one salesperson might have to do all three tasks.

___ 6. High-caliber order getters are essential in sales of business installations and accessory equipment.

___ 7. Sales representatives for progressive merchant wholesalers often serve as advisors to their customers--not just as order takers.

___ 8. Unsought consumer products often require order getters--to convince customers of the product's value.

___ 9. A wholesaler's order takers handle so many items that they usually will not--and probably should not--give special attention to any particular items.

___ 10. A consumer products manufacturer using an indirect channel system has little need to use missionary salespeople.

___ 11. A business products manufacturer may benefit considerably by using technical specialists, even though a direct channel of distribution and order getters are used.

___ 12. A major accounts sales force sells directly to very large accounts.

___ 13. Telemarketing has none of the benefits of a personal visit.

___ 14. The big advantage of telemarketing is that it saves time, but a disadvantage is that its costs are high.

___ 15. A sales territory is a geographic area that is the responsibility of one salesperson or several working together.

___ 16. The first step in deciding how may salespeople are needed is to estimate how much work can be done by one person in some time period.

___ 17. A good job description should not be too specific--since the nature of the sales job is always changing.

___ 18. All new salespeople should receive the same kind of sales training.

___ 19. A written job description can be helpful in setting the level of compensation for salespeople, because it shows whether any special skills or responsibilities are required that will command higher pay levels.

___ 20. A combination compensation plan will usually provide the greatest incentive for a salesperson to increase sales.

___ 21. The most popular compensation method is the straight commission plan.

22. A sales manager's control over a salesperson tends to vary directly with what proportion of his compensation is in the form of salary.

23. Many firms set different sales objectives--or sales quotas--to adjust the compensation plan to differences in potential in each territory.

24. Basically, prospecting involves following all the leads in the target market--and deciding how much time to spend on which prospects.

25. Some kind of priority system is needed to guide sales prospecting--because most salespeople will have too many prospects.

26. The prepared (canned) sales presentation probably would be appropriate for the majority of retail clerks employed by convenience stores.

27. A salesperson's request for an order is called a close.

28. The consultative selling approach requires less skill on the part of the salesperson than the prepared approach.

29. An effective office equipment salesperson might use a selling formula sales presentation.

30. The AIDA sequence is helpful for planning a consultative selling sales presentation--but not for a selling formula sales presentation.

Answers to True-False Questions

1. F, p. 486	11. T, p. 495	21. F, p. 502
2. F, p. 487	12. T, p. 497	22. T, pp. 502-3
3. T, p. 487	13. F, p. 497	23. T, p. 503
4. T, p. 488	14. F, p. 497	24. T, p. 505
5. T, p. 489	15. T, p. 498	25. T, p. 506
6. T, p. 490	16. T, pp. 498-9	26. T, p. 507
7. T, p. 491	17. F, p. 499	27. T, p. 507
8. T, p. 492	18. F, p. 501	28. F, p. 507
9. T, p. 493	19. T, p. 502	29. T, p. 508
10. F, p. 495	20. F, p. 502	30. F, p. 508

Multiple-Choice Questions (Circle the correct response)

1. Which of the following statements about personal selling is *true*?
   a. As a representative of his company, a salesperson's job is to sell the customer rather than to help him buy.
   b. Today's salesperson is really only responsible for "moving products."
   c. The modern salesperson's sole job is to communicate his company's story to customers.
   d. Some sales representatives are expected to be marketing managers in their own geographic territories.
   e. A beginning salesperson could not expect to be responsible for a sales volume as large as that achieved by many retail stores.

2. A salesperson might have to perform three basic sales tasks. Choose the *correct* description of these tasks from the following:
   a. *Supporting:* the routine completion of sales made regularly to the target customers.
   b. *Order getting:* confidently seeking out potential buyers with a well-organized sales presentation designed to sell a product.
   c. *Order taking:* purpose is to develop goodwill, stimulate demand, explain technical aspects of product, train the middleman's salespeople, and perform other specialized services aimed at obtaining sales in the long run.
   d. All of the above are correct.
   e. None of the above are correct.

3. Order-getting salespeople would be required for which one of the following jobs?
   a. Helping a buyer plan and install a computer system.
   b. Helping drug retailers find new ways to display and promote their products.
   c. Seeking orders from food retailers for a new brand of cake mix which has been added to the company's line.
   d. "Helping" an indecisive supermarket customer select the kind of meat she should buy for dinner.
   e. All of the jobs call for order takers.

4. Chemco, Inc., a three-year-old producer of chemicals, has just hired a manufacturers' agent. The agent
   a. is probably replacing a company order getter who built up the territory.
   b. should assume that Chemco won't ever hire its own sales force for the territory.
   c. may lose the business when the territory gets to the point where it can be handled by an order taker.
   d. All of the above are equally likely.
   e. None of the above is a good answer.

5. A large appliance manufacturer has adequate wholesale and retail distribution--but is concerned that the middlemen do not push its products aggressively enough--because they also carry competitive lines. The manufacturer should hire some:
   a. missionary salespeople.
   b. order getters.
   c. order takers.
   d. technical specialists.

6. Which of the following statements is *false*?
   a. Team selling involves different specialists--to handle different parts of the selling job.
   b. A major accounts sales force is used to sell to small retailers who are not covered by wholesalers in the channel.
   c. Carefully selected sales territories can reduce the cost of sales calls.
   d. The first step in deciding how many salespeople are needed is to estimate how much work can be done by one person in some time period.

7. With regard to the level of compensation for salespeople, a marketing manager should recognize that:
   a. order takers generally are paid more than order getters.
   b. the appropriate level of compensation should be suggested by the job descriptions.
   c. a good order getter will generally be worth less to a firm than a good technical specialist.
   d. the firm should attempt to pay all its salespeople at least the going market wage for order getters.
   e. salespeople should be the highest-paid employees in the firm.

8. The sales manager of the Bubba Beanbag Corp. wishes to compensate his sales force in a way which will provide some security, incentive, flexibility, and control. The company should offer its sales force:
   a. straight salaries.
   b. straight commissions.
   c. a combination plan.

9. Regardless of the sales volume, the least expensive type of sales force compensation system is always:
   a. straight salary.
   b. straight commission.
   c. a combination plan.
   d. None of the above.

10. Danny White sells life insurance for a large Texas firm. He locates customers by selecting names out of a telephone directory and calling to arrange an appointment. He begins each presentation by explaining the basic features and merits of his product--eventually bringing the customer into the conversation to clarify the customer's insurance needs. Then he tells how his insurance policy would satisfy the customer's needs and attempts to close the sale. Danny's sales presentation is based on the:
    a. consultative selling approach.
    b. selling formula approach.
    c. canned presentation approach.

Answers to Multiple-Choice Questions

1. d, pp. 487-89	5. a, p. 495	8. c, p. 502
2. b, p. 489	6. b, p. 497	9. d, pp. 503-4
3. c, pp. 489-91	7. b, p. 499	10. b, p. 508
4. c, p. 491		

Exercise 16-1

Analyzing the nature of the personal selling task

Introduction

Personal selling may involve three basic tasks: (1) *order getting*, (2) *order taking*, and (3) *supporting*. Each task may be done by different individuals—or the same person may do all three. While we use these terms to describe salespeople by referring to their *primary* task, it is important to keep in mind that many salespeople do all of the three tasks to some extent.

Consider, for example, a sales rep for a manufacturer of an established consumer good which is distributed through wholesalers. Since the product is established in the marketplace, the sales rep's primary task would probably be order taking—obtaining routine orders from regular wholesale customers. The same rep may also be expected to do other secondary tasks, however. For example, he may be expected to get orders from new wholesale customers—and so he wold also do order getting at times. Further, he might also spend part of his time helping the wholesaler's sales force—by informing retailers about his company's product, building special store displays, and so forth. In this case, the sales rep would be doing a supporting task.

This exercise focuses on the basic differences among the three selling tasks. In some cases, these differences may be rather clear. In other cases, the differences may be quite difficult to see. To determine what kind of sales rep is needed to handle a particular personal selling job, we will try to distinguish between the *primary* and *secondary* selling tasks. *Note: the words "primary" and "secondary" are used in this way in this exercise only—they do not appear in the text.*

Assignment

Six cases are presented below to show how the selling tasks may vary. In some of the cases, the sales rep will perform both primary and secondary selling tasks, while in others only the primary selling task will be discussed. Read each case and then indicate (a) the *primary* selling task *usually required to effectively carry out the specified job* and (b) any secondary selling task(s) which *may also be described in the case*. Then explain your answer in the space marked "Comments." The first case is answered for you as an example.

1. Jane Smith, a sophomore at Dominion University, works part time at the Campus Book Store. During the week, Jane works afternoons waiting on customers at the lunch counter. On weekends, she usually operates the cash register at the candy and cigarette counter—in addition to handling bills for public utilities. According to her boss, Jane is a very good worker.

    a. Primary selling task: <u>Order taking</u>

    b. Secondary selling task(s): <u>Possibly order getting</u>

Learning aid for use with

c. Comments: <u>No order getting is specifically mentioned, but she may do some occasionally.
For example: "Would you like to try some of our fresh strawberry pie today? It's
delicious!"</u>

2. Paul Sure is earning most of his own college expenses by selling Fuller Brush personal care
products door-to-door. At first, Paul did not like his job, but lately has been enjoying it
more—and doing very well. As Paul puts it, "Once you learn the knack of getting your foot in
the door, sales come easily and the commissions add up fast. After all, people like our
products and the convenience of in-home buying."

a. Primary selling task: _____

b. Secondary selling task(s): _____

c. Comments: _____

_____

_____

3. Jake Woo-lon is a "sales engineer" with Creative Packaging Corporation—which specializes
in foam and air "bubble" packaging materials. Producers use these packaging materials to
protect their products inside shipping cartons during shipping. Creative Packaging has a line
of standard products but also will produce custom packaging materials if that is what a
customer needs. The company does advertising in trade magazines, and each ad includes a
response card. When a prospect calls to inquire about Creative Packaging products, Woo-lon
is sent out to analyze the customer's packaging needs. He determines who much protection is
needed and which packaging product would be best. After finishing his work, Woo-lon
reports back to his sales manager—who assigns another sales rep to handle the rest of the
contacts with the customer.

a. Primary selling task: _____

b. Secondary selling task(s): _____

c. Comments: _____

_____

_____

4. Midwest Power Equipment (MPE) Company is a large merchant wholesaler that distributes
chain saws, lawn mowers, and other outdoor power equipment. MPE sells to retailers and also
sells direct to large end-users—such as golf courses, and cemeteries. Recently MPE decided
to target local government (city and county) buyers—who purchase equipment to maintain

parks, roadside areas, and public schools and hospitals. In the past, these buyers often just purchased equipment from local retailers. Jane Porter, a sales rep for MPE, was assigned responsibility for identifying who influenced these purchase decisions, and for persuading them either to buy from MPE or at least allow MPE to bid on their next order. In addition, Porter has been successful in getting MPE on the provincial government list of approved vendors. That means that various government agencies can select equipment from the MPE catalog and submit a purchase order without a lot of red tape. Porter follows up with the warehouse manager to make certain that these orders are shipped promptly.

a. Primary selling task: _____

b. Secondary selling task(s): _____

c. Comments: _____

  _____

  _____

5. Pat O'Brien, a marketing major in college, went to work for Campbell's Soup as soon as she graduated. While she hopes to become a brand manager some day, Pat is a district sales representative—calling on supermarkets, grocery stores, and convenience stores. Her job is to build special displays, inform store managers of new products, provide merchandising assistance, review customer complaints, and occasionally to suggest special orders for the stores she visits. Pat is paid a straight salary—plus a bonus when sales in her district are good. (Note: Campbell's uses merchant wholesalers to distribute its products.)

a. Primary selling task: _____

b. Secondary selling task(s): _____

c. Comments: _____

  _____

  _____

6. For twenty years, Chuck Hayes has been a manufacturers' agent. Based in Vancouver, British Columbia, he represents a variety of noncompeting manufacturers of parts and components used by small firms that customize vans and make recreational boats. For example, he calls on the many small producers of boats on the Gulf Coast and sells them the special water-resistant fabrics and chrome-plated hardware that they need for boat interiors. His other customers include a number of very large boating supply wholesalers. Chuck has worked at getting to know his customers really well. Because of the variety and complexity of the lines he represents, he spends much of his time checking his customers' parts inventories. This gives him continual customer contact—and provides a useful service. He also finds some time to seek new customers—and is always looking for new producers to represent. Recently,

however, Chuck found out from one of his customers that he has been cut "out of the loop" by one of the manufacturers that he represents. The manufacturer of cast deck fittings (brass and chrome-plated cleats and so on) has set up a toll-free line and has distributed catalogs to its existing customers, encouraging them to shop by phone. When he called the company sales office, the sales manager said: "I guess we should've told you. But, frankly, Chuck, you aren't bringing us many new accounts—it's the same old people ordering each year. They know who we are and we know who they are. And it comes down to this: I have inexpensive part-timers here who can answer the phones and take orders for a lot less than I have to pay you in commission."

a. Primary selling task:_____

b. Secondary selling task(s):_____

c. Comments:_____

   _____

   _____

Question for Discussion

Three different kinds of sales presentations are discussed in the text: the *prepared, consultative,* and *selling formula* presentations. Which of these three kinds of sales presentations would be most appropriate for each of the sales reps described in Exercise 16-1? Why?

Exercise 16-2

Selecting the appropriate kind of salesperson

Introduction

Many people believe that a good salesperson must always be an aggressive, extroverted type of individual with highly developed persuasive skills. Such is not the case, however. Studies have shown, for example, that middle-class shoppers often prefer salespeople who tend to be passive and impersonal. Thus--like all other ingredients of a firm's marketing mix--the kind of salesperson needed depends on the needs and attitudes of the firm's target market.

In addition, the firm must keep its basic promotion objectives in mind. The selling task is not always one of persuasion--but may involve informing or reminding target customers about the company's products and/or the company itself. Therefore, it is often desirable to use order takers--or supporting salespeople--rather than order getters.

Selecting the right kind of salesperson is an important strategy decision. Using the wrong kind of salesperson to handle a specific selling situation may do a firm more harm than good.

Assignment

This exercise will give you practice in selecting the appropriate kinds of salespersons. Several situations involving a need for personal selling are described below. For each situation, indicate which of the following kinds of salespeople would be *most* appropriate--and then explain *why* in the space provided.

> A. Order getter
> B. Order taker
> C. Missionary salespeople
> D. Technical specialist

The first situation is answered for you as an example.

Learning aid for use with

1.   A video rental store needs a person to operate its checkout counter.

a)   Type of salesperson: *Order taker*

b)   Reason: *The chief task is to complete transactions which the customers have begun by coming to the store and making a selection.*

2.   A group of IBM managers who have taken early retirement want to hire a salesperson to promote their new business which is performing "MIS Audits"--evaluating the expense and effectiveness of firms' current management information systems and offering suggestions for improvement. Some firms do this type of evaluation themselves, but many companies don't have the technical or management expertise to know about all of the alternative ways the MIS might be improved.

a)   Type of salesperson:

b)   Reason:

3.   A real estate developer is about to open the model homes for a new subdivision and wants to hire a salesperson who is experienced in new home sales.

a)   Type of salesperson:

b)   Reason:

4.   A glass manufacturer needs someone to call on automobile companies to determine their needs for new models and to work with the company's engineers and pricing staff to develop new proposals.

a)   Type of salesperson:

b)   Reason:

5.   A maker of industrial dishwashing machines (used by institutions and very large restaurants) wants to take advantage of lower freight tariffs to expand the market for its existing product line.

   a)   Type of salesperson:

   b)   Reason:

6.   A company that manufactures radio equipment for commercial aircraft wants to add a new salesperson to be responsible for global positioning satellite systems (a type of radio receiver which can compute a plane's position based on satellite signals) with its existing customers, a small number of very large commercial aircraft manufacturers.

   a)   Type of salesperson:

   b)   Reason:

7.   A distributor of "stock" steel (steel bars, pipes and so on, used by fabricators to make things out of steel) needs an "inside" counter salesperson. The duties are primarily telephone work, processing orders from existing customers, and helping "walk-in" customers.

   a)   Type of salesperson:

   b)   Reason:

8.   A group of lawyers wants to sell prepaid legal services to unions and other employee groups; although the idea has been popular in other areas of the country, they are the first law firm to offer this service in their city.

   a)   Type of salesperson:

   b)   Reason:

9.   A new firm that hopes to offer a series of "wellness" programs--including exercise classes, stress-reduction seminars, and diet plans--for employees of large companies needs a salesperson to call on the personnel managers of prospect firms, explain the service, and negotiate contracts.

   a)   Type of salesperson:

   b)   Reason:

Question for Discussion

What kind of sales compensation plan--straight salary, straight commission, or a combination plan--would be appropriate in the above situations? Why? What factors must be considered in choosing a sales compensation plan?

Chapter 17

Advertising

What This Chapter Is All About

Chapter 17 focuses on advertising—the main kind of mass selling—and the strategic decisions which must be made.

The importance of specifying advertising objectives is emphasized. Advertisements and advertising campaigns cannot be effective unless we know what we want done.
Next, the kinds of advertising which can be used to reach the objectives are explained. Then, how to deliver the message—via the "best" medium, and what is to be communicated—the copy thrust—is discussed.

Advertising agencies are treated also. They often handle the advertising details for advertisers—under the direction of the firm's advertising manager. Avoiding deceptive advertising is also treated. Increasingly, this has strategic importance—because of further government regulation.

Try to see how advertising would fit into a promotion blend—and be a part of a whole marketing strategy. Advertising is not an isolated topic. It can be a vital ingredient in a marketing strategy.

Important Terms

product advertising, p. 517
institutional advertising, p. 517
pioneering advertising, p. 517
competitive advertising, p. 518
direct type advertising, p. 518
indirect type advertising, p. 518

comparative advertising, p. 519
reminder advertising, p. 520
advertising allowances, p. 521
cooperative advertising, p. 521
copy thrust, p. 531
advertising agencies, p. 533

True-False Questions

___ 1. Although it is the most expensive form of promotion on a per-contact basis, advertising does permit communication to large numbers of potential customers at the same time.

___ 2. Canadian corporations spend an average of 20 percent of their sales on advertising—with the largest share of this going to television.

___ 3. Advertising objectives should be very specific—much more so than personal selling objectives.

___ 4. A firm whose objective is to help buyers make their purchasing decision should use institutional advertising.

___ 5. Pioneering advertising should be used in the market introduction stage of the product life cycle to develop selective demand for a specific brand.

___ 6. The objective of competitive advertising is to develop selective demand—demand for a specific brand.

___ 7. Direct competitive advertising involves making product comparisons with competitive brands, while indirect competitive advertising focuses solely on the advertiser's products.

___ 8. Because comparative advertising involves specific brand comparisons—using actual product names—it has been banned by Consumer and Corporate Affairs Canada.

___ 9. Reminder advertising probably should not be used unless the firm has achieved brand preference or brand insistence for its products.

___ 10. Advertising allowances are price reductions to firms further along in the channel to encourage them to advertise or otherwise promote the firm's products locally.

___ 11. The main reason cooperative advertising is used is that large manufacturers usually can get lower media rates than local retailers.

___ 12. Regardless of a firm's objectives, television advertising is generally more effective than newspaper or magazine advertising.

___ 13. A major limitation of using audience data which has been collected by the various media to aid in media selection is that the data seldom contain the market dimensions which a particular advertiser may feel are most important.

___ 14. A firm that wants to send a specific message to a clearly identified target market probably should seriously consider using direct-mail advertising.

___ 15. Copy thrust means what is to be communicated by written copy and illustration.

___ 16. The first job in message planning is determine how to get attention.

___ 17. Advertising agencies are specialists in planning and handling mass selling details for advertisers.

___ 18. Normally, media have two prices: one for national advertisers and a lower rate for local advertisers.

___ 19. Advertising effectiveness can be measured quite simply and accurately just by analyzing increases or decreases in sales.

___ 20. Unfortunately, no effort at self-regulation by advertises has ever been successful in either shaping advertising guidelines or in stopping problem ads.

___ 21. Consumer and Corporate Affairs Canada has the power to control deceptive or false advertising.

1. F, p. 514	8. F, pp. 519-520	15. T, p. 531
2. F, p. 514	9. T, p. 520	16. T, p. 531
3. T, p. 515	10. T, p. 521	17. T, p. 533
4. F, p. 517	11. F, p. 521	18. T, p. 534
5. F, p. 517	12. F, pp. 522-523	19. F, p. 537
6. T, p. 518	13. T, p. 524	20. F, p. 542
7. F, p. 518	14. T, pp. 528-529	21. T, p. 541

Multiple-Choice Questions (Circle the correct response)

1. The largest share of total advertising expenditures in Canada goes for:
   a. newspaper advertising
   b. television advertising
   c. magazine advertising
   d. direct-mail advertising
   e. radio advertising

2. Regarding "good" advertising objectives:
   a. Given no clearly specified objectives, advertising agencies may plan campaigns that will be of little benefit to advertisers.
   b. Advertising objectives often are not stated specifically enough to guide implementation.
   c. Advertising objectives should be more specific than personal selling objectives.
   d. The objectives should suggest which kinds of advertising are needed.
   e. All of the above are true.

3. Which of the following statements about advertising objectives is *false*?
   a. They should be as specific as possible.
   b. They should be more specific than personal selling objectives.
   c. They usually are quite clear from the nature and appearance of an advertisement.
   d. They should flow from the overall marketing strategy.
   e. They should set the framework for an advertising campaign.

4. Bill Smith developed an innovative machine to make a more effective and less expensive bottle cap. He found a backer, produced a model, photographed it, and placed an advertisement in a food canners magazine explaining how caps could be made as needed—right in the canner's plant. Much of the ad copy tried to sell the convenience and inventory cost-saving features of in-plant production as needed rather than purchasing large quantities. Smith's advertising was trying to develop:
   a. selective demand.
   b. primary demand.
   c. derived demand.
   d. elastic demand.

5. The message "Drink milk every day," is an example of which type of advertising?
   a. Pioneering
   b. Competitive
   c. Indirect action
   d. Reminder
   e. Direct action

Learning aid for use with

6. "Better things for better living through chemistry," is an example of:
   a. pioneering advertising.
   b. reminder advertising.
   c. competitive advertising.
   d. institutional advertising.
   e. cooperative advertising.

7. "Cooperative" advertising refers to the practice of:
   a. manufacturers and middlemen sharing in the cost of advertising which is done by the manufacturer.
   b. manufacturers doing some advertising and expecting their middlemen to cooperate by providing the rest of the promotion blend.
   c. the manufacturer paying for all of the advertising which is done by its middlemen.
   d. local retailers doing advertising which is partially paid for by a manufacturer.
   e. middlemen picking up the promotion theme of the manufacturer and carrying it through.

8. The choice of the "best" advertising medium depends upon:
   a. the promotion objectives.
   b. the budget available.
   c. the target markets.
   d. the characteristics of each medium.
   e. all of the above.

9. To communicate a very specific message to a very select, well-identified group of consumers—one probably should use:
   a. magazines aimed at special-interest groups.
   b. newspapers.
   c. television.
   d. direct mail.
   e. radio.

10. Which of the following statements about advertising agencies and compensation methods is true?
    a. The 15 percent commission system is no longer required—and some advertisers have obtained discounts or fee increases.
    b. Some agencies were quite dissatisfied with the traditional compensation arrangements between advertisers and agencies because their costs were rising—and some advertisers were demanding more services than could be provided profitably.
    c. Some advertisers—especially industrial goods manufacturers—were quite satisfied with the traditional compensation arrangements whereby the agency did the advertiser's advertising work in return for the normal discount allowed by the media.
    d. The agencies earn commission from media only when time or space is purchased at the national rate (as opposed to local rates).
    e. All of the above are true statements.

11. Which of the following statements about measuring advertising effectiveness is *false*?
    a. The most reliable approach is to check the size and composition of media audiences.
    b. Some progressive advertisers are now demanding laboratory or market tests to evaluate the effectiveness of advertisements.
    c. No single technique or approach has proven most effective.
    d. When specific advertising objectives are set, then marketing research may be able to provide feedback on the effectiveness of the advertising.
    e. Ideally, management should pretest advertising before it is run rather than relying solely on the judgment of creative people or advertising "experts."

Answers to Multiple-Choice Questions

1. a, p. 539
2. e, pp. 515-16
3. c, p. 516
4. b, p. 517

5. a, p. 517
6. d, p. 517
7. d, p. 521
8. e, pp. 522-523

9. d, pp. 528-529
10. e, pp. 534-536
11. a, pp. 537-538

Exercise 17-1

Identifying different kinds of advertising

Introduction

Perhaps because of the high cost of advertising, some companies try to use multi-purpose ads to reach several promotion objectives at the same time. Studies have shown, however, that such ads often fail to produce *any* of the desired effects. On the contrary, several special-purpose ads are much more likely to stimulate positive responses than a single multi-purpose ad. Thus, a marketing manager usually should use different kinds of advertising to accomplish different promotion objectives.

This exercise is designed to show the different kinds of advertising which can be used--and to show the various objectives an advertisement might have. While doing the assignment, you should see that promotion objectives may be only indirectly concerned with increasing sales--and that a firm may have other reasons for advertising. Try to guess what these "other reasons" are--and how they might relate to a company's overall marketing mix.

Assignment

Using recent magazines and newspapers, find advertisements to *final consumers* which illustrate the following kinds of advertising (as defined in the text):

> A. Institutional
> B. Pioneering
> C. Direct competitive
> D. Indirect competitive
> E. Comparative
> F. Reminder

Clip out the ads--and for each ad attach a separate sheet of paper indicating:

a) what kind of advertising the ad illustrates.
b) what target market, if any, the ad appears to be aimed at.
c) the general and specific objectives of each ad--e.g., to inform consumers (general) about three new product improvements (specific).
d) the name of the magazine or newspaper in which the ad appeared.

Question for Discussion

When one overall objective of a company's marketing activities must be to sell its products, why would advertisements have objectives such as those you indicated for your examples?

Learning aid for use with

Exercise 17-2

Determining advertising objectives and the appropriate kind of advertising

Introduction

About 1910 George Washington Hill--president of the American Tobacco Company--is said to have made this now-famous quote: "I am convinced that 50 percent of our advertising is sheer waste, but I can never find out which half." Today, there are many business executives who share Mr. Hill's feelings. Billions of dollars are spent each year creating clever--and sometimes annoying--ads which often appear to be poorly designed and largely ineffective.

Actually, it is extremely difficult to measure the effectiveness of advertising--because companies often lack clearly defined advertising objectives. In hopes of remaining competitive, advertisers often budget some fixed percent of their sales dollars to advertising without any specific objectives in mind--other than to just "promote the product."

Like all business expenditures, however, there is no reason for making advertising expenditures unless the company has some specific purpose in mind. Since the advertising objectives selected will largely determine the kind of advertising that is needed, companies should set specific advertising objectives which are tied to their overall marketing strategies.

Assignment

This exercise will give you some practice determining the kind of advertising that may be needed to obtain some specific advertising objectives. Described below are several situations in which some kind of advertising may be necessary or desirable. For each situation: (a) indicate what *general* (i.e., inform, persuade, and/or remind) and *specific* objectives the advertising probably would be meant to achieve; and (b) indicate which of the following kinds of advertising would be *most* appropriate to accomplish that objective.

        A.   Pioneering advertising
        B.   Direct competitive advertising
        C.   Indirect competitive advertising
        D.   Reminder advertising
        E.   Institutional advertising
        F.   Comparative advertising

The first situation is answered for you as an example.

1. A print ad shows an insurance adjuster with a clip-board in hand watched by a family with grateful expressions on their face. The only "copy" is a single line: "You're in good hands with Allstate."

    a) Advertising objectives: *Remind. This ad assumes that consumers already know that Allstate is in the domestic casualty insurance market and builds on other advertisements which have given greater details about product benefits.*

    b) Kind of advertising: *Reminder.*

2. General Motors takes out double page advertisements in national newspapers to announce the new multi-valve *Northstar* engine for its Cadillac division. The ad copy mentions the technical sophistication of the engine including its power and long time between tune-ups.

    a) Advertising objectives: _____

    _____

    _____

    b) Kind of advertising: _____

3. The metropolitan transportation district receives a grant from the coalition of local governments to advertise bus services to promote clean air by switching commuters from single-occupancy cars. Billboards and TV time are too expensive, so the bus company uses the money to purchase placard ads inside its own buses. The copy says: "Save gas--take the bus!"

    a) Advertising objectives: _____

    _____

    _____

    b) Kind of advertising: _____

4. Print advertisements for a producer of designer clothing simply feature the designer's "brand name" and a picture of scantily clad models frolicking in romantic situations.

    a) Advertising objectives: _____

    _____

    _____

    b) Kind of advertising: _____

5. A print advertisement for Rolls Royce automobiles features an attractive couple driving a Rolls convertible in front of New York's Plaza hotel. The driver of a Mercedes sedan looks on and there is also a Lincoln in the background. The ad copy is a single line: "Simply the best motor car in the world."

   a) Advertising objectives: _____

   _____

   _____

   b) Kind of advertising: _____

6. Qualitas, Ltd. is one of the leading producers of stereo speakers in Canada. Unlike the technological advances in other types of stereo components, there has been little change in speakers in the last 30 years. However, Qualitas has just patented a revolutionary new way to reproduce sound through a speaker. The new Qualitas speaker produces music that is significantly better. Some industry sources predict that by the year 2000 the new technology will capture 40 to 50 percent of the stereo speaker market.

   a) Advertising objectives: _____

   _____

   _____

   b) Kind of advertising: _____

7. After the re-unification of Germany, the German government ran print ads in business-news magazines in the U.S., Canada, and Japan with a map of all of Germany in the background and the headline: "Made in Germany." The copy described the education of German workers and their reputation for producing quality products, and also noted opportunities for new investments in factories in the enlarged Federal States.

   a) Advertising objectives: _____

   _____

   _____

   b) Kind of advertising: _____

8.　British Airways uses print advertisements which show a picture of the supersonic Concorde in flight, with the simple copy: "Until they come up with a way to fax people," and the tag line: "British Airways. The world's favorite airline."

　　a)　Advertising objectives: _____

　　　　_____

　　　　_____

　　b)　Kind of advertising: _____

9.　In an attempt to reposition its high performance PS/2 "ultimedia" computers towards the higher end of the microcomputer market, IBM's print ads include a table comparing product benefits of the "ultimedia " computer line with features and service of Compaq and Dell computers.

　　a)　Advertising objectives: _____

　　　　_____

　　　　_____

　　b)　Kind of advertising: _____

Question for Discussion

Would there be difficulties in evaluating the effectiveness of the media chosen for the situations mentioned in Exercise 17-2? Why?

Chapter 18

Pricing objectives and policies

What This Chapter Is About

Chapter 18 talks about the strategic decisions in the Price area. You should see that there is much more to Price than accepting the "equilibrium price" set by the interaction of supply and demand forces (as discussed in Appendix A). The actual price paid by customers depends on many factors. Some of these are discussed in the chapter. They include the trade, quantity, and cash discounts offered; trade-ins: who pays the transportation costs; and what actually is included in the marketing mix.

The chapter begins with a discussion of possible pricing objectives—which should guide price setting. Then, the marketing manager's decisions about price flexibility and price level over the product life cycle are discussed.

The marketing manager must also set prices which are legal. The chapter discusses what can and cannot be done legally.

Clearly, there is much more to pricing than the simple economic analysis which we used earlier to understand the nature of competition. Chapter 18 is an important chapter—and deserves very careful study.

Important Terms

price, p. 546
target return objective, p. 549
profit maximum objective, p. 549
sales-oriented objective, p. 550
status quo objectives, p. 551
nonprice competition, p. 551
administered prices, p. 551
one-price policy, p. 552
flexible-price policy, p. 552
skimming price policy, p. 553
penetration pricing policy, p. 554
introductory price dealing, p. 555
value pricing, p. 557
basic list prices, p. 558
discounts, p. 558
quantity discounts, p. 558
cumulative quantity discounts, p. 558
noncumulative quantity discounts, p. 559

seasonal discounts, p. 559
net, p. 559
cash discounts, p. 559
2/10, net 30, p. 560
trade (functional) discount, p. 560
sale price, p. 560
everyday low pricing, p. 561
allowances, p. 562
advertising allowances, p. 562
stocking allowances, p. 562
push money (or prize money) allowances, p. 562
trade-in allowance, p. 562
rebates, p. 564
F.O.B., p. 565
zone pricing, p. 566
uniform delivered pricing, p. 566
freight absorption pricing, p. 567
price fixing, p. 567

True-False Questions

___ 1. Any business transaction in our modern economy can be thought of as an exchange of money—the money being the Price—for something of greater value.

___ 2. The "something" that Price buys is different for consumers or users than it is for channel members.

___ 3. A target return objective is often used in a large company with several divisions for administrative convenience.

___ 4. Profit maximization objectives are undesirable from a social viewpoint, because profit maximization necessarily leads to high prices.

___ 5. Instead of setting profit-oriented objectives, a marketing manager should follow sales-oriented objectives because—in the long run—sales growth leads to big profits.

___ 6. Market share objectives provide a measurable objective—but an increase in market share does not always lead to higher profits.

___ 7. Status quo pricing objectives make it virtually impossible for a firm to implement an effective marketing strategy because of the non-price competition.

___ 8. Instead of letting daily market forces determine their prices, most firms (including all of those in monopolistic competition) set their own administered prices—sometimes holding them steady for long periods of time.

___ 9. A one-price policy means offering the same price to all customers who purchase goods under essentially the same conditions and in the same quantities.

___ 10. Flexible pricing is seldom used any more in Canada because it does not aid selling—and because flexible prices are generally illegal under Canadian legislation.

___ 11. A skimming pricing policy is especially desirable when economies of scale reduce costs greatly as volume expands—or when the firm expects strong competition very soon after introducing its new product.

___ 12. A penetration pricing policy might be indicated where there is no "elite" market—that is, where the whole demand curve is fairly elastic—even in the early stages of the product's life cycle.

___ 13. Introductory price dealing means the same thing as using a penetration pricing policy.

___ 14. Sellers who may appear to emphasize below-the-market prices in their marketing mixes may really be using different marketing strategies—not different price levels.

___ 15. Basic list prices are the prices final consumers (or industrial consumers) are normally asked to pay for products.

___ 16. Discounts from the list price may be granted by the seller to a buyer who either gives up some marketing function or provides the function for himself.

___ 17. Quantity discounts may help the seller to get more of a buyer's business or to reduce the seller's shipping and selling cost—but they usually also shift some of the storing function from the buyer back to the seller.

___ 18. Cumulative quantity discounts tend to encourage larger single orders than do noncumulative quantity discounts.

___ 19. Cash discounts are used to encourage buyers to pay their bills quickly—meaning they are granted to buyers who pay their bills by the due date.

___ 20. The following terms of sale appear on an invoice: 1/10, net 30. A buyer who fails to take advantage of this cash discount offer is—in effect—borrowing at an annual rate of 18 percent a year.

___ 21. A mass merchandiser that allows government employees to purchase goods at 10 percent below the store's normal selling prices is using a trade or functional discount.

___ 22. Allowances are typically given only to channel members who provide some service—such as additional selling effort.

___ 23. Trade-in allowances are price reductions given for used goods when similar new goods are bought.

___ 24. PMs or "spiffs" are given to retailers by manufacturers or wholesalers to pass on to their salespeople in return for aggressively selling particular items or lines.

___ 25. F.O.B. pricing simplifies a seller's pricing—but may narrow his target market because a customer located farther from the seller must pay more for his goods and might be inclined to buy from nearby suppliers.

___ 26. With zone pricing, an average freight charge is made to all buyers within certain geographic areas, thus lowering the chance of price competition in the channel and simplifying the figuring of transportation charges.

___ 27. Uniform delivered pricing—which is used when the seller wishes to sell his products in all geographic areas at one price—is most often used when transportation costs are relatively high.

___ 28. Freight absorption pricing means absorbing freight costs so that a firm's delivered price will meet the nearest competitors.

1. F, p. 546
2. T, p. 547
3. T, p. 549
4. F, pp. 549-550
5. F, p. 550
6. T, p. 551
7. F, p. 551
8. T, pp. 551-552
9. T, p. 552
10. F, pp. 552-553

11. F, p. 553
12. T, pp. 554-555
13. F, p. 555
14. T, p. 556
15. T, p. 558
16. T, p. 558
17. F, p. 558
18. F, pp. 558-559
19. F, p. 559
20. T, p. 560

21. F, p. 560
22. F, p. 562
23. T, p. 562
24. T, p. 562
25. T, p. 565
26. T, p. 566
27. F, p. 566
28. T, p. 567

Multiple-Choice Questions (Circle the correct response)

1. Which of the following would be least *likely* to be included in the "something" part of the "price equation" for channel members?
   a. Quantity discounts
   b. Rebates
   c. Price-level guarantees
   d. Sufficient margin to allow chance for profit
   e. Convenient packaging for handling

2. Which of the following price objectives would a marketing manager for a public utility be most likely to pursue?
   a. Status quo
   b. Market share
   c. Target return
   d. Profit maximization
   e. Sales growth

3. With respect to pricing objectives, a marketing manager should be aware that:
   a. profit maximization objectives generally result in high prices.
   b. status quo pricing objectives can be part of an extremely aggressive marketing strategy.
   c. target return objectives usually guarantee a substantial profit.
   d. sales-oriented objectives generally result in high profits.
   e. All of the above are true statements.

4. Prices are called "administered" when:
   a. they are determined through negotiations between buyers and sellers.
   b. they fall below the "suggested list price."
   c. a marketing manager has to change his strategy every time a customer asks about the price.
   d. government intervenes to ensure that prices fluctuate freely in response to market force.
   e. firms set their own prices for some period of time—rather than letting daily market forces determine their prices.

5. In contrast to flexible pricing, a one-price policy:
   a. means that the same price is offered to all customers who purchase goods under the same conditions.
   b. involves setting the price at the "right" level from the start— and holding it there.
   c. generally results in rigid prices which change very infrequently.
   d. means that delivered prices will be the same to all customers.
   e. All of the above.

6. Which of the following factors would be *least favorable* to a skimming price policy?
   a. The firm is a monopoly.
   b. The whole demand curve is fairly elastic.
   c. The product is in the market introduction stage of its life cycle.
   d. The firm follows a multiple target market approach.
   e. The firm has a unique, patented product.

7. The Gill Corp. is introducing a new "me-too" brand of shampoo in market maturity. To speed its entry into the market—without encouraging price competition with other shampoo manufacturers—Gill should consider using:
   a. a penetration pricing policy.
   b. a flexible-price policy.
   c. a skimming pricing policy.
   d. introductory price dealing.
   e. an above-the-market price-level policy.

8. The Stark Corporation purchases large quantities of iron castings from a well known producer. Stark receives a discount which increases as the total amount ordered during the year increases. What type of discount is involved here?
   a. Seasonal discount
   b. Cumulative quantity discount
   c. Brokerage allowance
   d. Noncumulative quantity discount
   e. Cash discount

9. The terms "3/20, net 60" mean that:
   a. in effect—the buyer will pay a 27 percent interest rate if he takes 60 days to pay the invoice.
   b. the buyer must make a 3 percent down payment—with the balance due in 20 to 60 days.
   c. a 3 percent discount off the face value of the value of the invoice is permitted if the bill is paid within 60 days—otherwise, the full face value is due within 20 days.
   d. the invoice is dated March 20 and must be paid within 60 days.
   e. None of the above is a true statement.

10. The Bowman Co., a manufacturer of sports equipment, gives its retailers a 2 percent price reduction on all goods with the expectation that the dealers will advertise the goods locally. Apparently, Bowman believes that local promotion will be more effective and economical than national promotion. This is an example of:
   a. "push" money.
   b. a brokerage allowance.
   c. a cash discount.
   d. a trade discount.
   e. an advertising allowance.

11. Some producers give _____ to retailers to pass on to the retailers' salesclerks in return for aggressively selling particular items or lines.
   a. brokerage commissions
   b. advertising allowances
   c. trade discounts
   d. "push money"
   e. cash discounts

12. A producer in Quebec sold some furniture to a firm in Toronto. If the seller wanted title to the goods to pass immediately—but still wanted to pay the freight bill—the invoice would read:
   a. F.O.B. delivered.
   b. F.O.B. seller's factory—freight prepaid.
   c. F.O.B. Toronto.
   d. F.O.B. seller's factory.
   e. F.O.b. buyer's warehouse.

13. If a buyer purchases a shipment of products from a seller in another city and the invoice reads "F.O.B. shipping point,"
   a. the seller pays the freight bill and keeps title to the products until they are delivered.
   b. the seller pays the freight bill but title to the products passes to the buyer at the point of loading.
   c. the buyer pays the freight but the seller keeps title to the products until delivery.
   d. the buyer pays the freight and gets title to the products at the point of loading.
   e. both a and c.

14. Which of the following statements about geographic pricing policies is true?
   a. Zone pricing penalizes buyers closest to the factory.
   b. Uniform delivered pricing is more practical when transportation costs are relatively low.
   c. Freight absorption pricing may increase the size of a firm's market territories.
   d. F.O.B. pricing tends to reduce the size of market territories.
   e. All of the above are true statements.

Answers to Multiple-Choice Questions

1. b, p. 547
2. c, p. 549
3. b, p. 551
4. e, pp. 551-552
5. a, p. 552

6. b, p. 553
7. d, p. 555
8. b, pp. 558-59
9. a, p. 560
10. e, p. 562

11. d, p. 562
12. b, p. 565
13. d, p. 565
14. e, pp. 565-567

Exercise 18-1

Using discounts and allowances to improve the marketing mix

Introduction

Most price structures have a basic list price from which various discounts and allowances are subtracted. *Discounts* (not to be confused with discount selling) are reductions from list price that are given by a seller to a buyer who either gives up some marketing function or provides the function himself. Several types of discounts are commonly used, including:

a) Cumulative quantity discounts
b) Noncumulative quantity discounts
c) Seasonal discounts
d) Cash discounts
e) Trade (functional) discounts

Allowances are similar to discounts. They are given to final consumers, customers or channel members for doing "something" or accepting less of "something." Different types of allowances include:

a) Advertising allowances
b) Push money or prize money allowances
c) Trade-in allowances
d) Stocking allowances

While many firms give discounts and allowances as a matter of custom, they should be viewed as highly useful tools for marketing strategy planning. As outlined in the text, each type is designed for a specific purpose. Thus, some firms offer buyers a choice of several discounts and allowances.

The purpose of this exercise is to illustrate how discounts and allowances can be used in marketing strategy planning. The emphasis will be on recognizing opportunities to improve a firm's marketing mix. In Exercise 18-2, we will discuss various legal restrictions which may affect a firm's policies regarding discounts and allowances.

Assignment

Presented below are five cases describing situations in which a firm *might* want to add or change some discount or allowance--as part of its marketing mix. Read each case carefully and then answer the questions which follow.

1. College Grove Apartment Complex offers two-bedroom apartments with the same basic "roommate" floor plan that is popular with other student-oriented apartments in the area. In August and early September, there is no difficulty in attracting tenants at the "going rate" of $650 per month rent. Although there is a penalty for breaking the lease, each year a number of unexpected vacancies occur at the end of the first semester when some students graduate or drop out of school, move to a dorm, or find someone new with whom to live. Of course, the same thing happens at other apartments, so in late December and early January there are always more empty apartments than new renters. As a result, competition for tenants is usually intense. In this "buyer's market," student renters look for the best deal--and apartment managers dread the idea of having an empty apartment that brings in no rent for the spring semester.

   a) What type of discount or allowance would you recommend in this situation? Why?

2. Athletic Footwear Company produces a high-quality line of Lightfoot brand men's and women's running shoes. Lightfoot shoes are distributed nationally through a network of carefully selected sporting stores and runners' stores. When jogging first became popular, Lightfoot sales grew rapidly—in pat because of its ongoing advertising in national magazines. Now, however, sales are flat—and in some areas falling. Most retailers now carry several competing brands of shoes—and the company is concerned about what it considers "a lack of adequate promotion support at the retail level."

   a. Could Athletic Footwear Company use discounts or allowances to obtain additional promotion support at the retail level? Why? If so, what type would you recommend? Why?

   b. What would be the advantages and limitations of your recommendation relative to other approaches?

Learning aid for use with

3. Yadadoto manufactures "intelligent" electronic keyboards for the home. Many parents buy a keyboard when their children start to take piano lessons. An electronic keyboard is less expensive than a regular piano, takes less space, and also offers advanced features not available on a piano. In fact, many parents are attracted to the keyboards because of these special features. For example, the keyboard can "memorize" and play back a song, provide accompaniment for "duets," or play the "left-hand" part of a piece while the student practices the "right hand"--and about thirty other features. All of this can help keep students interested in practicing and speed the learning process. However, many people return the instruments after a short period of time because they have trouble understanding how to get the keyboard to do the various things possible. Yadadoto is redesigning the keyboard to make it easier to use, but that will take quite some time. In the meantime, the marketing manager is considering offering a lower wholesale price to dealers who agree to give customers at least five one half-hour lessons when they buy a keyboard. That should ensure that kids and their parents know how to use the keyboard's special functions. Yadadoto plans to keep the same suggested retail list price in its catalogs and advertisements.

   a)   What kind of price adjustment is being proposed?

   b)   Why doesn't Yadadoto just cut its wholesale or retail list price to spur sales?

4. Sandy Delarocha is enjoying his new business as a finisher of hardwood floors. Homeowners who want their floors refinished pay "cash up front" when work begins, but with new construction Sandy bills the general contractor as soon as the work is complete. Most of the contractors will use any excuse to hold Sandy off until they have closed the sale of the house--and that's often three or four months after he's done his work! Sandy didn't give this problem much thought at first because he considered it a necessary nuisance if he wanted to get the new construction business. But, while preparing his taxes, Sandy realized that during the last year he had paid the bank more than $3,600 in interest charges on his line of credit. He has been using the bank loans to pay his workers--while he waits for the contractors to pay their accounts. When Sandy set his prices, he hadn't planned on having to pay that much interest expense--and the problem is really bothering him. He is also worried that contractors will use someone else if he raises his prices.

   a)   What would your recommend? Why?

5. Flagstone Oil Co. supplies heating oil to customers in a ski-resort area. Flagstone is not the lowest price distributor in the area, but the company offers a service in which its route drivers will check a residential customer's tank and "top it off" before it runs out--without the customer placing an order. This service is important to many customers in the area because their vacation homes are empty much of the time--but they want to leave some heat on to prevent damage from frozen pipes. It's expensive to send out trucks and drivers to check the tanks--many of which

don't need much oil, but Flagstone has used this service to attract customers. Recently, however, Flagstone has encountered a problem. A competing distributor has been promoting lower prices during the peak oil-use months (December, January and February) when home owners are in town. Many of Flagstone's customers have had the competitor fill their tanks. When the Flagstone drivers arrive they find the tanks full. Then in the fall and spring customers expect Flagstone to keep their tanks topped off.

a) Is there a way that Flagstone could use a discount or allowance to combat this problem? Explain your thinking.

b) Would your recommended solution be better than Flagstone simply adopting year-round low pricing?

6. The Trend-Setters Dress Shop has just purchased $20,000 worth of women's dresses from Fashion Manufacturing Company. The invoice for the dresses included the terms "3/10, net 60."

a) What do the terms 3/10, net 60 mean?

b) Suppose Trend-Setters pays the invoice 10 days after receipt. What amount should it pay Fashion Manufacturing?

c) If Trend-Setters does not pay the invoice until 60 days after receipt, it will in effect be borrowing money at a fairly high interest rate. Calculate what the effective interest rate would be in this case. (Assume a 360 day year.)

d) What conditions would make it sensible for Fashion Manufacturing to offer these terms?

Question for Discussion

Do discounts and allowances really offer marketing managers a great deal of flexibility in varying their marketing mixes? Explain.

Learning aid for use with

Exercise 18-2

How legislation affects pricing policies

Introduction

Pricing legislation is a very complex field and often even legal counsel cannot assure their clients of clear-cut advice in pricing matters. This is due in part to the vague and ambiguous way in which many laws have been phrased by legislators and in part to the fact that no two situations are ever exactly alike. It is up to the courts and administrative bodies to interpret pricing legislation, and their interpretation of laws has tended to vary considerably, depending on the political and social environment.

Nevertheless, a marketing manager should try to understand the legal environment and know how to work within it. Legislation and legal cases often tend to focus on pricing matters because prices are tangible and highly visible elements of the marketing mix. Businessmen have considerable freedom to charge whatever prices they choose, subject to the forces of competition, of course. But they must be aware of, and adhere to, the restrictions which do exist. Ignorance of the law is no excuse, and the penalty for violating pricing laws can be quite severe.

This exercise is designed to enhance your understanding of the Competition Act provisions which pertain to pricing matters. Here, the intent is not to make you a legal expert but rather to examine in detail the kinds of pricing activities which *might* be viewed as illegal in certain situations. A review of pages 133-37 of chapter 4 would be in order before you proceed.

Assignment

Described below are several situations involving pricing activities which might be judged illegal in certain circumstances. Study each situation carefully and then answer the questions which follow.

1. Jumping Jeans Ltd., a retail sportswear chain, has four locations in Toronto and plans to open its first store in Montreal next month. The Quebec sales manager has proposed a "two for the price of one" sale for the first week of Montreal operations. However, his proposal has run into some opposition from the president of Jeans who thinks that, since the same offer isn't being made in Toronto, the proposed sale may be illegal. The president is also afraid of being accused of "predatory pricing." The sales manager has assured him that such a sale would be legal, but the president refuses to give his blessing until he consults his lawyer.

    Do you think the sales manager or the president is correct in this case? Why? Do you think a "one-shot" deal of this nature should be subject to restrictive legislation? Why or why not?

2. Lazy Laundry Ltd. is a highly successful coin-operated laundry chain in Quebec. For several years it was the only laundry in Povungnituk but now another firm has opened up. At this location Lazy charges ten cents less per load for washing and five cents less for drying than is charged at its other Quebec outlets. Last week a complaint alleging "predatory pricing" was sent to the Restrictive Trade Practices Commission by the new competitor in Povungnituk. As far as the company is concerned, it maintains that lower prices are being charged at Povungnituk because the prospective customers are relatively poor. Also, the costs of operation are lower in this far northern community than in it is other locations.

   You have been asked to assist in preparing the defense to the predatory pricing complaint. Do you think the company can successfully defend its pricing policy for Povungnituk? Why or why not?

3. You have recently been hired as marketing consultant to a major U.S. cake mix company which wants to enter the Canadian market. It estimates that its start-up costs for Canada will be substantial, e.g., new packaging, national advertising campaign, etc. To help defray some of these expenses, it plans initially to limit its discounts to the following three types:

   a. A quantity discount of 10 percent but only on sales of more than ten cases.
   b. A 10 percent discount, over and above any quantity discount, on all sales to wholesalers, and
   c. An additional 5 percent cumulative quantity discount of all sales to retailers in a given year of over 100 cases.

   For Canadian purposes, you are asked to comment on the legality or illegality of each type of discount under the Competition Act as described in your text. Also, comment on whether you think functional, quantity and cumulative quantity discounts ought to be legal.

Learning aid for use with

4. As marketing manager for Carefree Carpet Retailers Ltd., you have been asked to approve the following copy for next week's newspaper ad:

Carefree Carpets Ltd. Charme Sales
Top Quality Broadloom $10.95 per yd.
Normally $15.95 per yd or more
Hurry! Limited quantity

You immediately telephone the sales manager for further details about the proposed sale stock. He advises you that over 75 yards are available for the sale. In addition, he has a substantial stock of similar broadloom which is regularly priced at $11.95 per yard. As well, the sales manager tells you that the broadloom to be advertised was priced at $16.95 per yard when it was first introduced four years ago. The $15.95 price applied as recently as last year when this broadloom was discontinued due to manufacturing irregularities.

Do you see any ethical or moral reason for not approving this advertisement? If you approve it, will Carefree be vulnerable to prosecution for false or deceptive advertising? Why or why not?

5. Gleam and Sheen is a new hair product which provides long-lasting highlights. It has been extremely successful since it was introduced into the market two months ago. This success is largely due to a national TV advertising campaign which began at the time of launch and has created a high degree of consumer awareness of this unique new product. Orders have temporarily exceeded supply, and the Montreal distributor learned today that a refusal to supply complaint has been filed against it with the Restrictive Trade Practice Commission. The complaint was filed by a Montreal discount drugstore which was one of the first firms to place its order for Gleam and Sheen. This order was placed within the first week of the TV campaign, and it has yet to be filled while other orders have been filled. The complaint alleges that sales of approximately $300 have been lost to date.

You are an investigator for the Restrictive Trade Practices commission and must determine whether or not remedial action is required in this matter. Do you have sufficient information to make the determination? If so, do you think remedial action is required? If you do not have sufficient information, what additional data is required?

6. The Better Business Bureau of Yourtown, Canada, recently received a telephone call from an irate customer who wished to voice a complaint about "Honest Sam's," a mass merchandiser with several stores in the surrounding area. It seems the customer had gone to "Honest Sam's" to take advantage of some bargain items that were featured in an "inventory clearance sale" advertisement. The first item on his shopping list was a compact stereo marked down from $150 to $99.95. Upon arrival at the store, he found only one of the featured stereos in stock—a floor model in very poor condition. The salesclerk apologized and suggested that he consider buying one of the store's other models at "regular everyday low pricing," ranging from $199 on up. The customer then went over to the clothing department to check on some men's blazers which, according to the ad, were "regularly priced from $50-$90" and "now reduced to only $39.99." He found a large array of cheap blazers, many of them out-of-style by several seasons, which were hardly worth the sale price let alone the prices quoted in the ad. An official from BBB sympathized with the customer and admitted that his agency had received many similar complaints about "Honest Sam's." He went on to say, however, that there was very little anyone could do about such merchandising tactics, other than to avoid shopping at such stores.

Comment on the Better Business Bureau's analysis of the above situation. Are "Honest Sam's" merchandising practices deceptive? Was the customer really deceived? Can anything be done in such situations?

Questions for Discussions

According to one point of view, the Competition Act benefits consumers by prohibiting pricing practices which may tend to injure competition. Another point of view, however, holds that the Act only serves to protect inefficient competitors and thus may actually be harmful to consumers. Which view to you agree with? Why? How can we determine which view is "right"?

Appendix C

Marketing arithmetic

What This Appendix Is About

Appendix C provides a brief introduction (or review) of some important accounting terms which are useful in analyzing marketing problems.

The content of an operating statement (profit-and-loss statement) is reviewed first. Accounting terms are used in a technical sense--rather than a layman's sense--and should be studied with this in mind. Accountants try to use words precisely--and usually try to place the same kinds of data in the same places in their statements. So try to capture the "model" which they are using. Basically, it is: sales minus costs equals profit.

It is also useful to be able to calculate stockturn rates, operating ratios, markups, markdowns, and ROI and ROA--to fully understand some of the concepts in the text chapters.

This material should be "easy review" for those who have had some accounting. But regardless of your background, it probably will be helpful to study this material--to deepen your understanding of accounting statements and tools. Familiarity with these ideas is assumed in the text!

Important Terms

operating statement, p. 573
gross sales, p. 575
return, p. 575
allowance, p. 575
net sales, p. 575
cost of sales, p. 576
gross margin (gross profit), p. 576
expenses, p. 576
net profit, p. 576

purchase discount, p. 577
stockturn rate, p. 578
operating ratios, p. 579
markup, p. 580
markdown ratio, p. 581
markdown, p. 582
return on investment (ROI), p. 582
balance sheet, p. 582
return on assets (ROA), p. 583

True-False Questions

___ 1. An operating statement is a simple summary of the financial results of a company's operation over a specified period of time.

___ 2. The three basic components of an operating statement are sales, costs, and return on investment.

___ 3. Net sales equals gross sales minus returns and allowances.

—   4.   The "cost of sales" is the total value (at cost) of the sales during the operating period.

—   5.   Gross margin (or gross profit) equals net sales minus operating expenses.

—   6.   Net profit equals net sales minus the cost of sales minus operating expenses.

—   7.   To calculate the net profit accurately, purchase discounts and freight charges should be added to the cost of sales.

—   8.   Expenses do not include the cost of sales.

—   9.   The stockturn rate is a measure of how long it takes a certain inventory of goods to be sold.

—   10.   Stockturn rate may be calculated as the cost of sales divided by the average inventory at cost.

—   11.   The various components of an operating statement should always be expressed in absolute numbers rather than in percentages.

—   12.   If a store takes a 50-cent markup on a certain product, then its net profit for that item is also 50 cents.

—   13.   A 25 percent markup on cost equals a 20 percent markup on selling price.

—   14.   A markdown ratio equals dollar markdowns divided by net sales; returns and allowances are not included.

—   15.   Markdowns are generally shown on a firm's operating statement.

—   16.   Return on investment is not shown on the firm's operating statement.

—   17.   To increase return on investment, a firm *must* increase sales.

—   18.   Although return on investment is calculated in the same way as return on assets, the two ratios are trying to show different things about the company's use of resources.

Answers to True-False Questions

1. T, p. 573	7. F, p. 576	13. T, p. 581
2. F, p. 573	8. T, p. 577	14. F, p. 582
3. T, p. 575	9. F, p. 578	15. F, p. 582
4. T, p. 576	10. T, p. 579	16. T, pp. 582-583
5. F, p. 576	11. F, pp. 579-580	17. F, p. 583
6. T, p. 576	12. F, p. 580	18. F, p. 583

Multiple-Choice Questions (Circle the correct response)

1. The primary purpose of the operating statement is:
   a. to determine which products or customers are most profitable.
   b. to determine the net profit figure for the company.
   c. to present data to support the net profit figure.
   d. to indicate the source of the firm's assets.
   e. both b and c above.

2. The essential components of an operating statement are:
   a. gross sales, gross margin, and net profit.
   b. net sales, cost of sales, and profit or loss.
   c. sales, costs, and profit or loss.
   d. gross sales, gross margin, expenses, and net profit.
   e. sales, markdowns, and ROI.

3. Which of the following statements is *true*?
   a. "Gross sales" is equal to revenue actually received and kept.
   b. "Cost of sales" means the cost value of goods on hand at any given time.
   c. Expenses are included in the "Cost of sales" section of the operating statement.
   d. "Gross margin" less the "Cost of sales" equals "Net profit."
   e. None of the above statements is true.

4. Given the following data for the XYZ Company for the year 199X, calculate XYZ's net profit.

Gross sales	$157,000
Returns	3,000
Allowances	4,000
Purchases	60,000
Beginning inventory	50,000
Freight-in	3,000
Cost of sales	100,000
Expenses	30,000

   a. $10,000
   b. $12,000
   c. $17,000
   d. $20,000
   e. $27,000

5. Which of the following statements is *false*?
   a. Stockturn rate equals cost of sales divided by average inventory at cost.
   b. Stockturn rate equals gross sales divided by average inventory at selling price.
   c. Stockturn rate equals net sales minus gross margin divided by average inventory at cost.
   d. Stockturn rate equals sales in units divided by average inventory in units.
   e. Stockturn rate equals net sales divided by average inventory at selling price.

Use the following data to answer questions 6 and 7.

Gross sales	$1,020,000	
Markdowns	50,000	
Cost of sales		50%
Beginning inventory	150,000	
Returns and allowances	20,000	
Expenses		30%
Purchases	400,000	

6. Calculate the net profit (or loss) for the firm described above.
    a. $150,000
    b. $190,000
    c. $204,000
    d. $200,000
    e. Cannot be determined without more information.

7. Assume that the average stockturn rate for this industry is 4. How does this firm compare to its competitors?
    a. The firm has an above-average turnover rate.
    b. The firm has a below-average turnover rate.
    c. The firm has an average turnover rate.
    d. Cannot be determined.

Use the following data from a company's last accounting period to answer questions 8-10.

Sales returns	$ 10,000	
Sales allowances	15,000	
Expenses		25%
Closing inventory at cost	50,000	
Markdowns	45,000	
Freight-in	5,000	
Purchases	150,000	
Net profit	30,000	10%

8. The cost of sales is:
    a. $225,000
    b. $105,000
    c. $145,000
    d. $195,000
    e. $ 75,000

9. The stockturn rate is:
    a. 6.0
    b. 3.9
    c. 4.3
    d. 2.8
    e. 1.5

10. The markdown ratio is:
    a. 20 percent
    b. 11 2/3 percent
    c. 18 1/3 percent
    d. 10 percent
    e. 15 percent

11. Joe's Shoe Store uses a traditional markup of 25 percent for all of its shoes. If a pair of shoes costs him $6, what should Joe *add* to this cost to determine his selling price?
    a. $1.50
    b. 33 1/3 percent of $6.00
    c. 125 percent of $6.00
    d. $3.00
    e. 25 percent of $6.00

12. Knowledge of departmental markdown ratios for a given period would be useful in:
    a. preparing an operating statement for that period.
    b. determining the value of goods on hand.
    c. measuring the efficiency of the various retail departments.
    d. computing the stockturn rate for that period.
    e. All of the above.

13. To increase its return on investment (ROI), a firm could:
    a. increase its profit margin.
    b. increase its sales.
    c. decrease its investment.
    d. increase its leveraging.
    e. All of the above.

14. *Given the following information, calculate the ABC Company's ROI.*

Net sales	$1,000,000
Gross margin	200,000
Markdowns	200,000
Assets	300,000
Net profit (after taxes)	10,000
Owner's investment	100,000

    a. 3.3 percent
    b. 1,000.0 percent
    c. 10.0 percent
    d. 2.5 percent
    e. 5.0 percent

15. In Question 14, the ABC Company's ROA was:
    a. 3.3 percent.
    b. 2.5 percent.
    c. 30.0 percent.
    d. 150.0 percent.
    e. Some negative number--because the assets were larger than the owners' investment.

Answers to Multiple-Choice Questions

1. e, p. 573
2. c, p. 573
3. e, pp. 575-576
4. d, pp. 574-576
5. b, pp. 578-579

6. d, pp. 579-580
7. a, pp. 578-579
8. d, pp. 576-577
9. d, pp. 578-579
10. a, pp. 581-582

11. b, pp. 580-581
12. c, p. 581
13. e, pp. 582-583
14. c, p. 583
15. a, p. 583

Exercise C-1

Marketing arithmetic

Introduction

A firm's financial records contain much useful information for a marketing manager. An effective marketing manager will make regular use of them in his planning. This exercise is designed to improve your understanding of the operating statement and the information it contains.

Assignment

1. Complete the ABC Corporation's Operating Statement (on the next page) by filling in the blank lines and then use the information in the financial statement to answer the following questions.

2. Calculate the stockturn rate (using cost figures).

3. Calculate the following operating ratios. (Round each answer to one decimal place.)

    a) Net sales   100%

    b) Cost of sales   _____

    c) Gross margin   _____

    d) Expenses   _____

    e) Net profit   _____

ABC CORPORATION
Operating Statement
For the Year Ending December 31, 199X

Gross sales			$52,000
Less: Returns and allowances			4,000
Net sales		a) _____	
Cost of sales			
Beginning inventory at cost			$12,000
Purchases at billed cost		$25,000	
Less: Purchase discounts		2,000	
Purchases at net cost	b) _____		
Plus freight-in		2,000	
Net cost of delivered purchases		c) _____	
Cost of goods available for sale		d) _____	
Less: Ending inventory at cost		8,000	
Cost of sales		e) _____	
Gross margin (gross profit)		f) _____	
Expenses			
Selling expense			
Sales salaries		7,000	
Advertising expense		2,200	
Delivery expense		2,300	
Total selling expenses		g) _____	
Administrative expense			
Office salaries		3,800	
Office supplies		900	
Miscellaneous		300	
Total admin. expense		h) _____	
General expense			
Rent expense		1,100	
Miscellaneous		100	
Total general expense		i) _____	
Total expense		j) _____	
Net profit from operation		k) _____	

Question for Discussion

What additional financial information would help the marketing manager of ABC Corporation to improve his operation?

Chapter 19

Price setting in the business world

What This Chapter Is About

Price setting is challenging--but deciding on the right price is crucial to the success of the whole marketing mix.

Chapter 19 treats cost-oriented pricing in detail--because it is commonly used and makes sense for some firms. But cost-oriented pricing doesn't always work well. You should study this approach carefully, so you can better understand its advantages and disadvantages.

Pay special attention to the relationships of the various cost curves. Notice how costs vary at different levels of operation.

Some business managers have recognized the problems with average-cost pricing and have tried to bring demand into their price-setting. Demand-oriented pricing requires some estimate of demand--and ideally a whole demand curve. But demand curves are not easy to estimate. This is one reason why demand-oriented pricing has not been widely used. But it is possible to *estimate* demand curves. And it is probably better to try to estimate a demand curve than ignore it. Some examples of how this is being done are presented at the end of the chapter.

By estimating demand, it is possible to estimate the likely profit of various quantities--and find the most profitable price and quantity. Although this approach is not as widely used as cost-oriented pricing, it deserves careful study. Demand must be considered when setting price--unless you are willing to leave making a profit to chance. Demand-oriented pricing can be done--and can be very useful in helping to carry out the marketing concept--that is, satisfying customers *at a profit*.

Important Terms

markup, p. 589
markup (percent), p. 589
markup chain, p. 591
stockturn rate, p. 591
average-cost pricing, p. 593
total fixed cost, p. 595
total variable cost, p. 595
total cost, p. 595
average cost (per unit), p. 595
average fixed cost (per unit), p. 595
average variable cost (per unit), p. 595
experience curve pricing, p. 598
target return pricing, p. 599
long-run target return pricing, p. 599
break-even analysis, p. 599
break-even point (BEP), p. 600
fixed-cost (FC) contribution per unit, p. 601
marginal analysis, p. 602
marginal revenue, p. 603

marginal cost, p. 603
rule for maximizing profit, p. 606
marginal profit, p. 608
price leader, p. 610
value in use pricing, p. 611
reference price, p. 611
leader pricing, p. 611
bait pricing, p. 612
psychological pricing, p. 612
odd-even pricing, p. 612
prestige pricing, p. 613
price lining, p. 614
demand-backward pricing, p. 615
full-line pricing, p. 616
complementary product pricing, p. 617
product-bundle pricing, p. 617
bid pricing, p. 617
negotiated price, p. 618

True-False Questions

___ 1. Markup (dollars) means the dollar amount added to cost of products to get the selling price-- or markup (percent) means a percentage of the selling price which is added to the cost to get the selling price.

___ 2. According to the definition of markup given in the text, a product which a retailer buys for $2.00 would be priced at $3.20 if the retailer applied a markup of 60 percent.

___ 3. Considering the large number of items the average retailer or wholesaler carries--and the small sales volume of any one item--a markup approach to pricing makes sense.

___ 4. A producer--whose product sells for $24--distributes its product through wholesalers and retailers who traditionally use a "markup chain" of 20 percent and 40 percent, respectively. Therefore, the retail selling price of this product is $50.

___ 5. A wholesaler or retailer concerned with increasing profits should consider using a smaller markup as a way of achieving a substantial increase in turnover.

___ 6. "Stockturn rate" means the number of times a firm's beginning inventory is sold in a year.

___ 7. Producers commonly use a cost-oriented pricing approach--adding a standard markup to obtain their selling price.

___ 8. Because average-cost pricing consists of adding a "reasonable" markup to the average cost of a product, it assures the producer of earning a profit at any level of output.

___ 9. Total fixed cost is the sum of those costs that are fixed in total--no matter how much is produced.

_ 10. Total variable cost would include items such as wages paid to workers, sales commissions, and salaries paid to top executives.

_ 11. The rate of growth of total cost as output increases is not affected by total fixed cost.

_ 12. Average cost is obtained by dividing total cost by the related total quantity.

_ 13. Average fixed cost increases as the total quantity produced increases.

_ 14. Average variable cost is obtained by dividing total variable cost by the number of units produced.

_ 15. Because of economies of scale, all average and total costs tend to decline as the quantity produced increases.

_ 16. Average-cost pricing works best when demand conditions are changing rapidly and substantially.

_ 17. Experience curve pricing is like average-cost pricing--except that prices are based on an estimate of future average costs.

_ 18. Unlike the average-cost curve approach, target return pricing assures that the target return is achieved--even if the quantity that is actually sold is less than the quantity used in setting the price.

_ 19. Those who use long-run target return pricing assume that short-run losses and above-normal profits will average out in the long run--thus allowing the firm to achieve its long-run target return objectives.

_ 20. Break-even analysis suggests that once a firm reaches its break-even point, profit will keep increasing with every additional unit sold.

_ 21. Although break-even analysis considers the relationship of total revenue and total cost, it may not solve the firm's pricing problem because the assumed price may not be tied to realistic demand estimates.

_ 22. The traditional goal of economic analysis--to maximize profits--is a reasonable one because if you know how to make the biggest profit, you can always adjust your price to pursue other objectives--while knowing how much profit you are giving up.

_ 23. Marginal analysis helps the marketing manager make the best pricing decision by focusing on the last unit which would be sold--to determine how total revenue and total cost would be affected.

_ 24. Since marginal revenue is the change in total revenue which results from the sale of one additional unit of a product--and since this extra unit will be sold while charging a positive price for all items--marginal revenue can never be negative.

_ 25. The marginal revenue curve is the same as the demand curve when the demand curve is down-sloping.

___ 26. Marginal cost--which is the change in total cost that results from producing one more unit--might also be defined as the change in total variable cost that results from producing one more unit.

___ 27. If an average-cost curve first drops and then rises, the related marginal cost curve would also start rising--but at a greater level of output.

___ 28. To maximize profit--the firm should produce that output where the difference between marginal revenue and marginal cost is the greatest.

___ 29. When using a graph to determine the most profitable output and price for a firm, the best price is obtained by going from the MR-MC intersection over to the price axis.

___ 30. Marginal analysis indicates that--to maximize profits--a firm should be willing to increase the quantity it will sell until the marginal profit of the last unit is at--or near--zero.

___ 31. If marginal costs can be covered in the short run--even though all fixed costs cannot--the firm should remain in operation.

___ 32. A firm in an oligopoly situation cannot use marginal analysis to maximize its profits because of the "kinked" demand curve facing the firm.

___ 33. A price leader in an oligopoly situation should have a very good understanding of its own and its competitors' cost structures--as well as an estimate of the industry demand curve.

___ 34. Value in use pricing is setting prices which will capture some of what customers will save by substituting the firm's product for the one currently being used.

___ 35. Reference prices do not vary from one customer to another for the same basic type of purchase (for example, paperback books).

___ 36. Leader pricing is most common in oligopoly situations--where most firms will raise or lower their price only after the industry leader raises or lowers its price.

___ 37. Items featured in "bait pricing" are real bargains priced low to get customers into the store to buy these and other items.

___ 38. Psychological pricing assumes that some price changes will not affect the quantity sold.

___ 39. Retailers who use "odd-even pricing" seem to assume that they face a rather jagged demand curve--that slightly higher prices will substantially reduce the quantity demanded.

___ 40. Prestige pricing is possible when target customers think that high prices mean high quality or high status--and the demand curve for this market slopes down for a while and then bends back to the left again.

___ 41. Although price lining may result in higher sales, faster turnover, and simplified buying--it also increases the retailer's total inventory requirements and often leads to greater markdowns.

___ 42. Henry Ford's decision to build a car for the "masses"--setting "a price so low as to force everybody to the highest point of efficiency"--is an example of demand-backward pricing.

Learning aid for use with

43. A producer that offers a complete line (or assortment) of products should not be overly concerned about full-line pricing if it is aiming at different target markets for each of its products.

44. Complementary product pricing is setting prices on several products as a group.

45. Firms that use product-bundle pricing usually set the overall price so that it's cheaper for the customer to buy the bundle than to buy each item separately.

46. The major job in bid pricing is assembling all of the costs--including the variable and fixed costs--that should apply to each job.

47. Bargaining may involve the whole marketing mix, not just the price level in arriving at a negotiated price.

Answers to True-False Questions

1. T, p. 589	17. T, p. 598	33. T, p. 610
2. F, pp. 589-590	18. F, p. 599	34. T, p. 611
3. T, p. 590	19. T, p. 599	35. F, p. 611
4. T, p. 591	20. T, p. 599-600	36. F, pp. 611-612
5. T, p. 591	21. T, pp. 600-601	37. F, p. 612
6. F, pp. 591-592	22. T, pp. 602	38. T, p. 612
7. T, p. 592	23. T, p. 602	39. T, p. 612
8. F, p. 594	24. F, p. 603	40. T, p. 613
9. T, p. 595	25. F, p. 603	41. F, p. 614
10. F, p. 595	26. T, pp. 603-604	42. T, p. 615
11. T, p. 595	27. F, pp. 604-605	43. T, p. 616
12. T, p. 595	28. F, p. 606	44. T, p. 617
13. F, p. 595	29. F, pp. 607-608	45. T, p. 617
14. T, p. 595	30. T, p. 608	46. T, p. 617
15. F, p. 595	31. T, p. 609	47. T, p. 618
16. F, p. 596	32. F, p. 609-610	

Multiple-Choice Questions (Circle the correct response)

1. A certain product retails for $100. How much does this product cost the retailer if his markup is 33 1/3 percent?
   a. $25.00
   b. $33.00
   c. $50.00
   d. $75.00
   e. $66.67

2. The markup approach to price setting used by most middlemen:
   a. makes little sense--given the large number of items carried and the small sales volume of any one item.
   b. is very inflexible because the same markup percent must be applied to all products.
   c. often uses the trade (functional) discount allowed by the manufacturer.
   d. is quite complicated--because each product has a different delivered cost.
   e. All of the above.

3. A certain item is sold at retail for $50. The retailer's markup is 25 percent *on cost*. The wholesaler's markup is 25 percent. What is the manufacturer's selling price?
   a. $30.00
   b. $32.00
   c. $28.10
   d. $35.11
   e. $25.00

4. With respect to markups and turnover, a marketing manager should be aware that:
   a. a low stockturn rate increases inventory carrying costs.
   b. depending on the industry, a stockturn rate of 1 or 2 may be quite profitable.
   c. high markups don't always mean big profits.
   d. speeding turnover often increases profits because the firm's operating costs are a function of time and the volume of goods sold.
   e. All of the above are true statements.

5. Which of the following statements about average-cost pricing is *true*?
   a. The chief merit of this approach is that it is based on well-researched pricing formulas.
   b. It consists of adding a "reasonable" markup to the average cost of a product.
   c. This method takes into consideration cost variations at different levels of output.
   d. It assumes that the average cost for the next period will be different from that of the last period.
   e. All of the above are true statements.

6. Average-cost pricing:
   a. consists of adding a "reasonable" markup to the average cost of a product.
   b. uses demand-oriented pricing formulas.
   c. does not allow for cost variations at different levels of output.
   d. focuses on the differences between fixed and variable costs.
   e. Both A and C are true.

7. Total cost usually:
   a. is zero at zero quantity.
   b. grows at a rate determined by increases in total variable cost.
   c. is the sum of total fixed and total marginal costs.
   d. grows at a rate determined by increases in total fixed cost.
   e. None of the above is a true statement.

8. The *major* weakness of average-cost pricing is that:
   a. it always leads to losses instead of profits.
   b. costs decline and rise at different levels of output.
   c. demand is ignored.
   d. average fixed cost increases as the quantity increases.
   e. All of the above.

9. Average cost pricing will result in *larger* than expected profit:
   a. most of the time.
   b. if the average fixed cost estimate is based on a quantity that is smaller than the actual quantity sold.
   c. if the average total cost is higher than expected.
   d. only if the manager makes arithmetic errors in computing average variable cost.
   e. None of the above is correct.

10. Trying to find the *most profitable* price and quantity to produce:
    a. requires average-cost pricing.
    b. requires an estimate of the firm's demand curve.
    c. is easy once the average fixed cost is known.
    d. is only sensible if demand estimates are exact.
    e. All of the above are true.

11. When a firm seeks to obtain some specific percentage return on its investment (or a specific total dollar return), it is using:
    a. break-even pricing.
    b. experience curve pricing.
    c. "what the traffic will bear" pricing.
    d. target return pricing.
    e. average-cost pricing.

12. A manufacturer who uses "target return" pricing sold 1,000 units of his product last year. He wants to earn a profit of at least $20,000 in the coming year. If his fixed costs are $40,000 and his variable costs equal $20 per unit, what price would he charge (assuming that he could still sell 1,000 units)?
    a. $60
    b. $40
    c. $80
    d. $120
    e. Cannot be determined with information given.

13. Break-even analysis assumes that:
    a. variable cost is constant per unit but varies in total.
    b. average fixed costs increases as quantity increases.
    c. the demand curve slopes downward and to the right.
    d. average variable cost first decreases and then increases as quantity increases.
    e. All of the above.

14. Assume that a producer's fixed costs amount to $240,000, its variable costs are $30 per unit, and it intends to sell its portable washer to wholesalers for $50. Given this information, the break-even point is:
    a. 8,000 units.
    b. 12,000 units.
    c. 14,000 units.
    d. 20,000 units.
    e. almost 50,000 units.

15. Given the following data, compute the BEP *in dollars*:
    Selling price = $1.25
    Variable cost = $ .75
    Fixed cost   = $45,000
    a. $36,000
    b. $60,000
    c. $90,000
    d. $112,500
    e. None of the above.

16. Break-even analysis can be used for:
    a. relating prices to potential demand.
    b. comparing various assumed pricing alternatives.
    c. finding the most profitable price.
    d. estimating future sales.
    e. All of the above.

17. A monopolistic competitor's "marginal revenue":
    a. is always positive.
    b. is always shown above the corresponding down-sloping demand curve on a graph.
    c. is the change in total revenue that results from the sale of one more unit of a product.
    d. All of the above are true statements.
    e. Only a and c above are true statements.

18. The change in total cost that results from producing one more unit is called:
    a. average variable cost.
    b. marginal cost.
    c. average fixed cost.
    d. total variable cost.
    e. average total cost.

19. To maximize profit, a firm should:
    a. produce that output where marginal revenue is at a maximum.
    b. produce that output where marginal cost is just less than or equal to marginal revenue.
    c. produce that output where marginal cost is greater than marginal revenue.
    d. try to maximize the difference between marginal revenue and marginal cost.
    e. produce that output where marginal profit is at a maximum.

20. A marketing manager should be aware that the most profitable level of output:
   a. is where total revenue equals total cost.
   b. is where the difference between marginal revenue and marginal cost is the greatest.
   c. is where the vertical difference between total revenue and total cost is the greatest.
   d. is where marginal revenue is at a maximum.
   e. Both b and c are correct.

Use the following figure to answer questions 21-23.

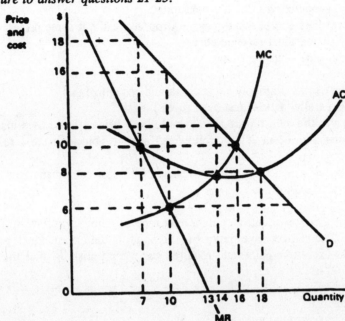

21. The most profitable quantity to sell would be:
   a. 7
   b. 10
   c. 13
   d. 14
   e. 18

22. The most profitable price would be:
   a. $6
   b. $8
   c. $10
   d. $16
   e. $18

23. The break-even point is:
   a. 10 units
   b. 13 units
   c. 14 units
   d. 16 units
   e. 18 units

24. In applying traditional economic analysis, a firm has discovered *two* break-even points--rather than a single break-even point. This means that:
   a. the firm's demand curve cannot be down-sloping.
   b. there is a profitable operating range which surrounds the point of maximum profit.
   c. seeking the maximum profit point is likely to prove fruitless.
   d. the firm has not experienced any economies or diseconomies of scale.
   e. None of the above--there can never be more than one break-even point.

25. Profit-maximizing oligopolists will find that their marginal cost curves intersect:
   a. marginal revenue curves that are horizontal.
   b. marginal revenue curves that appear to drop vertically at some prices.
   c. down-sloping marginal revenue curves.
   d. negative marginal revenue curves.

26. A "price leader" in an oligopoly situation should recognize that:
   a. "conscious parallel action" has been ruled illegal.
   b. other firms in the industry are sure to raise their prices if he raises his first.
   c. price cutting may occur if the "followers" are not able to make a reasonable profit at the market price.
   d. marginal analysis is not applicable because of the kinked demand curve.
   e. All of the above are true.

27. An equipment producer is introducing a new type of paint sprayer to sell to automobile body-repair shops. The sprayer saves labor time in painting the car, makes it possible to get as good a job with less expensive paint, and requires less work polishing after the car is painted. This company should use:
   a. leader pricing.
   b. bait pricing.
   c. complementary product pricing.
   d. odd-even pricing.
   e. value in use pricing.

28. The manager of Green's Dress Shop has concluded that her customers find certain prices very appealing. Between these prices are whole ranges where prices are apparently seen as roughly equal--and price cuts in these ranges generally do not increase the quantity sold (i.e., the demand curve tends to drop vertically within these price ranges). Therefore, the manager has decided to price her dresses as close as possible to the top of each price range. This is known as:
   a. prestige pricing.
   b. bait pricing.
   c. leader pricing.
   d. psychological pricing.
   e. odd-even pricing.

29. Setting relatively high prices on products with perceived high status is known as:
   a. price lining.
   b. odd-even pricing.
   c. leader pricing.
   d. prestige pricing.
   e. bait pricing.

30. The practice of setting different price levels for different quality classes of merchandise--with no prices between the classes--is called:
   a. full-line pricing.
   b. prestige pricing.
   c. price lining.
   d. odd-even pricing.
   e. psychological pricing.

31. "Demand-backward" pricing:
   a. is like leader pricing.
   b. has been called "market-minus" pricing.
   c. requires no demand estimates.
   d. is usually performed by retailers.
   e. All of the above are true statements.

32. Which of the following statements about "full-line pricing" is *true*?
   a. A marketing manager usually attempts to price products in the line so that the prices will seem logically related and make sense to potential customers.
   b. Most customers seem to feel that prices in a product line should be somewhat related to cost.
   c. The marketing manager must try to recover all his costs on the whole product line.
   d. Not all companies that produce a variety of products must use full-line pricing.
   e. All of the above are true statements.

33. With regard to bid pricing, a marketing manager should be aware that:
   a. the customer is always required to accept the lowest bid.
   b. since it costs very little to submit a bid, most firms try to bid for as many jobs as possible.
   c. the same overhead charges and profit rates usually apply to all bids.
   d. the major task is assembling all the costs--including the variable and fixed costs that apply to a particular job.
   e. All of the above are true statements.

Answers to Multiple-Choice Questions

1. e, pp. 589-590	12. c, p. 599	23. e, p. 608
2. c, pp. 589-590	13. a, pp. 599-600	24. b, p. 608
3. a, p. 591	14. b, pp. 600-601	25. b, p. 609
4. e, p. 591	15. d, p. 601	26. c, p. 610
5. b, p. 593	16. b, p. 601	27. e, p. 611
6. e, p. 594	17. c, p. 603	28. d, p. 612
7. b, p. 595	18. b, p. 603	29. d, p. 613
8. c, p. 596	19. b, pp. 605-606	30. c, p. 614
9. b, pp. 596-598	20. c, p. 606	31. b, p. 615
10. b, pp. 597-598	21. b, pp. 606-608	32. e, p. 616
11. d, p. 599	22. d, pp. 606-608	33. d, p. 617

Exercise 19-1

Elements of cost-oriented price setting

Introduction

This exercise is designed to familiarize you with the arithmetic of cost-oriented pricing. Because most firms use cost-oriented methods to set prices, it is important that you understand these methods. Retailers and wholesalers, for example, use traditional markups that they feel will yield a reasonable rate of profit. You should be aware of how markups are figured. And you should know how stock turnover is calculated. Further, you should understand how the various types of costs differ, how they relate to each other, and how they affect profits as the sales volume varies.

Note: It is highly recommended that you review Appendix C: Marketing Arithmetic on pages 572-584 of the text before starting this exercise.

Assignment

Answer the following set of problems. Show your work in the space provided.

1. The usual retail price of an item is $100.00. The manufacturer's cost to produce the item is $40.00. Retailers take a 50 percent markup and wholesalers take a 10 percent markup. (Note: markup is calculated on selling price, unless otherwise indicated.)

    a) What is the retailer's markup in dollars? _____

    b) What is the wholesale price? _____

    c) What is the manufacturer's price? _____

d)   What is the manufacturer's markup percentage? _____

e)   What is the manufacturer's markup percentage *on cost*? _____

2.   The Headen Manufacturing Company is trying to set its price on an item that will sell at retail for $80.00.

a)   For retailers to earn a markup of 25 percent, what should the wholesale price be? _____

b)   For the wholesalers in 2a to earn a markup of 10 percent, what should the manufacturer's price be? _____

3.   Complete the following table by filling in the blanks. *Hint:* start with the first column and work to the right, column by column.

Item	Quantity produced				
	0	1	2	3	4
Total Cost	____	____	____	____	$400
Total fixed cost	$120	____	____	____	____
Total variable cost	____	____	$140	____	____
Average cost	n/a*	____	____	$110	____
Average fixed cost	n/a*	____	____	____	____
Average variable cost	n/a*	$70	____	____	____

*Note: n/a means not applicable (because at zero output there is not an average cost per unit).

4.   a)   Using the data from Question 3, plot the total cost, total fixed cost, and total variable cost curves on the following graph.

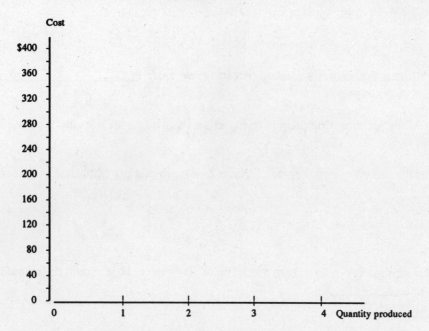

b) Using the data from Question 3, plot the average cost, average fixed cost, and average variable cost curves on the following graph.

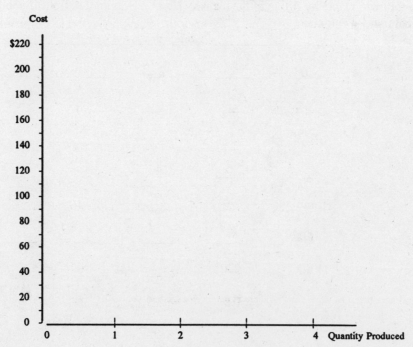

5.   Simplex Corp. has fixed costs of $2,000,000 and average variable costs of $100 per unit at all levels of output. It wishes to earn a profit of $300,000 this year--which is an increase of 10 percent over last year when Simplex sold 5,000 units of its product.

a)   Use the average-cost pricing method to determine what price Simplex should charge for its product.

b)   Suppose Simplex were only able to sell 4,000 units this year because of increased competition. What would its profit (or loss) be?

c)   Suppose Simplex's sales increased to 7,000 units this year. What would its profit (or loss) be?

d)   Based on your answers to parts a, b, and c, what do you conclude about the effectiveness of average-cost pricing?

6.   Suppose in Question 5 that Simplex had decided to use "target return" pricing instead of average-cost pricing. Suppose further that it wished to earn a 20 percent return on its investment of $500,000.

   a)   What price should Simplex charge for its product?

   b)   What would Simplex's return on investment be if it were only able to sell 4,000 units?

   c)   What would Simplex's return on investment be if its sales increased to 7,000 units?

Question for Discussion

Why do so many firms use cost-oriented pricing methods when such methods have so many obvious shortcomings?

Exercise 19-2

Using break-even analysis to evaluate alternative prices

Introduction

Break-even analysis can be a very useful tool for evaluating alternative prices--especially when the prices being considered are fairly realistic from a demand point of view. Break-even analysis shows how many units would have to be sold--or how much dollar volume would have to be achieved--to just cover the firm's costs at alternative prices. A realistic appraisal of the likelihood of achieving the break-even point associated with each alternative price might show that some prices are clearly unacceptable--that is, there would be no way that the firm could even reach the break-even point, let alone make a profit.

The mechanics of break-even analysis are relatively simple--once you understand the concepts and assumptions. This exercise reviews these ideas and then has you apply them to a fairly common decision-making situation.

Assignment

Read each of the following problems carefully--and fill in the blanks as you come to them. Where calculations are required, make them in the space provided--and show your calculations to aid review.

1. Study the break-even chart in Figure 19-2a on the next page and answer the following questions:

    a) According to Figure 19-2a, at what quantity, total revenue, and price will the firm break even?

        Quantity _____ Total Revenue _____ Price _____

    b) The firm's total fixed cost in this situation is: _____

    c) The firm's average variable cost (AVC) is: _____

FIGURE 19-2a
Break-Even Chart

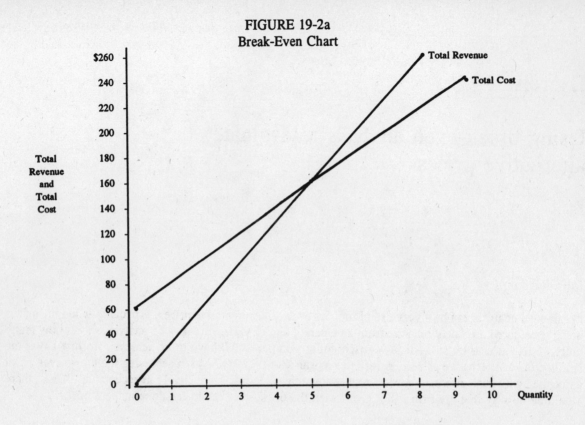

FIGURE 19-2b

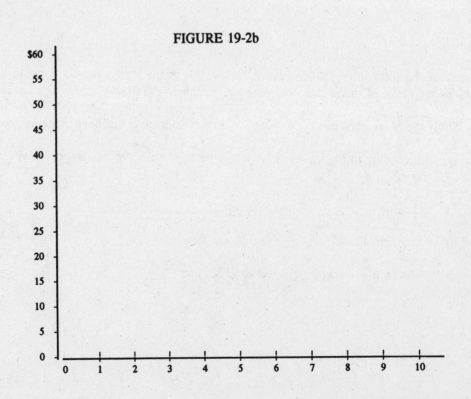

Learning aid for use with

d)   Using Figure 19-2a, draw the total revenue curve that would be relevant if the firm were considering a price of $50 per unit. Given this price of $50 per unit, at what quantity and total revenue would the firm break even?

Quantity _____   Total Revenue _____

e)   What price should the firm charge to maximize profits--the price you calculated in (a) or $50? Why?

2.   a)   Suppose you were considering going into the car-washing business and investing in a new kind of car-washing unit which is more mechanized than the usual ones--but also has higher fixed costs. Calculate the break-even point in dollars and units if the usual price of $4.00 per car were charged. The variable cost per car is estimated at $2.00. The total fixed cost per year (including depreciation, interest, taxes, fixed labor costs, and other fixed costs) is estimated at $320,000.

BEP in $ _____   BEP in units _____

b)   There is some possibility that there will be increased price cutting in your proposed market in the near future. Calculate the BEPs for the situation in (a) if the retail price drops to $3.50 per car.

BEP in $ _____   BEP in units _____

c) There is also a possibility that the new washing unit will deliver a better job for which some people will be willing to pay more. Calculate the new BEPs if it were possible to raise the retail price to $4.50.

BEP in $ _____ BEP in units _____

d) Should you go into the car-washing business in *any* of the above situations? Explain.

Question for Discussion

Looking at Figures 19-2a and 19-2b, what does break-even analysis assume about the nature of demand and about the competitive environment? Is break-even analysis relevant for monopolistic competition?

Learning aid for use with

Exercise 19-3

Setting the most profitable price and quantity to produce

Introduction

Demand must be considered when setting prices. Ignoring demand curves does not make them go away. Usually, a market will buy more at lower prices--so total revenue *may* increase if prices are lowered. But this probably won't continue as the price gets closer to zero. Further, total cost--and perhaps average costs--will increase as greater quantities are sold.

So, if a firm is at all interested in making a profit (or avoiding losses), it should consider demand and cost curves *together*. This exercise shows how this can be done--and emphasizes that not all prices will be profitable.

Assignment

Figure 19-3 shows the Fast Manufacturing Company's estimated total revenue and total cost curves for the coming year. Study this figure carefully and answer the questions which follow.

FIGURE 19-3

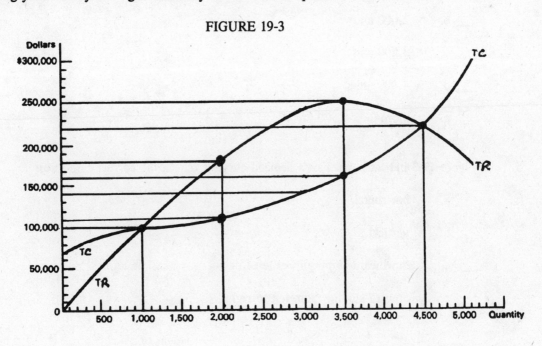

1. Complete the following chart by referring to Figure 19-3--the graph of Fast's total costs and revenues.

Quantity	Total Cost	Average Cost	Total Revenue	Price*	Total Profit (Loss)
1,000	——	——	——	——	——
2,000	——	——	——	——	——
3,500	——	——	——	——	——
4,500	——	——	——	——	——

*Remember: Total Revenue = Price x Quantity
            Total Profit = Total Revenue - Total Cost

Using the information from Question 1, and Figure 19-3, answer Questions 2-9.

2. The maximum amount of profit Fast can earn is: $ _____

3. Fast has total fixed costs of: $ _____

4. To maximize its *total revenue*, Fast should sell (check the correct response):

___ a.   1,000 units.

___ b.   2,000 units.

___ c.   3,500 units.

___ d.   4,000 units.

___ e.   more than 4,500 units.

5. Figure 19-3 indicates that Fast's demand curve is (check the correct response):

___ a.   horizontal.

___ b.   vertical.

___ c.   downward-sloping from left to right.

___ d.   upward-sloping from left to right.

Learning aid for use with

6. Fast's demand curve is (check the correct response):

   ___ a.   elastic.

   ___ b.   inelastic.

   ___ c.   unitary elastic.

   ___ d.   elastic up to 3,500 units and inelastic beyond 3,500 units.

   ___ e.   inelastic up to 3,500 units and elastic beyond 3,500 units.

7. Fast's *average* cost curve is (check the correct response):

   ___ a.   horizontal.

   ___ b.   U-shaped.

   ___ c.   vertical.

   ___ d.   upward-sloping from left to right.

8. Fast will *lose money* if it sells (check the correct response):

   ___ a.   less than 1,000 units.

   ___ b.   less than 4,500 units.

   ___ c.   more than 3,500 units.

   ___ d.   more than 4,500 units.

   ___ e.   both a and d are correct.

9. Fast will *break even* if it sells (check the correct response):

   ___ a.   1,000 units.

   ___ b.   2,000 units.

   ___ c.   3,500 units.

   ___ d.   4,500 units.

   ___ e.   both a and d are correct.

10.   To *maximize profit*, Fast should sell (check the correct response):

   ___ a.   1,000 units.

   ___ b.   2,000 units.

   ___ c.   3,500 units.

   ___ d.   4,500 units.

   ___ e.   more than 4,500 units.

Question for Discussion

Should a firm in monopolistic competition try to sell as many units as it can produce? Why or why not? State your assumptions.

Exercise 19-4

Using marginal analysis to set the most profitable price and quantity to produce

Introduction

Too many firms seem to ignore demand--depending almost blindly on cost-oriented pricing. A firm might operate quite profitably using cost-oriented pricing--but could it earn larger profits by charging a different price? The firm has no way of answering this question unless it also takes demand into consideration. When both costs and demand are known (or estimated), marginal analysis can be used to determine the most profitable price and the most profitable quantity to produce. Of course, in the short run the firm's objective may *not* be to maximize profit. In this case, marginal analysis can be used to show how much profit is "lost" when the firm pursues some other objective--such as maximizing sales.

This exercise uses the graphic approach to marginal analysis. You are asked to interpret—from a graph—the relationships among demand, price, quantity, average cost, marginal cost, and marginal revenue. (See pages 602-10 in the text.)

Assignment

Use Figure 19-4 on the next page to answer the following questions:

1. At what price would 184 units be sold? _____

2. How many units would be sold if the firm priced its product at $24? _____

3. At what output (quantity) _____ and price _____ would the average cost per unit be *minimized*?

4. At what output _____ and price _____ would the firm break even?

5. At what output _____ and price _____ would the firm maximize its *total revenue*?

6. At what output _____ and price _____ would the firm maximize its *total profit*?

7. What will the average profit per unit be when the firm maximizes its total profit? _____

8. What is the maximum amount of profit this firm can earn? _____

FIGURE 19-4

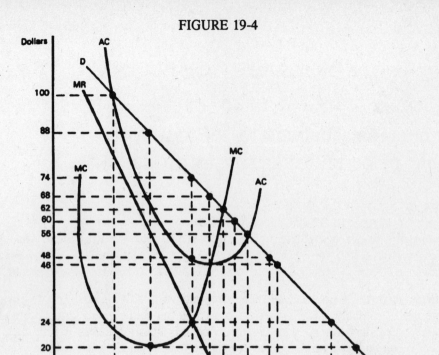

Question for Discussion

Why do so few firms use demand-oriented pricing? Is it an impossible task?

Learning aid for use with

Chapter 20

Planning and implementing quality marketing programs

What This Chapter Is About

Chapter 20 emphasizes that marketing strategy planning requires creative *blending* of all the ingredients of the marketing mix. And, eventually, a marketing manager must develop a time-related *plan* that spells out the implementation details for a strategy. Then, since most companies have more than one strategy, marketing managers should develop a whole marketing *program* which integrates the various plans.

You need an estimate of potential sales to know if a marketing plan will be profitable. So this chapter explains different methods for forecasting sales. You should become familiar with the different methods and their likely accuracy--because each has advantages *and* disadvantages. Some firms make several forecasts on the way to developing one final estimate of future sales.

Sales forecasting must consider not only market potential but also the firm's (and competitors') marketing plans--and how customers might respond to those plans.

Since Chapter 9, we have been discussing various aspects of the four Ps. The product classes and the product life cycle are integrating themes which have been running through these chapters. This chapter highlights these ideas. A product's class and stage in the life cycle can suggest some "typical" marketing mixes, but typical is not always desirable.

Chapter 20 also highlights the types of opportunities that are available in international marketing. The typical evolution of corporate involvement in international marketing is explained. It is noted that some corporations become so deeply involved with international marketing that they become "multinational corporations."

Following selection of a firm's marketing program, use of project scheduling and related techniques can help the implementation effort. Finally, we discuss ways to build quality into the implementation effort. Total quality management means more than offering customers products that don't have defects. Because marketing is dynamic, managers must seek ways to continually improve the marketing strategy and how it is implemented. Total quality management approaches--ranging from application of techniques such as fishbone diagrams and Pareto charts to empowerment and training of service employees--are proving to be important ways to implement quality marketing programs.

Important Terms

market potential, p. 627
sales forecast, p. 627
trend extension, p. 628
factor method, p. 629
factor, p. 629
time series, p. 633
leading series, p. 633
indices, p. 633
jury of executive opinion, p. 634
spreadsheet analysis, p. 639
exporting, p. 641
licensing, p. 642

contract manufacturing, p. 642
management contracting, p. 642
joint venturing, p. 642
wholly-owned subsidiary, p. 643
multinational corporations, p. 643
task method, p. 647
total quality management (TQM), p. 650
continuous improvement, p. 651
Pareto chart, p. 652
fishbone diagram, p. 652
empowerment, p. 654

True-False Questions

___ 1. A marketing strategy is a "big picture" of what a firm will do in some target market--while a marketing plan includes the time-related details for that strategy--and a marketing program is a combination of the firm's marketing plans.

___ 2. Market potential is an estimate of how much a whole market segment might buy.

___ 3. National economic forecasts available in business and government publications are often of limited value in forecasting the potential of a specific market segment.

___ 4. A major limitation of trend extension is that it assumes that conditions in the past will continue unchanged into the future.

___ 5. The factor method of sales forecasting tries to find a relation between a company's sales and some other factor which is readily available.

___ 6. A factor is a variable which shows the relation of some other variable to the item being forecasted.

___ 7. The main problem with the "buying power index" (BPI) is that it is based on just one factor--population.

___ 8. A leading series is a time series which, for some reason, changes in the opposite direction but ahead of the series to be forecasted.

___ 9. Indices are statistical combinations of several time series.

___ 10. "Trend-projecting" forecasting techniques should probably be supplemented by a "jury of executive opinion" or some other type of judgmental approach.

___ 11. Instead of relying heavily on salespeople to estimate customers' intentions, it may be desirable for a firm to use marketing research techniques such as surveys, panels, and market tests.

___ 12. Even if you don't know as much as you would like about potential customers' needs and attitudes, knowing how they would classify your product--in terms of the product classes--can give you a starting point in developing a marketing mix.

___ 13. When marketers fully understand the needs and attitudes of their target markets, they may be able to develop marketing mixes which are obviously superior to "competitive" mixes.

___ 14. Typically, marketing variables should change during a product's life cycle.

___ 15. A spreadsheet analysis is a useful tool for demonstrating how sales and profits change over a range of prices.

___ 16. When a manufacturer moves into exporting, it usually is primarily concerned with selling some of what the firm is currently producing to foreign markets.

___ 17. Licensing is a relatively easy--but risky--way to enter foreign markets.

___ 18. Management contracting--in international marketing--means turning over production to others, while retaining the marketing process.

___ 19. A domestic firm wishing to enter international marketing can use a joint venture--which simply involves entering into a partnership with a foreign firm.

___ 20. If a foreign market looked really promising, multinational corporations might set up a wholly-owned subsidiary--which is a separate firm owned by a parent company.

___ 21. A multinational company is one that earns over 30 percent of its total sales or profits by exporting domestic production to foreign markets.

___ 22. Finding the best marketing program requires some juggling among the various plans--comparing profitability versus resources needed and available.

___ 23. Budgeting for marketing expenditures as a percentage of either past or forecasted sales leads to larger marketing expenditures when business is good and sales are rising--and to reduced spending when business is poor.

___ 24. The most sensible approach to budgeting marketing expenditures is the "task method."

___ 25. Marketing program implementation efforts can be greatly aided by use of PERT--which stands for Product Evaluation and Rating Techniques.

___ 26. Total quality management works because everyone in the firm is concerned about quality.

___ 27. The commitment to constantly make things better one step at a time is called continuous improvement.

___ 28. In a Pareto chart, problem causes are ordered from least frequent to most frequent.

___ 29. The fishbone diagram is a visual aid that helps managers figure out why things go wrong.

1. c, p. 625	11. T, p. 634	21. F, p. 643
2. a, p. 627	12. T, p. 635	22. T, p. 645
3. c, p. 627	13. T, p. 636	23. T, p. 647
4. b, p. 628	14. T, pp. 637-638	24. T, pp. 647-648
5. d, p. 628	15. T, p. 639	25. T, p. 649
6. d, p. 629	16. T, p. 641	26. T, p. 650
7. d, p. 629-632	17. F, p. 642	27. T, p. 651
8. c, p. 633	18. F, p. 642	28. F, p. 652
9. c, p. 634	19. T, pp. 642-643	29. T, pp. 652-653
10. a, p. 634	20. T, p. 643	

Multiple-Choice Questions (Circle the correct response)

1. The main difference between a "strategy" and a "marketing plan" is:
    a. that a plan does not consider the firm's target market.
    b. that a plan includes several strategies.
    c. that time-related details are included in a plan.
    d. that resource commitments are made more clear in a strategy.
    e. There is no difference.

2. As defined in the text, market potential is:
    a. what a market segment might buy (from all suppliers).
    b. how much a firm can hope to sell to a market segment.
    c. how much the firm sold to a market segment in the last year.
    d. the size of national income for the coming year.

3. A good marketing manager knows that:
    a. market potential is an estimate of how much a firm can hope to sell to a particular market segment.
    b. sales forecasts should be developed BEFORE marketing strategies are planned.
    c. a firm's sales forecast probably will be less than the estimated market potential.
    d. sales forecasts are estimates of what a whole market segment might buy.
    e. All of the above are true.

4. You have been asked to develop a sales forecast for one of your company's major products. What would be the most logical *starting point?*
    a. Determine why the company's sales fluctuate the way they do.
    b. Consider the prospects for the economy as a whole.
    c. Determine your industry's prospects for the near future.
    d. Analyze regional sales for this product for last year.
    e. Perform marketing research into consumer buying habits.

5. The trend-extension method often can be useful for forecasting annual sales, but it depends upon the assumption that:
   a. the forecast is for a new product.
   b. sales during the coming period will be about the same as the previous period.
   c. there will be big changes in market conditions.
   d. the general growth (or decline) which has been seen in the past will continue in the future.
   e. the firm will continue to improve its marketing mixes.

6. *Sales & Marketing Management* magazine's "Buying Power Index" is based on:
   a. each market's share of the total Canadian population.
   b. each market's share of the total income in Canada.
   c. each market's share of the total retail sales in Canada.
   d. All of the above.
   e. Only a and b above.

7. Given the complexity of buyer behavior, sales forecasts for established products are likely to prove more accurate if based on:
   a. the opinion of the sales staff.
   b. trend extension.
   c. a single factor.
   d. several factors.

8. Sales forecasters often try to find business indicators which change before sales and thus will help predict future sales. These indicators are called:
   a. correlation coefficients.
   b. time series.
   c. leading series.
   d. trend extenders.
   e. input-output measures.

9. Palladin Specialist, Inc. has developed a new product about which it is quite excited. Which of the following sales forecasting methods would be *least appropriate*?
   a. Market tests
   b. Sales force estimates
   c. Trend extension
   d. Jury of executive opinion
   e. A survey of customers

10. Which of the following sales forecasting techniques would be most useful for the marketing manager of an business products manufacturer facing intense competition?
    a. Sales force estimates
    b. Jury of executive opinion
    c. Use of a national economic forecast
    d. Trend extension of past sales
    e. Multiple-factor method

11. A company which wants to *objectively* estimate the reaction of customers to possible changes in its marketing mix should use:
   a. trend extension.
   b. jury of executive opinion.
   c. sales force estimates.
   d. surveys, panels, and market tests.
   e. None of the above.

12. Developing a "marketing plan":
   a. means selecting a target market and developing a marketing mix.
   b. involves nothing more than assembling the four Ps better than your competitors.
   c. is easy--and profits are virtually guaranteed--provided that a firm fully understands the needs and attitudes of its target market.
   d. All of the above are true statements.
   e. None of the above is a true statement.

13. A manufacturer of a consumer product is trying to establish brand recognition and preference in monopolistic competition. The firm places considerable emphasis on channel development and is becoming somewhat less selective in its choice of middlemen. Promotion is both informative and persuasive--as the firm is seeking to increase both primary and selective demand. Prices in the industry are competitive--but there has been little price-cutting to date. What stage of the product life cycle is this firm's situation characteristic of?
   a. Market introduction
   b. Market growth
   c. Market maturity
   d. Sales decline

14. When a business firm in one country sells a firm in another country the right to use some process, trademark, or patent for a fee or royalty--this practice is called:
   a. exporting.
   b. contract manufacturing.
   c. joint ventures.
   d. licensing.
   e. management contracting.

15. To minimize its own risks, the Stampede Petroleum Corp. of Calgary, Alberta operates a South American oil refinery which is wholly owned by residents of that country. Stampede is engaged in an activity known as:
   a. management contracting.
   b. a joint venture.
   c. exporting.
   d. licensing.
   e. contract manufacturing.

16. A multinational corporation:
   a. is one which sells the right to use some process, trademark, patent, or other right for a fee or royalty to foreign firms.
   b. is a worldwide enterprise which makes major decisions on a global basis.
   c. is any firm which earns over 30 percent of its sales and profits in foreign markets.
   d. All of the above are true statements.

Learning aid for use with

17. A marketing program can be best described as consisting of several:
    a. marketing plans.
    b. advertising campaigns.
    c. marketing mixes.
    d. operational decisions.
    e. target markets.

18. Which of the following is the most sensible approach to budgeting for marketing programs?
    a. Budget expenditures as a percentage of either past or forecasted sales.
    b. Set aside all uncommitted sales revenue--perhaps including budgeted profits.
    c. Base the budget on the amount required to reach predetermined objectives.
    d. Match expenditures with competitors.
    e. Set the budget at a certain number of cents or dollars per sales unit--using the past year or estimated year ahead as a base for comparison.

19. Flow-charting techniques such as CPM and PERT:
    a. require that all marketing activities must be done in sequence.
    b. do not indicate how long a project will actually take to complete.
    c. identify the tasks which must be performed to achieve predetermined objectives.
    d. require complex mathematical tools and analysis.

20. Total quality management:
    a. requires that everyone in the organization be concerned with improving quality.
    b. means more than just using statistical controls to reduce manufacturing defects.
    c. views the cost of lost customers as an important result of quality problems.
    d. applies to service producers as well as manufacturers.
    e. all of the above are correct.

21. Using total quality management to improve the implementation of a marketing program is likely to include:
    a. the use of Pareto charts to determine the critical path for scheduling marketing activities.
    b. the use of fishbone diagrams to show which problems are most important.
    c. an emphasis on treating routine customer problems and unusual ones in the same way--because every problem is equally important.
    d. training and empowerment of employees to identify and solve customer problems.
    e. all of the above are correct.

Answers to Multiple-Choice Questions

1. c, p. 625	8. c, p. 633	15. a, p. 642
2. a, p. 627	9. c, p. 634	16. b, p. 643
3. c, p. 627	10. a, p. 634	17. a, p. 644
4. b, p. 628	11. d, p. 634	18. c, pp. 646-647
5. d, p. 628	12. e, pp. 635-636	19. c, p. 649
6. d, p. 629	13. b, p. 638	20. e, pp. 650-654
7. d, p. 629	14. d, p. 642	21. d, pp. 650-654

Exercise 20-1

Using the "Survey of Buying Power" to estimate market and sales potential

Introduction

All marketers are faced with the ongoing problem of forecasting market and sales potentials. Forecasting is as much an art as it is a science, and there are many different forecasting methods that can be used. Regardless of which method is used, the forecast should be based on data that is accurate, reliable, and up to date.

Many forecasters rely very heavily on market data published in *Sales and Marketing Management's* annual "Survey of Buying Power." The "Survey" provides data on three important market characteristics—population, "Effective Buying Income," and retail sales. Both total and household population are given. "Effective Buying Income" (comparable to disposable income) is broken down into five income groups, and retail sales are shown for nine categories. Further, the data is broken down geographically according to Census Metropolitan Areas, counties, and cities.

While there is usually a lengthy time lag in the publication of Canadian census data, the "Survey of Buying Power" is carefully updated and published each year. Moreover, "Survey" data has been shown to correlate very highly with the census data on which it is based. A disadvantage, however, is that "Survey" data, like all published data, may not be available in the exact form a particular firm desires—and thus may not be directly applicable. Most firms find it necessary to modify the data, or supplement it with other data—before making their forecasts.

Probably the most widely used aspect of the "Survey" is the "Buying Power Index" (BPI), a weighted index of three variables—population, Effective Buying Income, and retail sales—which measures a market's ability to buy and expresses it as a percentage of the total Canadian potential. The BPI is calculated by giving a weight of 5 to the market's percent of the Canadian Effective Buying Income, a weight of 3 to its percent of Canadian retail sales, and a weight of 2 to its percent of the Canadian population. The sum of these weighted percents is then divided by 10 to arrive at the BPI.

For example, suppose Anytown, Canada, had about 5 percent of the total Canadian Effective Buying Income, about 4 percent of Canadian retail sales, and about 1 percent of the Canadian population. Then the BPI for Anytown would be:

$$\frac{5\,(5) + 3\,(4) + 2\,(1)}{19} = 3.9$$

Thus Anytown's market potential, relative to the Canadian, in total, would be 3.9 percent. So if Canadians were expected to buy $10,000,000 worth of "widgets" during the coming year, the population of Anytown might be expected to buy 3.9 percent x $10,000,000 or $390,000 worth of widgets.

FIGURE 20-1 Sample Tables from Sales and Marketing Management's "Survey of Buying Power"

Ont. (cont.) S&MM ESTIMATES County City	Metro Area Code	POPULATION 12/31/83 Total Pop (thousands)	% Of Canada	House-holds (thousands)	% Of Canada	RETAIL SALES BY STORE GROUP—1983 Total Retail Sales ($000)	% Of Canada	Food ($000)	Eating & Drinking Places ($000)	General Mdse. ($000)	Apparel & Accessories ($000)	Furniture/ Furnish./ Appliance ($000)	Auto-motive ($000)	Gas Stations ($000)	Hard-ware ($000)	Drug ($000)	SALES/ ADVERTISING INDEXES Sales Activity	Buying Power	Quality
Essex	536	300.1	1.2316	113.8	1.2335	1,418,458	1.4067	398,634	159,510	202,832	85,691	82,528	309,033	112,765	8,424	62,326	114	1.2462	104
▲Windsor		193.4	.7731	69.6	.7544	1,339,481	1.1642	333,551	137,754	191,516	77,537	70,083	241,050	89,676	4,711	50,853	151	.8814	114
Frontenac	510	111.2	.4446	43.2	.4482	685,437	.5957	166,795	47,583	101,645	35,431	28,669	119,484	63,773	2,116	24,881	134	.5285	119
△Kingston		51.1	.2043	21.6	.2341	382,803	.3327	94,889	40,291	42,745	31,962	20,704	53,198	25,338	1,402	15,137	163	.2868	140
Glengarry		19.7	.0787	6.7	.0726	63,849	.0555	14,873	7,596	2,759	2,638	1,421	16,407	7,272	814	539	71	.0818	104
Grenville		26.5	.1060	9.5	.1030	71,924	.0625	18,465	6,578	5,981	2,667	4,062	13,903	8,557	835	2,341	59	.0713	67
Grey		76.8	.3070	29.0	.3143	420,709	.3657	100,497	28,492	44,992	19,984	21,699	92,445	38,627	6,466	17,374	119	.3195	104
Haldimand-Norfolk Reg. Mun.		91.4	.2661	33.0	.2577	509,998	.4432	128,135	38,544	30,792	21,902	22,081	141,078	39,016	6,021	16,521	121	.3974	109
Haliburton		11.4	.0456	4.7	.0509	82,748	.0720	19,394	1,044	11,606	2,318	2,478	15,083	11,182	362	4,346	158	.0604	132
Halton Reg. Mun.	532	269.3	1.0766	92.5	1.0026	1,579,265	1.3726	362,643	130,369	145,276	75,429	54,025	407,479	126,010	8,742	79,113	127	1.4708	137
Burlington		116.5	.4737	41.7	.4520	791,540	.6879	194,872	57,568	103,667	42,142	23,223	189,115	57,708	3,639	38,677	145	.6768	143
Halton Hills		36.9	.1475	13.0	.1409	193,208	.1679	41,129	22,640	9,454	8,491	8,083	56,534	11,754	1,315	9,229	114	.1954	132
Milton		30.3	.1211	9.9	.1073	103,654	.0901	20,520	10,332	1,965	4,455	1,694	33,417	10,074	299	4,468	74	.1435	118
Oakville		82.5	.3298	27.9	.3024	490,963	.4267	106,122	39,829	30,190	20,341	21,025	128,413	46,474	3,489	26,739	129	.4542	130
Hamilton-Wentworth Reg. Mun.	507	424.3	1.6962	162.1	1.7569	1,942,490	1.6883	527,029	159,894	316,676	83,515	85,713	285,926	145,322	10,099	73,117	100	1.6874	99
▲Hamilton		301.9	1.2069	117.5	1.2735	1,672,003	1.4532	410,702	134,431	297,368	76,920	79,405	261,643	120,711	7,984	59,563	120	1.2547	104
Stoney Creek		37.6	.1503	12.3	.1333	120,543	.1048	44,764	17,802	2,201	2,163	2,140	24,030	10,871	335	4,210	70	.1251	83
Hastings		111.4	.4453	41.8	.4531	474,035	.4120	111,036	33,231	52,537	20,292	17,290	115,539	38,634	2,781	16,444	93	.4003	90
Belleville		36.2	.1447	13.4	.1474	194,722	.1692	44,086	14,393	21,236	11,251	10,645	46,094	9,574	1,043	7,776	117	.1378	95
Huron		57.8	.2311	20.7	.2243	331,063	.2877	72,300	21,013	25,255	12,416	12,814	97,952	20,233	4,234	9,198	124	.2464	107
Kenora Terr. Dist.		53.6	.2342	22.0	.2383	213,516	.1854	50,406	13,511	28,894	6,179	4,542	26,686	18,380	1,448	4,643	73	.2381	94
Kent		105.9	.4233	39.1	.4238	520,110	.4520	123,909	40,547	51,971	24,983	28,252	109,644	48,504	3,157	29,794	107	.4510	107
Lambton	525	41.9	.1675	13.4	.1452	273,038	.2373	64,822	27,103	41,736	17,061	15,276	50,684	16,494	1,040	16,276	142	.1851	111
Chatham		134.2	.5365	50.0	.5419	390,969	.3398	95,196	33,441	56,187	18,551	15,544	77,519	25,903	2,299	13,435	63	.4740	88
△Sarnia		34.3	.2179	21.1	.2287	239,356	.2080	57,717	16,638	36,299	12,937	12,208	54,360	9,971	933	6,335	95	.2208	101
Lanark		50.6	.2023	18.6	.2016	144,131	.1253	28,723	8,399	13,944	5,925	4,140	37,144	13,475	1,738	4,787	62	.1244	67
Leeds		53.7	.2147	20.6	.2233	172,201	.1497	33,291	14,900	17,180	5,389	5,964	28,042	17,816	1,629	6,275	70	.1645	78
Lennox & Addington		33.7	.1347	11.9	.1290	94,751	.0823	24,259	7,544	8,097	3,713	2,995	18,299	14,569	932	3,576	61	.1340	99
Manitoulin Terr. Dist.		11.0	.0440	4.0	.0433	59,712	.0519	9,186	2,441	12,153	629	1,743	12,454	6,485	1,316	2,915	139	.0420	95
Middlesex	512	326.0	1.3032	130.1	1.4101	2,064,090	1.8114	517,271	198,499	363,093	100,620	77,370	381,133	146,023	8,716	55,180	139	1.7211	132
▲London		264.7	1.0587	106.4	1.1534	1,902,999	1.6539	476,505	190,174	287,330	97,164	71,471	341,365	130,745	6,593	46,525	156	1.4552	138
Muskoka Dist. Mun.		40.2	.1607	15.7	.1702	339,885	.2953	94,034	33,571	25,482	12,520	18,079	54,475	40,012	3,721	13,236	104	.2195	137
Niagara Reg. Mun.	522	370.2	1.4799	138.9	1.5055	1,451,716	1.2617	374,984	152,510	173,902	74,486	57,704	262,635	102,019	6,758	49,903	85	1.3996	95
Fort Erie		23.1	.1003	11.7	.1268	75,903	.0660	20,404	14,153	3,329	2,063	3,468	12,788	4,953	458	3,753	66	.0980	98
▲Niagara Falls		72.6	.2902	25.7	.2786	321,949	.2798	81,151	55,735	28,485	12,939	12,384	50,294	21,576	1,229	15,076	96	.2617	90

FIGURE 20-1 (concluded)

Port Colborne	19.6	.0784	7.6	.0824	91,094	.0792	30,622	7,196	8,087	4,247	3,172	16,364	6,409	438	3,447	101	.0760	97
St. Catharines	127.1	.5081	47.4	.5137	631,832	.5491	162,426	44,322	112,818	42,258	23,891	111,330	41,873	2,694	13,065	108	.5267	104
Welland	47.8	.1911	16.5	.1788	224,399	.1950	57,613	15,671	15,102	11,376	11,054	50,373	19,851	372	8,685	102	.1673	88
Nipissing Terr. Dist. .515	50.0	.3198	28.9	.3132	403,489	.3507	97,419	41,019	56,252	17,203	15,003	76,199	36,731	2,526	10,277	110	.3110	97
△North Bay	50.9	.2035	16.5	.1788	292,358	.2541	72,235	25,737	46,624	12,328	12,079	54,176	23,922	1,849	7,356	125	.1987	96
Northumberland	67.6	.2702	24.8	.2648	349,402	.2037	90,192	29,744	27,656	12,925	14,737	60,666	50,739	3,565	7,825	112	.3282	121
Ottawa-Carleton Reg. Mun. .517	570.1	2.2791	230.4	2.4972	2,016,896	2.4462	687,128	275,594	500,986	137,177	104,451	435,737	148,777	19,330	87,298	107	2.0948	127
△Ottawa	301.0	1.2033	126.5	1.3711	2,272,756	1.9753	511,759	237,034	411,687	132,715	88,993	371,711	88,213	8,790	64,370	164	1.4924	124
Oxford	80.2	.3526	31.2	.3382	444,936	.3867	98,615	32,197	48,698	18,077	21,104	126,887	42,351	3,648	10,961	110	.3693	105
Woodstock	26.0	.1039	8.9	.0965	218,878	.1902	56,725	14,441	24,941	10,665	8,797	57,245	15,698	1,376	6,026	183	.1408	134
Perry Sound Terr. Dist.	34.6	.1383	13.1	.1419	134,140	.1166	32,799	9,298	8,470	2,920	3,713	28,518	19,929	1,818	3,237	84	.1051	76
Peel Reg. Mun. .532	535.7	2.1415	172.6	1.8708	2,381,200	2.0906	642,093	240,536	148,527	79,997	88,695	516,864	242,406	13,135	110,550	97	2.2751	106
Brampton	171.4	.6852	53.4	.5788	784,796	.6821	213,018	49,388	57,286	31,374	27,169	182,158	84,029	4,013	36,896	100	.7489	109
Caledon	34.9	.1395	10.1	.1095	120,431	.1047	37,922	9,855	6,319	2,642	3,292	23,603	10,692	443	7,753	75	.1236	89
Mississauga	328.9	1.3148	109.1	1.1825	1,475,973	1.2828	391,153	181,293	84,922	45,981	58,434	311,107	145,685	8,679	65,901	98	1.4022	107
Perth	68.7	.2746	23.0	.2709	284,091	.2444	65,325	24,196	33,239	16,549	13,737	15,292	34,725	2,437	9,934	90	.2426	84
Stratford	28.3	.1131	10.5	.1138	184,904	.1607	57,569	16,240	26,761	10,518	7,623	8,475	18,537	1,206	7,000	142	.1252	111
Peterborough .518	104.7	.4186	46.6	.4401	694,043	.6032	173,517	57,736	98,159	31,483	31,685	123,642	50,641	3,349	19,725	144	.5954	139
△Peterborough	61.4	.2455	23.2	.2515	555,573	.4829	145,917	34,376	91,320	30,115	26,694	97,438	27,116	3,019	16,031	197	.3401	99
Prescott	20.3	.1211	18.4	.1127	128,195	.1114	29,099	14,144	14,637	8,634	5,118	23,238	13,239	1,664	1,761	92	.1186	91
Prince Edward	22.7	.0908	6.4	.0911	84,489	.0735	24,014	4,690	4,963	2,836	2,010	23,981	8,079	810	1,971	81	.0927	91
Rainy River Terr. Dist.	23.6	.0943	6.7	.0943	76,555	.0646	20,940	5,999	6,302	3,620	3,403	15,295	6,228	515	2,576	7?	.0944	7??
Renfrew .517	89.5	.3578	32.0	.3440	546,638	.4751	141,861	22,844	58,324	27,196	18,367	137,018	81,247	4,194	22,400	13?	.4163	116
Russell	23.7	.0947	7.5	.0813	99,535	.0787	19,946	7,202	13,288	2,138	5,249	27,437	5,247	401	844	8..	.0718	76
Simcoe	233.7	.9343	83.0	.9096	1,334,843	1.1619	322,903	126,696	146,437	44,269	54,311	281,021	104,541	16,739	49,659	121	1.0412	111
Barrie	41.1	.1643	13.7	.1485	460,161	.3999	101,248	29,649	34,793	16,051	19,398	128,126	28,146	3,255	15,302	2?3	.2431	148
Orillia	25.1	.1003	8.8	.0954	226,136	.1965	60,811	19,290	34,296	9,471	11,015	41,696	14,488	1,840	9,284	1?6	.1320	132
Stormont	63.8	.2550	23.6	.2558	339,233	.2948	86,664	28,267	41,448	16,029	15,804	68,335	27,695	849	11,181	116	.2509	9?
Cornwall	47.0	.1879	16.0	.1734	307,871	.2676	75,472	24,798	40,008	15,912	14,680	54,939	22,714	700	10,724	141	.1950	164
Sudbury Reg. Mun. .529	160.4	.6412	54.4	.6113	683,400	.5940	192,341	57,954	76,888	36,840	27,356	129,437	48,724	3,610	17,568	93	.5832	81
△Sudbury	91.2	.3646	32.8	.3555	580,376	.5044	163,295	45,005	73,744	33,863	22,705	111,073	36,089	2,626	14,063	1?8	.5666	159
Sudbury Terr. Dist.	26.4	.1054	9.8	.0975	64,058	.0557	20,844	4,659	9,323	1,613	1,008	4,282	16,127	753	1,959	?3	.0697	64
Thunder Bay Terr. Dist. .531	156.5	.4256	57.7	.4254	743,600	.6636	199,611	61,974	119,482	26,324	20,837	128,391	63,520	3,129	22,325	106	.6300	101
△Thunder Bay	113.3	.4329	42.3	.4585	613,634	.5333	172,702	41,332	94,412	23,545	17,072	104,812	39,896	2,638	28,920	18	.4913	108
Timiskaming Terr. Dist.	42.1	.1683	15.7	.1702	177,045	.1539	54,119	14,700	13,478	9,610	5,633	33,451	16,843	1,894	5,820	91	.1356	81
Toronto Met. Mun. .532	2,127.9	8.5065	835.4	9.0545	9,595,167	8.3396	2,318,126	1,114,123	1,286,961	539,451	375,277	1,814,436	590,879	40,434	389,543	98	8.7261	163
△Toronto	586.3	2.3438	238.9	2.5893	3,857,134	3.352	857,195	600,366	655,855	279,771	180,927	567,063	142,202	16,598	135,748	143	2.8306	121
Victoria	50.2	.2007	19.3	.2092	347,723	.3022	98,090	26,191	22,164	12,292	17,195	67,201	28,994	4,440	12,058	151	.2482	124
Waterloo Reg. Mun. .611	321.3	1.2844	118.3	1.2822	2,029,174	1.7637	438,500	162,904	359,790	99,971	87,973	464,235	140,873	9,233	49,238	137	1.6812	129
△Cambridge	90.8	.3230	28.0	.3033	437,437	.3807	109,814	44,032	23,529	18,163	18,205	112,404	32,071	2,073	13,113	118	.2769	117
△Kitchener	149.2	.5964	56.0	.4070	1,087,930	.9455	200,743	77,116	229,443	67,177	51,303	235,127	78,919	2,575	26,884	159	.8237	138
Waterloo	49.0	.1959	20.6	.2233	332,891	.2893	94,049	28,946	47,548	11,874	11,509	65,957	21,333	2,033	8,250	148	.2979	132
Wellington .566	136.7	.5465	49.6	.5376	626,806	.5447	142,009	50,267	75,181	32,134	27,139	137,505	44,591	3,492	29,316	100	.6448	102
△Guelph	78.5	.3138	28.3	.3067	462,174	.4017	118,390	32,606	59,305	28,973	21,629	98,734	32,367	1,184	20,909	128	.3569	114

It should be noted that there is nothing sacred or necessarily valid about the weights used to calculate the BPI. Many firms tailor the index to their own needs by applying a different set of weights or adding additional variables to the index based on their past experience. A manufacturer of snowmobiles, for example, might add a weather variable, such as average inches of snowfall, to the BPI. Another pitfall in applying the BPI is that because it is broadly based, the BPI is said to be most useful for "mass products sold at popular prices." Thus, for more expensive products, the BPI may need to be modified by taking additional buying factors into account.

Assignment

The purpose of this exercise is to familiarize you with the Buying Power Index and show you its use in forecasting market and sales potentials. Answer each of the following questions and show your work in the space provided.

1. Suppose that Yourtown, Canada, accounts for 5 percent of the Canadian population, 6 percent of the nation's Effective Buying Income, and 3 percent of Canadian retail sales. Calculate Yourtown's "Buying Power Index."

2. Reading from Figure 20-1, what is the Buying Power Index for:
   a. the city of Toronto: _____

   b. Metro Toronto area: _____

3. a. About 700,000 electric toasters are sold in Canada each year. Based on the Buying Power Index, estimate the number of toasters that are sold in the Toronto metropolitan area each year.

   b. Assume that your firm has captured a 20 percent share of the electric toaster market. About how many electric toasters should your firm sell in the Toronto metropolitan area?

   c. Suppose your firm sold 1,000 electric toasters last year in the Metro Toronto area. Considering your answer to part (b) above, what does this fact indicate?

4. Assume that a firm with annual sales of $2,000,000 sells its products only in the Metro Toronto area. In order to allocate its sales force to different cities within the Metro Toronto area, the firm's sales manager wants to know what volume of sales the firm can expect in each city. Use the BPI to estimate the firm's sales volume in dollars for the city of Toronto only. (Hint: Although the percentages reflected in the BPI are relevant for all of Canada—not just the Toronto area—the relative positions of the different cities within this area remain the same.) Explain your answer.

5. Suppose a national manufacturer of expensive mink coats wanted to estimate its sales potential in the Metro Toronto area. Would the BPI be useful for this purpose? Why or why not?

Question for Discussion

Would the "Survey of Buying Power," data be more useful to "mass marketers" or "target marketers"? Why?

Learning aid for use with

Exercise 20-2

Adjusting marketing strategies over the product life cycle

Introduction

A marketing manager must take a dynamic approach to marketing strategy planning. Markets are continually changing--and today's successful strategy may be tomorrow's failure. Competitive advantages are often achieved and maintained by firms who are best able to anticipate and respond positively to changes in their marketing environment. Some changes may be completely unpredictable, of course--but other changes may be somewhat predictable and should be planned for in advance. Otherwise, by the time the planner realizes that some important changes have taken place, it may be too late to adjust an existing strategy or, if necessary, to plan a new strategy.

Among the changes that are more predictable—and which should be considered when developing marketing plans—are the typical changes in marketing mix variables which are often made over the course of a product life cycle. Exhibit 20-6 on page 638 of the text shows some of these typical changes.

Assignment

This exercise stresses how marketing strategies may need to be adjusted over the product life cycle. Read the following case and follow the instructions.

INNOTECH FOOD PROCESSOR

Innotech, Inc. manufactures a broad line of electric equipment for industrial buyers. Its sales and profits have stopped growing in recent years--and the firm's top executives are anxious to diversify into the consumer products market. However, they do not want to enter a new market with just another "me too" product. Instead, they hope to discover a real "breakthrough opportunity"--an unsatisfied market with large profit potential.

For several years, Innotech's marketing research and product planning departments have been working together in search of an innovative new product for the firm's entry into the consumer market. Now, the top executives believe that they have finally found such a product. The new product is a "freeze-dry unit" for foods. The unit makes it easy for consumers to make instant versions of just about any food-- just as freeze-dried coffee makes great instant coffee. The unit can process almost any type of food (ranging from eggs and hamburger to oatmeal, rice, and fruits) which are available at any supermarket. It has the capacity to cook up to two-pound batches of a food product and convert it to freeze-dried "pellets." Whenever the consumer is ready, the freeze-dried pellets can be put in a microwave oven with water and heated to produce fresh-tasting soups, sauces, gravy, drinks--and hundreds of other items which

Figure 20-2
Planned Changes in Marketing Strategy for Innotech
Over the Course of Its Product Life Cycle

Item	Market Introduction Stage
Target Market Dimensions	
Nature of Competition	
Product	
Place	
Promotion	
Price	

Learning aid for use with

Market Growth Stage	Market Maturity Stage

are otherwise time consuming to cook in small quantities. With the unit, a gourmet cook would be able to make fancy sauces on an impulse, an office worker could create a favorite type of homemade soup to take to work without the mess, and busy singles could keep pellets ready for when there's no time to go to the store or cook something from scratch. At first the new product idea seemed strange--perhaps even hard to believe--but in tests with consumers it has generated a very favorable response. Moreover, the freeze-dry unit is inexpensive and easy-to-operate, and it is expected to retail for about $100.

Innotech's marketing manager believes the new product will appeal to convenience-oriented families--and also health-conscious people who want to make their own "instant" foods but with more nutritious ingredients and without the preservatives typically found in packages at the store. The marketing manager feels the product has almost unlimited potential--citing the rapid growth of prepared and instant foods and the wide use of microwave ovens. Further, the firm's research and development staff is sure that it will take any potential competitors at least two years to introduce a similar product.

The electric freeze-dry unit is really a revolutionary new concept--and will probably require a major promotion effort to gain consumer acceptance. Moreover, Innotech has no established channels of distribution in the consumer products market--and middlemen may be reluctant to handle an unproven product which lacks a well-known brand name. Also, the firm is not sure what pricing policies to adopt, because it has no previous experience in the consumer products market.

To further complicate the strategy planning efforts, Innotech's marketing manager recognizes that the marketing strategy will need to be modified over time--as the new product passes through the various stages of its life cycle. So that the firm will be in a position to adjust quickly to changing market conditions, the president has asked the marketing manager for an overview of future marketing strategies for the freeze-dry unit--as well as the beginning strategy.

1.   Assume the role of marketing manager for Innotech, Inc. and fill in Figure 20-2 to show how your marketing strategy for the electric freeze-dry unit would vary over the stages of its product life cycle. (See Exhibit 20-6 on page 638 of the text for some general ideas about what you might include in your answers.) Be specific.

Question for Discussion

What kind of product will the "freeze-dry" unit be--that is, what product class--and what type of marketing mix would be typical for such a product? Are there any other factors that should be taken into account in planning the marketing mix for this product?

Exercise 20-3

Total quality management

Introduction

Marketing strategy planning is important to the success of every firm. Yet, a firm that doesn't do a good job implementing its strategy is likely to find itself losing customers and profits.

Many firms are finding that *total quality management* approaches can help them not just with reducing defects in production but also in implementing all aspects of a marketing program. As discussed in the text, total quality management approaches can be adapted to firms of any size and for all classes of products.

There are many technical details on how to use statistical techniques as part of a total quality management process. In the text, you get an introduction to two of these—fishbone diagrams and Pareto charts. But, even more than the techniques is the basic philosophy that motivates total quality management. In that regard, learning about and understanding the basic ideas and concepts (see pages 649-55) of total quality management is an important first step in using the approaches.

The purpose of this exercise is to give you practice analyzing different marketing problems from a total quality management perspective.

Assignment

In each of the following situations, a firm is having difficulty in reliably satisfying customer needs. In each situation, identify the most important problem (or problems) and make recommendations for how the firm can improve the implementation of its marketing plan. Be specific in relating your diagnosis and recommendations to the quality management concepts and techniques discussed in the text. The first question is answered for you as an example.

1. Security Bank is interested in shifting its emphasis from commercial lending to lending to consumers--especially in the area of residential mortgages. The bank has the "back office" capacity to handle the business and, with interests rates coming down, there is growing demand for new mortgages. Security's ad agency developed an effective series of radio and TV ads, and the bank president was pleased to learn that the new thrust seemed to be working. At the end of two months, mortgage applications were up 300 percent over the same period the year before. It wasn't long, however, before there were signs of trouble. Several customers complained about the slow turn-around time for loan approvals and the problems the delays had caused them. When the president checked on the matter, she found that there were many such cases--and she was even more surprised to find that the number of loans actually completed had decreased relative to the previous year. When she asked the head of the loan processing group for an explanation, he said "It's no one single bottleneck. Sometimes the appraisal is late coming in.

Other times there's some problem with the credit report or customers haven't completed the forms correctly. Sometimes the title insurance company holds us up on some detail. So, it's hard to say." The bank president said, "Well, I'm not happy about it. We'll just have to work harder until we can catch up. In the meantime, I hope it doesn't hurt our reputation."

a) Problem: *Neither the head of the loan processing group nor the president are coming to grips with the problem. They are not actively looking for ways to make continuous improvements. To make real improvements and do a better job of meeting customer needs, they will need to sort out the causes and effects for the things that have gone wrong (the delays in processing.) Some of the delays are interrelated because parts of the process depend on completion of work by other people--the applicants, title company, appraisers.*

b) Solution: *Security can begin to get a handle on the delays by developing a simple fishbone diagram to understand which parts of the system are causing delays. Then after some simple data collection, a Pareto Chart would help to identify which problems should be attacked first--for example, improving the application forms so consumers don't have trouble filling them out, and developing closer coordination with the appraisers and title insurance companies. Satisfying the customer is--or at least should be--important to them too.*

2. Wally Kuralt's objective is to build a profitable chain of book stores, so he's pleased that a literary critic for a local paper has written a very favorable review of the selection of books in his first store. However, while Wally was out to lunch a young woman approached the checkout counter at the store and told the sales clerk, "I don't have my receipt with me, but I bought this book here yesterday and, as you can see, one whole section is just blank pages. I've checked the shelf and the other two copies have the same problem. I'd like my money back." The clerk replied, "I'm very sorry for the problem, but it's store policy that only the manager can approve a refund without a receipt--and he's on his lunch break. Can you come back in a couple of hours?" The irritated customer replied, "I came here on my lunch break just to get this straight." The clerk responds, "I really regret the inconvenience. Would it be helpful if I had the manager call you when he comes back?"

a) Problem:

b) Solution:

3. Panther Automobile Co. has a reputation for producing elegant—but notoriously unreliable—sports sedans. One writer in the automotive press suggested that there was nothing finer than a Sunday afternoon spin in a Panther—as long as you could afford a "chase car" to follow behind with a mechanic and spare parts. In the face of aggressive new competition from Japanese and German manufacturers of luxury sedans, Panther has been losing market share. To counter this trend, Nigel Althorpe, Panther's director of marketing, announces to a convention of Panther dealers that the marketing mix will be adjusted. "For the new model year, leather upholstery and lambswool carpets

will no longer be extra-cost options, but instead will be included in the base price of the car. We have also increased the horsepower of the engine and made a number of other changes that will make it clear to customers that we have improved the quality of our cars."

a) Problem:

b) Solution:

4. The University cashier's office is open from 8 until 5 every day and students can come to pay their tuition and fees, take care of campus parking tickets, get a bus pass, sign up to rent a dorm room, and handle just about everything else that involves money. There are two service windows that work on a "first come, first served" basis and most of the time students only need to wait in line a few minutes to get help. However, sometimes there are long delays. As one student recently complained, "All I wanted to do was pay a fine for a lost library book, and it took nearly an hour because the computer had accidently unenrolled the guy in front of me in line--and they couldn't get it straight. The line at the other window wasn't moving either--they couldn't figure out how much to refund a student who had to drop out of school because of an accident. There must have been twenty people behind me in the line."

a) Problem:

b) Solution:

5. Pine Knoll is a well known summer camp for girls. Many campers return year after year and most of the promotion is handled by direct mail responses to word-of-mouth referrals. The camp has a unique coastal location and special boating facilities, and its superior reputation means that each year the camp has a waiting list. The camp has been owned by Richard Iverson's family for three generations. Prices at Pine Knoll have always been set by the Iverson family by "what seems fair," and there has never been any customer resistance to price raises. This summer Mr.

Iverson has received two notes and one phone call from parents complaining that the college and high-school age counselors don't seem quite as involved with the campers. When asked for specifics, parents find it hard to define their complaints, but one notes: "Nowadays, they all seem to bring cars with them to Pine Knoll, and as soon as they have time off, they're out of there." When Mr. Iverson asked the head counselor, Catherine Swaim, about the parents' complaint, Swaim responded, "That's true. A lot of them have boyfriends back in the city and they're commuting back to see them every chance they get. I guess we've just got a bad crop this year. Next year we'll get a better group of counselors--and be back to the old Pine Knoll!"

a) Problem:

b) Solution:

6.   Roller-King manufactures recreational roller skates. Its new in-line design has turned out to be much more popular than expected--and demand far exceeds production capacity. The only glitch is that there have been some problems with the wheels on some of the skates; after a short period of use the bearings in the wheel break and skates don't roll properly. The chief of production wants to change to a new assembly procedure that will eliminate the problem altogether, but he acknowledges that it will reduce output somewhat. The sales manager doesn't think that makes sense, however, because "the problem isn't very common, and it will be cheaper and easier to fix any problem skates under warranty."

a) Problem:

b) Solution:

Question for Discussion

If a firm has really adopted the marketing concept, why should it need to worry about having some sort of total quality management program?

Learning aid for use with

Chapter 21

Controlling marketing plans and programs

What This Chapter Is About

Chapter 21 shows that a wealth of information may be available from a firm's own records. But it will be useless unless the marketing manager knows how it can be obtained and used--and then asks for it!

Various sales and cost analysis techniques are presented in this chapter. They can be useful for evaluating and controlling the marketing activities of a firm. These techniques are not really complicated. They require only simple arithmetic, and perhaps a computer if a large volume of adding and subtracting is required.

Be sure to distinguish between straightforward sales or cost analysis and performance analysis. Also, be sure to distinguish between the full-cost approach and the contribution-margin approach to cost analysis. Each can be useful in certain situations. But uncritical use of either method might lead to the wrong decision.

This is an important chapter. Marketing plans are not always easy to implement. The marketing manager must know how to use these control-related tools. They help keep a plan on course--and point to situations where a new plan is needed.

Important Terms

control, p. 666
sales analysis, p. 667
performance analysis, p. 668
performance index, p. 670
iceberg principle, p. 674

natural accounts, p. 676
functional accounts, p. 676
full-cost approach, p. 681
contribution-margin approach, p. 682
marketing audit, p. 688

True-False Questions

___ 1. Control is the feedback process that helps the marketing manager learn how ongoing plans are working and how to plan for the future.

___ 2. Because of the 80/20 rule--traditional accounting reports are usually of great help to marketing managers in controlling their plans and programs.

___ 3. Routine sales analyses are best done by manually reviewing data stored in sales invoice files.

___ 4. The best way to analyze sales data is to break it down by geographic region and customer type.

_____ 5. Simple sales analysis provides a detailed breakdown of company sales records, but with no attempt to compare them against standards. Performance analysis seeks exceptions or variations from planned performance.

_____ 6. A performance index is a number--such as a baseball batting average--which shows the relation of one value to another.

_____ 7. A well-designed performance analysis will not only solve marketing problems--but may also be used to forecast sales.

_____ 8. The "iceberg principle" suggests that while averaging and summarizing data can be helpful to managers--they should be sure that these summaries do not hide more than they reveal.

_____ 9. Because most marketing expenditures are made for the general purpose of "increasing sales," detailed marketing cost analysis is all but impossible--and most marketing expenditures should be treated as general overhead costs.

_____ 10. While _functional_ accounts are the categories to which various costs are charged in the normal accounting cycle--_natural_ accounts are set up to indicate the _purpose_ for which the expenditures are made.

_____ 11. The first step in marketing cost analysis is to reclassify all the dollar cost entries in the functional accounts into natural accounts.

_____ 12. Marketing cost analysis can be used to analyze not only total company profitability--but also the profitability of territories, products, customers, salespeople, or any other breakdowns desired.

_____ 13. Marketing cost analysis is NOT performance analysis--but if the marketing manager has budgeted costs to various tasks, it would be possible to extend the cost analysis to a performance analysis.

_____ 14. The full-cost approach requires that difficult-to-allocate costs be split on some basis.

_____ 15. Although the contribution-margin approach focuses management attention on variable cost--rather than total cost--it is likely to lead to the same marketing decisions as the full-cost approach.

_____ 16. While full-cost analysis is especially useful for evaluating alternatives, the contribution-margin approach does a better job of showing individuals within the firm how much they have actually contributed to general overhead and profit.

_____ 17. For most firms, the biggest obstacle to using marketing cost analysis is not the amount of data processing that is required--but rather the need for marketing managers to insist that the necessary data be collected.

_____ 18. Ideally, a marketing audit should not be necessary because a good manager should continually evaluate the effectiveness of his operation--but, in practice, a marketing audit is probably needed because too many managers are "so close to the trees that they can't see the forest."

1. T, p. 666	7. F, pp. 671-672	13. T, p. 681
2. F, p. 666	8. T, pp. 674-675	14. T, p. 681
3. F, p. 667	9. F, pp. 675-676	15. F, p. 682
4. F, p. 668	10. F, p. 676	16. F, p. 685
5. T, p. 668	11. F, p. 676	17. T, p. 687
6. T, p. 668	12. T, pp. 677-678	18. T, p. 688

Multiple-Choice Questions (Circle the correct response)

1. According to the "80/20 rule":
   a. marketing accounts for 80 percent of the consumer's dollar.
   b. only 20 out of every 100 firms use formal marketing control programs.
   c. about 20 percent of a typical firm's customers are unprofitable to serve.
   d. even though a firm might be showing a profit, 80 percent of its business might be coming from only 20 percent of its products or customers.

2. A marketing manager who wants to analyze his firm's sales should be aware that:
   a. sales invoice files contain little useful information.
   b. the best way to analyze sales data is according to geographic regions.
   c. sales analysis involves a detailed breakdown of a company's sales forecasts.
   d. sales analysis may not be possible unless he has made arrangements for collecting the necessary data.
   e. a manager can never have too much data.

3. Performance analysis differs from sales analysis in that performance analysis involves:
   a. detailed breakdowns of a company's sales records.
   b. analyzing only the performance of sales representatives.
   c. comparing performance against standards--looking for exceptions or variations.
   d. analyzing only people--not products or territories.
   e. budgeting for marketing expenditures on the basis of contribution margins.

4. If Salesperson X had a performance index of 80 and Salesperson Y had a performance index of 120, then:
   a. Salesperson X may be having some problems and his sales performance should be investigated.
   b. the two would average out to 100--and this would suggest that "all is well."
   c. Salesperson X's performance should be investigated as a guide to improving everyone's performance.
   d. Salesperson Y probably should be fired.
   e. Salesperson Y obviously had higher sales than Salesperson X.

5. Which of the following statements best describes the "iceberg principle"?
   a. Problems in one area may be offset by good performances in other areas--and thus the problems may not be visible on the surface.
   b. Ten percent of the items in inventory usually account for 80 percent of the sales.
   c. Within a company's sales force there are usually one or two sales reps who don't carry their weight.
   d. Many sales reps do not make their quotas because they ignore certain clients.
   e. Airfreight is less risky than shipping by boat.

6. Marketing cost analysis
   a. uses the "natural" accounting categories commonly used for financial analysis.
   b. focuses on the purpose for which marketing money is spent.
   c. is not very accurate, since it is almost impossible to link marketing costs to specific sales.
   d. is done more frequently than analysis of manufacturing costs.
   e. None of the above is true.

7. Which of the following statements regarding marketing cost analysis is *false*?
   a. Functional accounts include items such as salaries, social security, taxes, raw materials, and advertising.
   b. The costs allocated to the functional accounts will be equal in total to those in the natural accounts.
   c. Functional accounts can be used to show the profitability of territories, products, customers, sales representatives, and so on.
   d. Cost analysis is not performance analysis.
   e. Traditional accounting methods do not show the purpose for which marketing expenditures are made.

8. A good marketing manager knows that:
   a. the costs allocated to functional accounts during a marketing cost analysis should equal--in total--those in the natural accounts.
   b. the "contribution-margin approach" considers only those costs which are directly related to each alternative.
   c. using the "full-cost" and "contribution-margin" approaches may suggest different actions.
   d. functional accounts usually are needed for determining the profitability of customers or products.
   e. All of the above are true.

9. If one were using the "full-cost" approach to marketing cost analysis, then allocating fixed costs on the basis of sales volume would:
   a. make some customers appear more profitable than they actually are.
   b. not be done--because only variable costs would be analyzed.
   c. make some products appear less profitable than they actually are.
   d. decrease the profitability of the whole business.
   e. Both a and c are true statements.

10. Which of the following statements about the contribution-margin approach is *false*?
    a. It is concerned with the amount contributed by an item or group of items toward covering fixed costs.
    b. This approach suggests that it is not necessary to consider all functional costs in all situations.
    c. Top management almost always finds this approach more useful than full-cost analysis.
    d. This approach frequently leads to data which suggest a different decision than might be indicated by the full-cost approach.
    e. It focuses on controllable costs--rather than on total costs.

11. Which of the following statements about a "marketing audit" is *true*?
    a. A marketing audit should be conducted only when some crisis arises.
    b. It probably should be conducted by someone inside the marketing department who is familiar with the whole program.
    c. A marketing audit should evaluate the company's whole marketing program--not just some parts of it.
    d. A marketing audit should be handled by the specialist most familiar with each of the marketing plans in the program.
    e. All of the above are true statements.

Answers to Multiple-Choice Questions

1. d, p. 666
2. d, p. 667
3. c, p. 668
4. a, pp. 670-671

5. a, pp. 674-675
6. b, pp. 675-676
7. a, p. 676
8. e, pp. 675-83

9. e, p. 681
10. c, pp. 682-685
11. c, pp. 688-91

Exercise 21-1

Sales and performance analysis

Introduction

This exercise shows how sales analysis and performance analysis might be used to help plan and control marketing programs. *Sales analysis* begins with a detailed breakdown of the company's sales records and can take many forms--since there is no one best way to analyze sales data. As outlined in the text, any one of several sales breakdowns may be appropriate--depending on the nature of the company, its products, and which strategies are being evaluated.

Performance analysis seeks exceptions or variations from planned performance. In contrast to simple sales analysis--where facts and figures are merely listed--performance analysis involves the use of predetermined standards against which actual results are compared. Here, the purpose is to determine where--and why--performance was better or worse than expected.

Sales analysis and performance analysis can be useful in pinpointing operating problems which may require corrective action--or in identifying areas in which the company may be performing exceptionally well. Such analyses will *not* reveal *what* is causing a given problem--nor will they provide a *solution* to the problem. This requires sound management judgment--both in interpreting the data and in developing solutions. By using sales and performance analyses, however, marketing managers can rely on factual evidence--rather than guesswork--when problems do arise--and thereby improve the quality of their decision making. Better yet, by continually auditing their marketing programs--by analysis of well-chosen data--they may be able to anticipate problems and take action *before* they become serious.

Assignment

Assume you are the marketing manager for a small manufacturer of electrical products. Your company's products are sold by five sales reps--each serving a separate territory--who earn a straight commission of 12 percent of sales. The company's accountant has just given you the data shown on the next page describing last year's sales. Actual sales were less than expected, so you decide to analyze the data further to help you decide what to do.

TABLE 21-1a

Sales Territory	Sales Quota	Actual Sales	Total Calls	Total Orders	Total Customers
A	750,000	900,000	1,300	1,000	400
B	500,000	500,000	1,100	650	250
C	600,000	300,000	400	250	300
D	$ 800,000	$ 400,000	1,000	300	350
E	300,000	450,000	600	300	100
Total	$2,950,000	$2,550,000	4,400	2,500	1,400

1. a)   Calculate a *sales performance index* for each sales territory. Show your work. One answer is provided as an example:

Territory A: ($900,000 / 750,000) X 100 = 120.0

Territory B:

Territory C:

Territory D:

Territory E:

b)   What do the performance indexes indicate about the relative selling performance of each salesperson? One answer is provided as an example.

Territory A: This salesperson's actual sales were much higher than expected for some reason. We should try to find out why.

Territory B:

Territory C:

Territory D:

Territory E:

2.   Some additional sales analysis would be desirable to help you decide *why* the sales reps performed as they did. Therefore, using the data in Table 21-1a make the necessary calculations to complete the following table. Some answers have been provided as a check on your work.

TABLE 21-1b

Sales Territory	Order/Call Ratio	Average Sale per Order	Average Sale per Customer	Sales Commission
A	76.9			
B				$60,000
C			$1,000	
D		$1,333		
E				
Average for All Territories	56.8			

3.   On the basis of your sales and performance analyses, what do you conclude about the sales performance of each salesperson? What factors would you want to investigate further before taking any corrective action?

Territory A:

Territory B:

Territory C:

Territory D:

Territory E:

Question for Discussion

Does the above analysis suggest any specific management action which was not clearly indicated by a review of Table 21-1a? How does this illustrate the "iceberg principle"?

Exercise 21-2

Marketing cost analysis for controlling marketing plans and programs

Introduction

This exercise shows the importance of marketing cost analysis in controlling marketing plans and programs. Our focus will be on analyzing the profitability of different *customers*--but marketing cost analysis could also be used to determine the profitability of different *products*. (Try it!)

The first step in marketing cost analysis is to reclassify all the dollar cost entries in the natural accounts into functional cost accounts. This has already been done for you in this exercise--to simplify your work. The next step is to reallocate the functional costs to those customers (or products) for which the expenditures were made. Here, careful judgment is required--because although no single basis of allocation is "correct," in some cases one may be better (i.e., make more sense) than others. Further, the basis of allocation selected can have a very significant effect on the profitability of a customer (or product).

Assignment

1.   Using the data in Tables 21-2a and 21-2b, calculate profit and loss statements for each of three customers. Show your answers in Table 21-2c. Where you must make allocations of costs to products or customers, indicate under "Comments" the basis of allocation you selected and why. (See the examples on pages 676-681 of the text for suggestions.)

TABLE 21-2a
Sales by Product

Product	Cost/Unit	Selling Price per Unit	Number of Units Sold	Items/Unit	Items Packaged
A	$11	$22	5,000	1	5,000
B	6	12	10,000	3	30,000
C	10	17	6,000	2	12,000

TABLE 21-2b
Sales by Customer

Customer	Number of Sales Calls	Number of Orders	Number of Units of Each Product Ordered		
			A	B	C
1	20	10	500	4,000	1,000
2	25	20	2,000	3,500	3,000
3	15	10	2,500	2,500	2,000
Total	60	40	5,000	10,000	6,000

Other expenses from functional cost accounts:

Administrative expenses	$36,000
Sales salaries	48,000
Clerical expenses (order and billing)	12,000
Advertising	33,000
Packaging expenses	11,750

Comments:

TABLE 21-2c
Profit and Loss Statement by Customer

	Customer 1	Customer 2	Customer 3	Whole Company
Net Sales:				
Product A:	_____	_____	_____	_____
Product B:	_____	_____	_____	_____
Product C:	_____	_____	_____	_____
Total Sales	_____	_____	_____	_____
Cost of Sales				
Product A:	_____	_____	_____	_____
Product B:	_____	_____	_____	_____
Product C:	_____	_____	_____	_____
Total Cost of Sales	_____	_____	_____	_____
Gross Margin	_____		_____	_____
Expenses:				
Sales Salaries	_____	_____	_____	_____
Clerical Expenses	_____	_____	_____	_____
Advertising	_____	_____		_____
Packaging Expense:				
Product A	_____	_____	_____	_____
Product B	_____	_____	_____	_____
Product C	_____	_____	_____	_____
TOTAL EXPENSE	_____	_____		_____
Net Profit (or loss)	_____	_____	_____	_____

2.   What do you conclude from your analysis? Should any of the customers be dropped? Why or why not? What factors must you consider in answering this question?

Question for Discussion

Which of the two basic approaches to cost analysis--full cost or contribution margin--was used in the above exercise? Would your conclusions have been different if the other approach had been used? If so, which approach is "correct"?

Chapter 22

Ethical marketing in a consumer-oriented world: appraisal and challenges

What This Chapter Is About

Chapter 22 provides an evaluation of the effectiveness of both micro- and macro-marketing. The text explains the authors' views, but their answers are far less important than their reasoning. It is extremely important to understand the arguments both pro and con--because the effectiveness of marketing is a vital issue. How well you understand this material--and how you react to it--may affect your own feelings about the value of business and the contribution you can make in the business world. Do not try to memorize the "right" answers. Rather, try to understand and evaluate the authors' reasoning. Then, develop your own answers.

When you have studied this chapter, you should be able to defend your feelings about the worth of marketing--using reasoned arguments rather than just "gut feelings." Further, you should have some suggestions about how to improve marketing--if you feel there are any weaknesses. Perhaps you yourself--as a producer and/or consumer--can help improve our market-directed system.

True-False Questions

___ 1. Although our economic objectives may change in the future, at the present time marketing probably should be evaluated according to the basic objective of the North American economic system—which is to satisfy consumer needs—as *consumers see them*.

___ 2. Since individual consumer satisfaction is a very personal concept, it probably does not provide a very good standard for evaluating macro-marketing effectiveness.

___ 3. At the micro-level, marketing effectiveness can be measured--at least roughly--by the profitability of individual marketers.

___ 4. According to the text, macro-marketing does not cost too much, but micro-marketing frequently does cost too much, given the present objective of the American economic system--consumer satisfaction.

___ 5. One reason why micro-marketing often costs too much is that many firms are still production-oriented and not nearly as efficient as they might be.

___ 6. Marketing inefficiencies are generally due to a lack of interest in the customer, improper blending of the four Ps, or a lack of understanding of the marketing environment.

___ 7. According to the text, greater use of cost-plus pricing would result in better, more efficient, micro-marketing decisions.

8. Despite the fact that the marketing concept is now applied universally, marketing does cost too much in most firms.

___ 9. Despite its cost, advertising can actually *lower* prices to the consumer.

___ 10. According to the text, it is probably fair to criticize the marketplace for fulfilling consumers' "false tastes" because marketing creates most popular tastes and social values.

___ 11. A good business manager might find it useful to follow the following rule: "Do unto others as you would have others do unto you."

___ 12. Because of the consumerism movement, the majority of consumers are now socially responsible.

___ 13. Given the role that business is supposed to play in our market-directed system, it seems reasonable to conclude that a marketing manager should be expected to improve and expand the range of goods and services made available to consumers.

___ 14. The text suggests that socially responsible marketing managers should try to limit consumers' freedom of choice for the good of society.

___ 15. Market-oriented business managers may be even more necessary in the future if the marketing system is expected to satisfy more subtle needs--such as for the "good life."

Answers to True-False Questions

1. T, p. 696	6. T, p. 699	11. T, p. 708
2. T, p. 697	7. F, p. 700	12. F, p. 712
3. T, p. 698	8. F, p. 700	13. T, p. 712
4. T, p. 698	9. T, p. 701	14. F, p. 713
5. T, p. 698	10. F, pp. 702-705	15. T, p. 713

Multiple-Choice Questions (Circle the correct response)

1. Consumer satisfaction:
   a. is the basic objective of all economic systems.
   b. is easier to measure at the macro-level than at the micro-level.
   c. depends on one's own expectations and aspirations.
   d. is hard to define.
   e. is totally unrelated to company profits.

2. Which of the following statements about marketing does the text make?
   a. Micro-marketing never costs too much.
   b. Macro-marketing does not cost too much.
   c. Marketing is not needed in all modern economies.
   d. Micro-marketing always costs too much.
   e. Macro-marketing does cost too much.

3. According to the text, micro-marketing may cost too much because:
   a. some marketers don't understand their markets.
   b. prices are frequently set on a cost-plus basis.
   c. promotion is sometimes seen as a substitute for product quality.
   d. All of the above are true statements.
   e. None of the above--marketing never costs too much!

4. Which of the following does NOT support the idea that "MICRO-marketing often DOES cost too much"?
   a. Many firms focus exclusively on their own internal problems.
   b. Distribution channels may be selected on the basis of personal preferences.
   c. Product planners frequently develop "me-too" products.
   d. Costly promotion may try to compensate for a weak marketing mix.
   e. Many firms try to maximize profits.

5. The text concludes that:
   a. advertising is a poor use of resources.
   b. advertising can actually lower prices to the consumer.
   c. marketing makes people buy things they don't need.
   d. marketing makes people materialistic.
   e. marketing's job is just to satisfy the consumer wants which exist at any point in time.

6. Which of the following is not a current trend affecting marketing strategy planning?
   a. growth of computer-to-computer ordering.
   b. less use of scanner data.
   c. more attention to quality.
   d. growth of just-in-time.
   e. collapse of communism.

7. The future poses many challenges for marketing managers because:
   a. new technologies are making it easier to abuse consumers' rights to privacy.
   b. the marketing concept has become obsolete.
   c. it is marketing managers who have full responsibility to preserve our macro-marketing system.
   d. social responsibility applies only to firms--not to consumers.
   e. ultimately it is marketing managers who must determine which products are in the best interests of consumers.

Answers to Multiple-Choice Questions

1. c, p. 697   4. e, pp. 699-700   7. a, p. 711
2. b, p. 700   5. b, p. 701
3. d, p. 699   6. b, p. 707

Learning aid for use with

Exercise 22-1

Does micro-marketing cost too much?

Introduction

One reason that micro-marketing often *does* cost too much is that some production-oriented firms insist on clinging to their traditional ways of doing things--ignoring new marketing mixes and strategies. In a dynamic market, this can lead to higher than necessary costs--and perhaps even to the bankruptcy of the firm.

This can easily be seen in channels of distribution--where many inefficient and high-cost channels exist even today. High-cost channels are not *necessarily* evidence of inefficiency, however. If some target markets really do want some special service which is relatively expensive--then perhaps that is the best channel system for them. But this possible reason for "high-cost" channels of distribution does not explain all such systems. Some do appear to be more expensive than necessary because the established firms insist on buying from and selling to their usual sources and customers--even though other available channels would do as good a job (or maybe better), at lower cost.

This exercise shows how the use of alternative channels of distribution might lead to different--and in some cases higher--prices to final consumers. You are asked to calculate the probable *retail* prices which would result if a manufacturer were to use several different channels to distribute its product.

Assignment

1. A manufacturer of a new toothpaste is planning to use several different channels of distribution, as listed below. Each middleman in each of the alternative channels uses a cost-plus approach to pricing. That is, each firm takes a markup on its selling price to cover operating expenses plus profit. The manufacturer sells the toothpaste to the *next* member of each channel for $1.10 per "large" tube.

    Using the data shown on the next page for markup estimates, calculate the *retail* selling price in each channel of distribution. Show your work in the space provided. The price for the first channel is calculated for you as an example.

	Operating Expenses*	Profit Margin*
Retail		
Small drugstores	39%	2%
Supermarkets	20%	1%
Chain drugstores	33%	3%
Mass-merchandisers	29%	2%
Wholesale		
Merchant wholesalers	13%	2%
Rack jobbers	18%	2%

*Note: operating expenses and profit margin are given as a percentage of sales

---

a) Manufacturer to merchant wholesalers who sell to small drugstores:

$$13\% + 2\% = 15\% \quad = \text{Merchant wholesalers' markup on selling price}$$

$$\frac{\$1.10}{100\% - 15\%} = \$1.29 = \text{Price to retailers}$$

$$39\% + 2\% = 41\% \quad = \text{Retailers' markup on selling price}$$

$$\frac{\$1.29}{100\% - 41\%} = \$2.19 = \text{Retail price}$$

b) Manufacturer directly to a national chain of drugstores:

c)   Manufacturer to merchant wholesalers who sell to supermarkets:

d)   Manufacturer directly to a regional chain of mass-merchandisers:

e)   Manufacturer to rack jobbers who sell to supermarkets:

2.   Consider the different retail prices that you calculated for Question 1. Assuming that it wanted to maximize profit, which channel(s) should the manufacturer choose to develop an effective marketing strategy or strategies? Why?

3.   Assume that each of the five channels in Question 1 were to survive in the marketplace. From a *macro* viewpoint, should the "high-cost" channels be made illegal to "protect" consumers--and develop a "fair and efficient" marketing system? Why or why not?

Question for Discussion

What other reasons besides "tradition" help explain why micro-marketing often *does* cost too much? What can (should) be done to make sure that micro-marketing does *not* cost too much in the future?

Learning aid for use with

Exercise 22-2

Does macro-marketing cost too much?

Introduction

All economic systems *must* have a macro-marketing system. The systems may take many forms, but al must have some way of deciding *what* and *how much* is to be produced and distributed *by whom, when,* and *to whom.*

Our macro-marketing system is basically a market-directed system. The key decisions are made fairly automatically and democratically--through the micro-level decisions made by individual producers and consumers. Together these individual decisions determine the macro-level decisions--and provide direction for the whole economy.

Does our macro-marketing system work in an efficient and fair way which achieves our social objectives? This question is very subjective, and we usually analyze the performance of our marketing system in terms of how well it satisfies consumer needs--as consumers see them. But remember that not all consumers have the same needs!

The marketing concept suggests that a firm should try to satisfy the needs of *some* consumers (at a profit). But what is "good" for some producers or consumers may not be "good" for the whole society. This is the "micro-macro dilemma." It means that in running our macro-marketing system, some compromises must be made to balance the needs of society and the needs of individual producers and consumers. Making these compromises and still protecting individual freedom of choice is not easy. This exercise will help you understand the difficulty of resolving micro-macro dilemmas.

Assignment

Listed below are several imaginary situations which might be classified as "micro-macro dilemmas." For each situation, identify both sides of the dilemma--i.e., who benefits and who suffers in each situation-- and state what action you would recommend.

1.   Due to recent terrorism in the airline industry, the government is considering a proposal that stricter regulations be enforced regarding passenger luggage that is stowed beneath the plane. In this proposal, all luggage on overseas flights will be searched for dangerous objects such as bombs or guns.

2.   Wanting to slow the flow from Toronto to its suburbs by making the city more attractive to live in, some Ontario legislators are proposing that any "large retailers" wanting to open a new store in the suburbs must also open one within the city.

3.   The release of chlorofluorocarbons into the atmosphere may be causing long-term damaging changes in the protective ozone layer--and plans are underway to stop producing fluorocarbons. As a result, manufacturers are trying to find other gases to use in products such as refrigerators and automobile air-conditioners. Although reputable scientific authorities disagree on the matter, some are arguing that any man-made gas may disrupt the environment, and thus manufacturers should only use gases "harvested" from the atmosphere, so accidental release would just return the environment to the status quo. But legislation banning the use of man-made gases might increase the cost of an average household refrigerator by more than $1,000.

4.   In the U.S., large hospitals often end up treating "uninsureds"—people who do not carry health insurance and who are not covered under any government program. To make up this loss, hospitals

Learning aid for use with

routinely increase the fees charged to patients who *do* have insurance, a process known as "cost shifting." Cost shifting increases the prices of medical insurance by 15 percent or more.

5.   Wanting to see more "equality of income," some Canadian legislators have introduced a bill proposing that all annual income over $200,000 be taxed at the rate of 100 percent.

6.   Parliament is considering a law that would ban the sale of "fortified" (high alcohol content) wines. Studies reveal that the potent, low-cost wines are sold primarily to alcoholics—especially homeless "winos."

7.   The federal government is considering a proposal to stop all television advertising for beer. Critics charge that the ads are primarily targeted at young people, including those under legal drinking age, and that the ads portray beer drinkers as living more interesting, exciting lives.

8.	To reduce the pressure on land fills and related environmental problems, a provincial parliament is considering a law to ban the sale of certain disposable products and packages—including disposable diapers. Companies would have two years before the law went into effect—to allow time for appropriate adjustments.

9.	Eager for new sources of revenue to reduce the federal deficit, but equally eager to avoid the appearance of raising tax rates, some legislators are interested in eliminating certain "allowable business expenses." One proposal argues that advertising expenses should no longer be tax deductible. This would have the net effect of making advertising much more expensive.

Question for Discussion

Can "micro-macro dilemmas" such as those discussed above be resolved in any workable way? How? Be specific. Would "micro-macro dilemmas" be better resolved in a market-directed or a planned economic system? What implication does this have for answering the question: "Does macro-marketing cost too much?"

Learning aid for use with